Global Unemployment

BY THE SAME AUTHOR:

Planning for Basic Needs in Kenya, with Dharam Ghai and Franklin Lisk, (ILO, Geneva, 1979)

Essays on Employment in Kenya, with Dharam Ghai, ed., (Nairobi, 1979)

Politics, Economics and Technical Training. A Kenyan Case Study, with G.C.M. Mutiso, (Nairobi, 1979)

The Struggle for Development: National Strategies in an International Context, with Manfred Bienefeld, ed., (John Wiley, 1983)

A World of Differentials: African Pay Structures in a Transnational Context, with others, (Hodder and Stoughton, 1983)

Global Unemployment:

The New Challenge to Economic Theory

Martin Godfrey
Fellow, Institute of Development Studies
at the University of Sussex

Wheatsheaf Books

DISTRIBUTED BY HARVESTER PRESS

First published in Great Britain in 1986 by
WHEATSHEAF BOOKS LTD
A MEMBER OF THE HARVESTER PRESS PUBLISHING GROUP
Publisher: John Spiers
Director of Publications: Edward Elgar
16 Ship Street, Brighton, Sussex

British Library Cataloguing in Publication Data
Godfrey, Martin
Global unemployment: the new challenge to economic theory.
1. Unemployment
I. Title
331.13'7 HD5707.5
ISBN 0-7450-0005-3
ISBN 0-7450-0046-0 Pbk

Typeset in 11 on 12-point Times by Gwynne Printers Ltd.,
Hurstpierpoint, Sussex

Printed and bound in Great Britain by
Biddles Ltd, Guildford and King's Lynn

THE HARVESTER PRESS PUBLISHING GROUP

The Harvester Press Publishing Group comprises Harvester Press Limited (chiefly publishing literature, fiction, philosophy, psychology, and science and trade books), Harvester Press Microform Publications Limited (publishing in microform unpublished archives, scarce printed sources, and indexes to these collections) and Wheatsheaf Books Limited (a wholly independent company chiefly publishing in economics, international politics, sociology and related social sciences), whose books are distributed by The Harvester Press Limited and its agencies throughout the world.

For Rosie

Contents

List of Tables

List of Figures

Preface

This book represents an attempt to combine a review of theorising about the nature, causes and consequences of unemployment and under-utilisation of labour in both industrialised and underdeveloped economies with a consideration of the implications for such theories of recent changes in the world economy. The hope in the review (in Chapters Two to Eight) is not so much to achieve comprehensive coverage, impossible in the space available, as to capture the *essence* of the approach of each of the various schools.

The problem in any such attempt at classification is that there are many ways in which the cake could be cut. Some, for instance, may dispute the need for a separate chapter on 'demand-side' development economics (Chapter Seven). Others may prefer a different schema for post-classical employment theorising in industrialised economies. For instance, David Evans has suggested that it would be preferable to use conceptualisation of the social or political economy as the criterion for separating two broad schools of thought. Thus from British classical political economy there would follow the general equilibrium theorising of Walras, Jevons, Menger, etc., with its social conceptualisation and continued acceptance of Say's Law. Keynes would be seen as being in the tradition of this school, with the single exception that he does not accept Say's Law, while the modern believers in voluntary unemployment would trace their lineage back to it via Pigou and Marshall. The other broad stream, he suggests, would flow through Marx to Kalecki, whose rejection of Say's Law is combined with some conceptualisation of the social/political economy. This schema differs from ours (in Chapter Three) primarily in its separation of Keynes from Kalecki rather than of both of them from the neoclassical economists. This makes a lot of sense in itself on the criterion suggested and is also a useful reminder that different taxonomies will be relevant for different purposes. At any rate it is hoped that ours is sufficiently clear to enable readers to make their own rearrangements as required.

The recent changes in the world economy on which attention is concentrated are: the increasing location of industrial production for the world market in the underdeveloped economies of the South as well as the industrialised economies of the North; the extensive use made by Northern employers of Southern migrant labour; and, more recently, the growth of unemployment in the North to levels and rates unheard of since the 1930s. An attempt is made, in the light of these changes and building on the review, to chart (rather than to explore in detail) new directions for theory which would break down the barrier between short-run theorising for industrialised and long-run for underdeveloped economies and analyse processes at a global as well as a national level. The focus throughout is primarily on theory and, while it is recognised that theory cannot be discussed in isolation from history and policy, it is also recognised that two volumes would have been necessary to give adequate treatment to these aspects. Wherever possible readers are given references which will enable them to pursue the issues further.

Various debts must be acknowledged. The heaviest are owed to Philip Leeson and Manfred Bienefeld. Philip's word-of-mouth reputation as the wisest of development economists and the most generous commenter on colleagues' work is richly deserved; he is the hidden co-author of many books, this one included (the usual disclaimers notwithstanding). Manfred has been the co-author with me of several papers and collaborator in many academic ventures over the past ten years, all of which have been drawn on heavily. Helpful comments and advice have also been received from many colleagues, including Christopher Colclough, Philip Daniel, David Evans, Raphael Kaplinsky, David Metcalf, Jerzy Osiatinski, Ennio Rodriguez, Hubert Schmitz, Dudley Seers, Hans Singer, Sheila Smith and Guy Standing. Thanks are also due to Boyd Gilman, for research assistance, and to Danielle Hodges and Beverley Harries, for processing the words.

1 The Nature of the Problem: Concepts, Measures and Trends

THE ONSET OF GLOBAL UNEMPLOYMENT

When the International Labour office launched its ambitious World Employment Programme in 1969 it saw the problem primarily as one of unemployment and underemployment in less-developed countries. As the preface to one of is early pilot country missions put it:

> unemployment has now become chronic and intractable in nearly every developing country. Whereas the industrial countries have mostly reduced open unemployment to about 3 to 6 per cent of their labour force, the comparable figure for other parts of the world is frequently over 10 per cent, and on top of this there is a range of other serious employment problems (ILO 1972: xi).

Since then the world has changed. The employment problems of the developing countries have not disappeared. They have, rather, been overlaid and potentially aggravated by the growth of unemployment in the industrialised countries to unprecedented post-war levels.

During the 1960s and the first three years of the 1970s, North America, Western Europe and Japan did indeed appear to have found the secret of full employment, with unemployment rates varying between 4 and 7 per cent in North America and rising no higher than 3 per cent in most European countries and in Japan. Table 1.1 shows how things have changed since then. The average unemployment rate in the member countries of the Organisation for Economic Cooperation and Development (which had stayed below 3 per cent during the 1960s) has climbed in the ten years since 1973 to almost 9 per cent, representing a total of 32.3 million people out of work. In some European economies (e.g. Belgium, Italy, the Netherlands and the UK) unemployment rates in 1983 were higher than or comparable with those at the height of the world depression fifty years earlier. The rate for OECD Europe as a whole was over 10 per cent. Several non-European countries not covered by Table 1.1 also had unprecedentedly high unemployment rates in 1983, for instance Australia's 10 per cent and Canada's 12 per cent.

Table 1.1 Unemployment Rates, Selected OECD Countries

	Percentage of total labour force						
	1933	*1959–67*	*1973*	*1975*	*1980*	*1982*	*1983*
Belgium	10.6	2.4	2.9	5.1	9.0	18.1	14.5
Denmark	14.5	1.4	0.7	4.9	6.5	9.9	10.7
France	—	0.7	1.8	4.1	6.3	8.0	8.0
W. Germany	14.8	1.2	1.0	3.6	3.0	6.1	8.0
Ireland	—	4.6	5.6	6.4	6.1	10.7	13.8
Italy	5.9	6.2	4.9	5.8	7.4	8.9	9.7
Japan	—	1.4	1.2	1.9	2.0	2.4	2.6
Netherlands	9.7	0.9	2.3	3.9	4.7	11.4	13.7
UK	13.9	1.8	2.5	4.7	7.0	12.3	13.1
USA	20.5	5.3	4.9	8.3	7.0	9.5	9.5

Sources: Freeman, Clark and Soete (1982); OECD, *Labour Force Statistics, Quarterly Labour Statistics* and *Employment Outlook,* 1983 and 1984.

At the same time as the level of unemployment in OECD countries has risen its structure and composition has been changing. The number of people experiencing long-term unemployment (for twelve months or more) has increased, particularly in Europe, and the rise in unemployment among young people of 24 or less and among ethnic minorities has been disproportionately fast. Until 1979 female unemployment was rising faster than that of males; since then it has been the other way round and by 1982 there was very little difference between male and female unemployment rates in the seven major OECD countries. Information about unemployment rates and trends in the developing countries outside the OECD is, unfortunately, less detailed and comprehensive. Table 1.2 summarises the situation in the relatively small number of such countries for which regular information is available.

Table 1.2 Unemployment Rates in Selected Developing Countries

	Percentage of labour force					
	1965	*1970*	*1975*	*1980*	*1981*	*1982*
Africa:						
Egypt	1.9[a]	2.4	2.5	5.2	—	—
Middle East:						
Syria	7.4	6.4	4.8	3.8[b]	—	—
Asia:						
S. Korea	7.4	4.5	4.1	5.2	4.6	4.4
Philippines	8.2	6.0	4.4	4.8	5.1	5.3
Latin America and Caribbean:						
Argentina	5.3	4.8	2.3	2.3	4.5	5.7
Chile[c]	5.4	4.1	15.0	10.4	11.3	20.0
Colombia[d]	8.9	8.2	10.5	9.9	8.1	—
Panama	7.6	7.1	6.4	8.8[e]	—	—
Peru[f]	—	4.7	4.9	7.0	6.8	7.0
Trinidad and Tobago	14.0	12.5	15.0	10.0	12.2	—
Uruguay[g]	7.2[h]	7.5	8.1[i]	7.3	6.6	—
Venezuela[j]	7.7[k]	6.3	7.6[l]	6.0	6.2	7.1

[a]1964, [b]1979, [c]Gran Santiago, [d]Bogota, [e]1979, [f]Lima Callao, [g]Montevideo, [h]1967, [i]1974, [j]urban, [k]1967, [l]1976.

Sources: Gregory (1980) and ILO, *Yearbooks of Labour Statistics.*

In general this table suggests that there has been no dramatic improvement in the employment situation in the third world to offset the deterioration in industrialised countries. Yet, at first sight, the table has some surprising features. Only in one case (Chile) has the unemployment rate increased in recent years on anything like the scale experienced by most of the OECD members covered by Table 1.1, and most developing countries now appear to have lower unemployment rates than most industrialised countries. Consider, for instance, the Philippines, a classic labour-surplus economy, which exports workers all over the world and where queues of job-seekers form outside cheap-labour factories in export-processing zones and domestic outworkers compete to produce garments at cutthroat rates. In 1982 its unemployment rate was 5.3 per cent, not only lower than those of the chronically sick men of Europe such as the UK, the Netherlands, Ireland and Belgium, but lower than those of all OECD member countries except Japan,

Norway, Sweden and Switzerland. To judge from Tables 1.1 and 1.2 Filipino job-seekers would have a better chance of getting a job at home than if they took their job search to the United States.

This impression is confirmed by the estimates of unemployment rates in the various developing regions of the world in 1980, based on a special ILO survey of 61 countries, shown in Table 1.3. Not only do the figures show little change from similar ILO estimates of five years earlier (when the average for Africa was put at 7.1 per cent, for Asia 3.9 per cent and for Latin America 5.1 per cent). They also compare relatively favourably with the 7.1 per cent unemployment rate in North America and that of 6.2 per cent in OECD Europe in ther same year (see Table 1.1). Only the low-income countries of Africa and (to a lesser extent) of Latin America and the Caribbean appear, on this measure, to have had a worse employment problem than the industrialised countries in 1980. Since 1980 this contrast is likely to have become further accentuated.

Table 1.3 Open Unemployment: Developing regions, Percentage of Labour Force, 1980

Group	*Total*	*Male*	*Female*
All developing countries[a]	6.0	5.2	7.8
Latin America and Caribbean (low-income countries)	8.1	7.4	10.3
Latin America and Caribbean (middle-income countries)	5.6	7.8	8.4
India	4.6	3.3	7.3
Asia (other low income countries)[a]	4.5	2.3	10.2
Asia (middle-income countries)[a]	3.4	3.4	3.4
Africa and Middle East (low-income countries)	14.8	15.9	12.6
Africa and Middle East (middle-income countries)	7.7	4.7	8.7
Africa and Middle East (capital surplus oil producers)	5.4	6.1	4.0

[a]Excluding China.

Source: ILO, *World Labour Report 1*, 1984.

Within developing countries, also, open unemployment seems to be primarily an urban rather than a rural problem, as Table 1.4 shows. Only in the case of Iran was the rural unemployment rate higher than the urban. More recent, scattered statistics suggest that this urban–rural contrast has persisted. In short, the message of unemployment statistics in the first half of the 1980s seems to be that industrialised economies such as Britain and the United States have a worse unemployment problem than do economies normally accredited with massive surplus labour such as India and the Philippines; and that rural areas of the third world have virtually no unemployment problem at all.

Table 1.4 Urban and Rural Unemployment Rates in Selected Developing Economics

Economy	*Year*	*Unemployment rate (%)* Urban	Rural	*Ratio of urban to rural unemployment rates*
Korea, Republic of	1965	12.7	3.1	4.1
Panama	1967	9.3	2.8	3.3
Chile	1968	6.1	2.0	3.1
Indonesia	1971	4.8	1.8	2.7
Taiwan	1968	3.5	1.4	2.5
Venezuela	1968	6.5	3.1	2.1
Philippines	1967	13.1	6.9	1.9
Trinidad and Tobago	1971	16.5	8.7	1.9
Tanzania	1965	7.0	3.9	1.8
India	1972–73	6.7	3.9	1.7
Malaysia	1967	11.6	7.4	1.6
Syria	1967	7.3	4.6	1.6
Sri Lanka	1968	14.8	10.4	1.4
Iran	1966	5.5	11.3	0.5

Source: Squire (1981).

PROBLEMS WITH THE STANDARD DEFINITION OF UNEMPLOYMENT

This apparent paradox is a reflection of the extremely restrictive nature of the standard international definition of unemployment, which until very recently was that adopted by the international conference of labour statisticians in 1954, as follows:

> (1) Persons in unemployment consist of all persons above a specified age who, on the specified day or for a specified week, were in the following categories:
> (a) workers available for employment whose contract of employment had been terminated or temporarily suspended and who were without a job and seeking work for pay or profit;
> (b) persons who were available for work (except for minor illness) during the specified period and were seeking work for pay or profit, who were never previously employed or whose most recent status was other than that of employee) i.e. former employers, etc.) or who had been in retirement;
> (c) persons without a job and currently available for work who had made arrangements to start a new job at a date subsequent to the specified period;
> (d) persons on temporary or indefinite lay-off without pay.
> (2) The following categories of persons are not considered to be unemployed:
> (a) persons intending to establish their own business or farm, but who had not yet arranged to do so, who were not seeking work for pay or profit;
> (b) former unpaid family workers not at work and not seeking work.

In short this definition demands of those to be categorised as unemployed that they be (a) 'not working' and (b) 'seeking work', a combination which is particularly difficult to sustain in a developing economy. As Sen comments: 'it is . . . a bit amazing that people qualifying in the [Indian] census as "unemployed" manage to get a living' (Sen 1975: 121). The definition only covers the area of overlap between the two circles of those not working and those seeking work which, in a third-world city such as Calcutta, as in Figure 1.1 (adapted

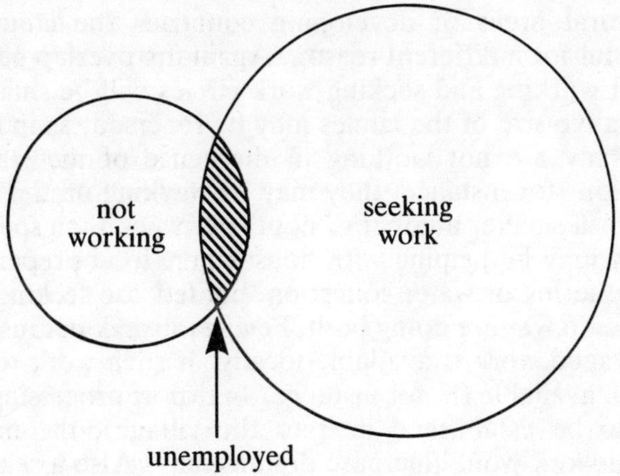

Figure 1.1: The Standard Definition of Unemployment Applied to a Third-World City
Source: Sen (1975)

from Sen's Figure 1.1), is likely to be very small. In a city such as Calcutta many will be seeking work, but few will be not working and even fewer will be doing both. It is not surprising that the unemployment rate on this definition is smaller in Calcutta or Manila than in London or New York. In the absence of a social security system most people cannot afford to be *both* not working *and* seeking work. Most of those who are seeking work have to find some way of keeping themselves alive which may place them outside the ranks of the unemployed on the standard definition. Many of those who are 'not working' will be women engaged in unpaid housework, working extremely hard but not counted as economically active by the statisticians unless they are also seeking work and therefore unemployed. Most of those who can afford to be wholly unemployed are likely to be relatively well educated and from relatively prosperous families (see Chapter Four for further discussion, particularly pages 112-13). Thus the concept of open unemployment is not very helpful in a third-world city.

In rural areas of developing countries the concept is unhelpful for a different reason. Again the overlap between the not-working and seeking-work circles will be small, but the relative size of the circles may be reversed, as in Figure 1.2. Many are not working in the sense of the standard definition (for instance, they may be working on the family farm for a smaller number of hours per week than specified[1] or they may be helping with housework, food preparation, fuel-gathering or water collection, but few are seeking work and even fewer are doing both. Few seek work because very little waged work is available locally. If such work were to become available (if, for instance, an export processing zone were to be established next to the village), the number seeking work would increase dramatically. Also a relatively large number is not working because the rural household offers subsistence even to those of its members whose contribution escapes the net of the labour statisticians.

In an industrialised economy such as the United States or Britain, similar conceptual problems exist, but the overlap between the two circles is likely to be larger, as in Figure 1.3,

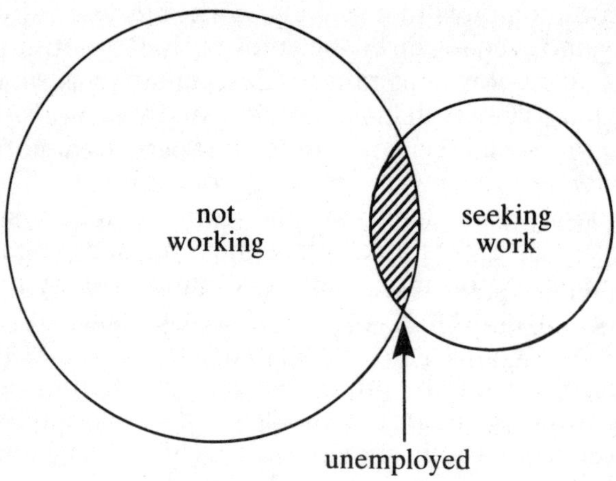

Figure 1.2: The Standard Definition of Unemployment Applied to a Rural Area in a Developing Country
Source: Sen (1975)

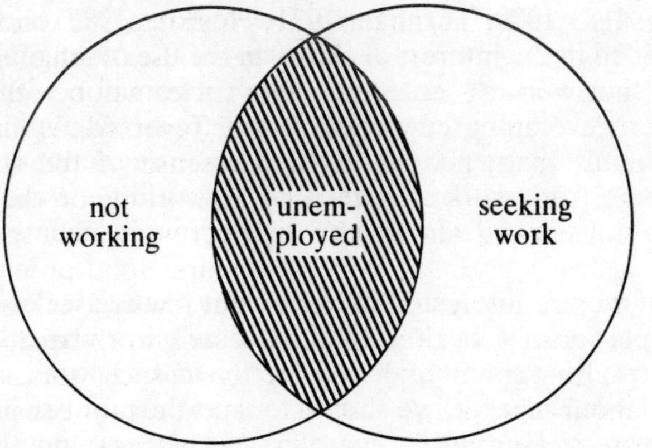

Figure 1.3: The Standard Definition of Unemployment Applied to an Industrialised Country
Source: Sen (1975)

because the availability of social security payments enables those who are not working to survive while seeking work. Again a large proportion of those not working will be hardworking housewives not counted as economically active unless they are also seeking work and therefore unemployed.

This discussion suggests that different measures of underutilisation of labour are needed for different purposes, as follows:

1. If we are interested in how much income people are losing as a result of not having a job, we should look at the number of those who are not working,[2] or working fewer hours than they are capable of, regardless of whether or not they are seeking work. This is what Sen would call the *income* aspect of underutilisation of labour. It has nothing necessarily to do with poverty as such. An unemployed person from a rich family could be deprived of income-from-work while enjoying a high standard of living as a result of transfers of income from other members of the family. Thus measures which define all those below a certain income level as 'unemployed' or 'underemployed'

(e.g. ILO 1970, Turnham 1971, Hopkins 1983) should be avoided in the interest of clarity in the use of language. On this 'not working' criterion India (in common with many other developing countries) has a lot of surplus labour. There are many people, particularly in rural areas, whose income from work is lower than if would be if they were fully utilised and who live by sharing family income.

2. If we are interested in the extent of the availability of people for new work even at extremely low wages, and in the resulting extent of dissatisfaction and demoralisation in the labour market, we should look at the number of those who are *seeking work*, regardless of whether or not they are not working. This is what Sen would call the *recognition* aspect of underutilisation of labour. Many (but not all) of those working for low incomes in low-productivity jobs which they regard as inadequate or below their potential may think of themselves, and even describe themselves to enumerators, as 'unemployed'. They are, according to the standard definition, working, but are vigorously seeking what they regard as a proper job. On this criterion, also, India has a lot of surplus labour. Many people, particularly in the cities, are looking for work even though 'employed'.

3. If we are interested in the extent of the loss of output which results from underutilisation of labour, we should look at the removable labour surplus, particularly in agriculture and perhaps in the bureaucracy. This is what Sen would call the *production* aspect of underutilisation, involving not idleness but waste—a level of output that is lower than it otherwise might be. The suggestion is that it would be possible to remove a certain number of people from their current activities in the labour force without affecting output, and to reallocate them to other activities. These disguised unemployed from the production point of view may or may not also be unemployed from the income point of view. If the income they receive on the farm is conditional on their helping in the family's work, then the income approach yields different results from the production approach. The distinction is important because

> of its implications both for income distribution and for the supply price of labour (see Sen 1975: 36 for further discussion). On this production criterion, also, many (but not all) economists would agree that India has a lot of surplus labour, i.e. that a large proportion of the labour force could be removed from agriculture without affecting output.

Thus even though its unemployment rate is low, India in common with many other labour-surplus economies does suffer from underutilisation of labour in all three of the sense identified by Sen. The fact that unemployment rates in developing economies have risen less sharply and are in general lower than those in industrialised economies does not mean that unemployment is now only a Northern problem. Indeed, recognition of the huge and growing scale of underutilisation of labour in developing economies seems to be increasing. For instance, Lipton, who contributed to the sceptical view taken by *Asian Drama* (Myrdal 1968: 2041–61; 2203–21) of unemployment and underemployment, now believes not only that unemployment[3] is 'probably a more important component of poverty than is generally believed' but also that 'its relative importance is probably increasing' (Lipton 1983: 66). He bases this view partly on evidence from Africa and Asia and partly on the following logic:

> In most Asian and some African LDCs, a growing proportion of rural people are deriving most of their income from hired labour. This . . . is because (with little good uncultivated land) inheritance and population growth steadily increase the proportion of families which, at equilibrium levels of income and effort, are net hirers-out of labour from the home farm. The supply of unskilled agricultural labour is rising; demand rises much more slowly than population growth; the scope for adjustment without changing the levels of employment is limited; and avoidance of *falls* in employment, by means of switches of labour supply into non-agriculture, is limited by the associated higher unemployment rates in urban areas. As education raises skill levels—so that some jobs once done by unskilled labourers are done (better) by those whose parents could afford the direct and opportunity costs of their education—unemployment shifts even further towards the unskilled, undereducated poor and poorest (ibid: 65).

THE SEARCH FOR MORE USEFUL DEFINITIONS

Relaxing the Seeking-Work Criterion

The conceptual clarification due to Sen's approach is to be welcomed, but the task of translating it into measurement practice largely remains[4]. That statisticians are aware of the problems is shown by recent relaxations in the international standard definition of unemployment. At the thirteenth international conference of labour statisticians in 1982 a resolution on unemployment spelled out the meaning of 'seeking work'. It should cover those who 'had taken specific steps in a specified recent period to seek paid employment or self-employment. The specific steps may include registration at a public or private employment exchange; application to employers; checking out worksites, farms, factory gates, market or other assembly places; placing or answering newspaper advertisements; seeking assistance of friends or relatives; looking for land, building, machinery or equipment to establish own enterprise; arranging for financial resources; applying for permits and licences, etc.' This is distinctly more liberal than actual measurement practice in most countries. Even more so is the concession that 'in situations where the conventional means of seeking work are of limited relevance, where the labour market is largely unorganised or of limited scope, where labour absorption is, at the time, inadequate, or where the labour force is largely self-employed, the standard definition of unemployment . . . may be applied by relaxing the criterion of seeking work.'

The quantitative significance of relaxing the seeking-work criterion (which could be seen as reaching towards coverage of Sen's income aspect of underutilisation of labour) can be judged from the 1979 Labour Force Survey in Malaysia which used two definitions of unemployment, 'active' and 'inactive'. The actively unemployed are those who did not work during the reference period and were actively seeking work on the usual criteria. The inactively unemployed are those 'who were not looking for work because they believed no work was available, or if available they were not qualified, and those who would have looked for work if they had not been temporarily ill or had it not been for bad weather, and those who were waiting to report for work within thirty days from the date of interview, those waiting for answers to job applications and those who have looked for work prior to the reference week' (Report of the Labour Force Survey 1979 Department of Statistics, Kuala Lumpur: 16). The effect of this relaxation on urban, rural, male, female and overall unemployment rates in Peninsular Malaysia can be seen in Table 1.5. As can be seen, active unemployment rates as normally defined are extremely low by international standards in both urban and rural areas. Relaxation of the seeking-work criterion more than doubles the overall unemployment rate, with the most spectacular impact (as would be expected from the earlier analysis) on the rate for rural women.

Table 1.5 *The Effect of Relaxing the Seeking-Work Criterion, Peninsular Malaysia, 1979*

	Both Sexes	*Male*	*Female*
Active Unemployment Rates (%)			
Overall	2.2	2.2	2.2
Urban	3.0	2.9	3.3
Rural	1.7	1.8	1.7
Inactive Unemployment Rates (%)			
Overall	3.6	2.6	5.2
Urban	2.9	2.5	3.8
Rural	3.9	2.7	5.9
Total Unemployment Rates (%)			
Overall	5.7	4.8	7.4
Urban	6.0	5.4	7.1
Rural	5.6	4.5	7.5

Source: 1979 Labour Force Survey, Malaysia.

Relaxing the Not-Working Criterion

Another route towards a more useful definition of unemployment now being explored is that of relaxing the 'not-working' criterion. At their 1982 conference the labour statisticians gave official recognition (in resolution 1, paras 14–20) to the concept of 'visible underemployment' which includes 'all persons in paid or self-employment whether at work or not at work, involuntarily working less than the normal duration of work determined for the activity, who were seeking or available for additional work during the reference period'. On this definition, Squire (1981: 72) reports rates of visible underemployment of 2, 5 and 28 per cent for urban areas of Colombia, Tanzania and Chile respectively during the 1960s and early 1970s. This could be seen as expanding the area of overlap between the not-working and seeking-work circles or, if the seeking-work condition were also dropped, as increasing the number considered to be exposed to the income aspect of unemployment.

More in line with Sen's recognition aspect, which covers those who are working a full normal week while desperately looking for a 'real' job, is the statisticians' concept of 'invisible underemployment', 'characteristic symptoms' of which 'might be low income, under-utilisation of skill, low productivity'. It is reminiscent of the term 'disguised unemployment', used by Joan Robinson to describe the situation in Britain in the 1930s; the disguised unemployed were those individuals whose incomes, productivity and degree of skill utilisation were lower than they had been prior to the onset of the depression (Robinson 1937). In this case the norm with which the current situation was being compared was at least clear and realistic, even though the measurement problems can be seen to be formidable.

More recent work on invisible underemployment in developing countries has suffered from an absence of clear and realistic norms of the Robinson type. For instance, Squire (1981: 72) reports estimates of rates of invisible underemployment of between 14 and 60 per cent in a wide range of countries in the 1960s and early 1970s on varying definitions, including the following; those earning less than Ksh 200 per monthy (Kenya); those earning less than the 'considered absolute minimum' (El Salvador); those earning less than the official minimum wage (Brazil, Peru and Tanzania); and those working short hours or earning less than the official minimum wage and most unpaid family workers (Mexico). Tokman (1983: 154) suggests as an indicator of the intensity of underemployment the proportion of the economically active population represented by the self-employed and unpaid family members—estimated at 41 per cent in 1950 and 36 per cent in 1970 for Latin America as a whole.

Most ambitious of all is Hopkins' attempt to estimate the number of underemployed workers in developing countries, i.e. those 'who do not earn enough to provide either themselves or their families with an adequate standard of living because they are unable to find work of a sufficiently remunerative and productive nature' (Hopkins 1983: 473). He estimates the total number of such underemployed in developing countries (excluding China) at 448 million in 1982 (51 per cent of the total labour force), of whom 23 million were in middle-income Latin America (an 'underemployment rate' of 27 per cent), 11 million in low-income Latin America (29 per cent), 17 million in oil-producing Middle East and Africa (24 per cent), 294 million in Asia excluding China (57 per cent), 27 million in arid Africa (44 per cent), and 76 million in tropical Africa (91 per cent).

These figures are useful as an indicator of the relative extent of poverty in the different regions of the developing world. But as measures of under-utilisation of labour they must be in doubt. As already emphasised they do not measure the income aspect of unemployment, which covers those whose income *from work* is below a certain level. Nor do they measure the recognition aspect of unemployment, which covers those who are dissatisfied with the work that they are doing, to the extent of nor regarding it as real employment, and using it only as a base for job-seeking; income will be one of the factors influencing such attitudes, but only one and not necessarily the most important.

In short, the labour statisticians can be forgiven for describing invisible underemployment as 'primarily an analytical concept' not amenable to statistical measurement. This does not mean that it is not important. Indeed, as should already be obvious, it may be one of the main forms that under-utilisation of labour takes in countries without state social security systems, particularly in urban areas.

Measuring the Removable Labour Surplus

The third area in which the search for a more useful definition of under-utilisation of labour has been extended has been relatively well-trodden, although less so in more recent years than in the 1950s and 1960s. This is the pursuit of Sen's production aspect of under-utilisation through attempts to measure the removable labour surplus, usually in agriculture.

Nurkse (discussed fully in Chapter Seven) was one of the first to claim that in densely populated peasant economies 'the marginal productivity of labour over a wide range is zero' (Nurkse 1953: 33). As Sen has pointed out (1962: 13), this claim implies, if taken literally, that agriculturalists are applying their labour beyond the point that would be rational (assuming that work has some disutility). However, zero marginal productivity of *workers* rather than of *labour* is a more plausible possibility, as Sen's well-known diagram (reproduced here as Figure 1.4) shows. Any application of labour beyond point L_1, where marginal productivity of labour becomes zero, would not make sense, but extra *workers* could still be taken on; indeed, a constant number of labour hours might be applied by a continually increasing number of workers. Thus, in terms of Figure 1.4, if OP_1 workers, each working 'normal' hours $\frac{OL_1}{OP_1}$ could produce the current level of output but the actual number of workers is OP_2, each working shorter than normal hours $\frac{OL_1}{OP_2}$, then P_1 P_2 workers could be removed from agriculture without affecting output. In other words, over this range marginal productivity of workers is zero, as long as the strict *ceteris-paribus* assumption is relaxed to the extent that man-hours per worker in agriculture rise after surplus workers have been removed.

It might still be objected that the expenditure of effort by workers, however many there were, would cease well before marginal productivity of labour fell to zero—at the point, in fact, when the marginal productivity of labour was matched by the positive marginal disutility of effort. However, even if this were the case, the possibility of a 'zero-marginal-product' surplus of workers would still arise, as Sen has more recently pointed out (1975: 33-35). For instance, in Figure 1.4, if we merely shift the total product curve to the right, so that the

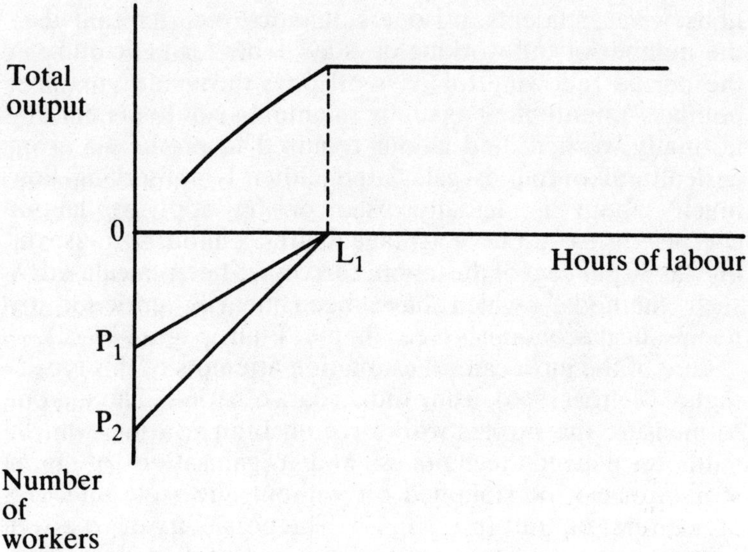

Figure 1.4: Zero Marginal Productivity of Labour and of Workers
Source: Sen (1962: 14)

dotted vertical line drawn from OL_1 cuts the curve at a point where it is still rising, the rest of our analysis is unaffected. Marginal productivity of labour is positive at this point but $P_1 P_2$ workers can still be removed from agriculture without affecting output as long as man-hours per worker are allowed to rise[5].

If further relaxations in the *ceteris-paribus* assumption were allowed, an even larger removable surplus of workers than $P_1 P_2$ would be implied. Indeed, the size of the surplus in any particular case would depend on the extent of the reorganisation of work practices and of use of additional fixed and variable capital that one considers likely and/or desirable as workers leave agriculture.

The usual method of measuring the removable labour surplus is broadly as follows. The surplus in man-hours is defined as the difference between labour avaiable and labour required where labour consists of the total agricultural population, less those too old or too young to work, housewives, students, prisoners, lunatics, etc., multiplied by the number of full working days available for agriculture in the period (allowing for days off on Sundays and national holidays!), multiplied again by the number of hours per day normally worked; and labour required to produce a given agricultural output is calculated either by observing how much labour is actually used or by applying labour coefficients to output or acreage figures. Labour surpluses as high as 30 per cent of the labour force have been calculated by such methods,[6] which have been heavily criticised by neoclassical economists (see Chapter Four, pages 110-12).

One of the most careful estimation attempts of this type is that of Mehra (1966), using Indian data of 1956-7. She sets out to measure the surplus workforce on Indian farms, 'which, with unchanged techniques and organisation of farm structure, can be siphoned off without adversely affecting agricultural output' (*op. cit:* 35). The possibility of an effect on non-agricultural output is recognised but not taken account of in the measurement method. The surplus is defined as 'the excess of actual over and above the required workforce on farms' and the number of required workers as 'that which is required at the peak time of agricultural operations'; the surplus, therefore, does not include seasonally unemployed workers.

Mehra avoids the problems of those who have used labour coefficients of various kinds to estimate requirements by, first of all, identifying farms on which surplus labour can be assumed not to exist. Given that 'there can be no surplus labour on a farm where at least one hired labourer is employed', Mehra suggests that this can be assumed about the farms in the largest size group, which have the highest ratio of hired to total labour force. The number of workers per acre in this group of farms is then used as the basis for calculating the required number of workers per acre in all farms, adjusting for differences in labour intensity per acre between farms of different sizes.

By this method Mehra estimates that in 1956/7, Indian agriculture was harbouring surplus labour representing between 6 and 29 per cent of its total workforce, depending on the view taken about the possibility of farm mergers or of exchanges of labour (to allow for the removal of fractions of working years). For India as a whole the mean ratio (between these two extremes) is 17 per cent and for some states it is almost 40 per cent. This suggests that, in addition to labour which is not utilised in off-seasons (not counted in this measure) there is a huge amount of surplus labour available for local work not involving geographical transfer (the 29 per cent maximum is the relevant figure here) and that, even for permanent work away from home, a smaller but still sizeable surplus of labour is available.[7].

'Available' is perhaps the wrong word to describe a labour surplus estimated by such a method, which implicitly assumes that all those working fewer hours or days than the norm do so involuntarily.[8] It is, in fact, labour *capacity* that is being measured by this method, not necessarily labour availability. As Sen puts it (1975: 132): 'for calculating the "availability" of a labour force to work outside their own farms, the production approach in itself is not sufficient, and one has to look into the income aspect and the recognition aspect. The recognition aspect influences a person's decision to seek or accept work elsewhere, and the income aspect is significant in the determination of the wage rate for such employment.' Thus, for an economy to fall into the 'unlimited-labour-supply' category described by Lewis (discussed in Chapter Five below), labour in the subsistence sector must not only be technically in surplus but must also be willing to move permanently to the capitalist sector at a given supply price.

We would agree, then, with Myrdal (1968: 2,059) that 'there is, and can be, no labour reserve *in abstracto*, independent of the time allowed, the foreseen changes and particular government policies'; and with Cumper (1954) that 'perhaps one shyould define one's categories of surplus afresh for each contemplated operation', since 'to persuade a village to apply its surplus labour, in the season of low labour demand in agriculture, to local public works is a very different proposition from persuading part of the farm labour force to remove to the towns to seek wage employment'. This makes measurement difficult. But that, again, does not render this aspect of under-utilisation of labour unimportant. The significant unused labour capacity in agriculture in a large part of the third world not only represents waste in countries that can ill afford it. It also represents a huge latent supply of labour to other sectors of the economy that is likely to become available at extremely low wages, with reverberations beyond the borders of the country concerned.[9]

UNEMPLOYMENT—DO OFFICIAL STATISTICS MEAN WHAT THEY PRETEND TO SAY?

Conceptual doubts about the standard definition of unemployment are compounded by doubts about measurement practice. How far do the unemployment statistics regularly published by governments give an accurate picture of the number of people who are both not working and seeking work and of the corresponding unemployment rates?[10]

There are important variations between countries in both definitions and instruments used. These include: the means of measurement, whether registrations at employment offices or labour force surveys; the base for the unemployment rate, whether the total labour force or only the civilian or waged and salaried labour force; the duration of the reference period; and whether or not the following categories are included in the unemployed—the laid-off, the not actively seeking work, the temporarily ill, students seeking work, those who did some work in the reference period but are looking for more, and unpaid family members working less than fifteen hours in a week.

Of the major industrialised economies the United States and Japan get closest to the ILO definition. Divergences from that definition raised huge problems of non-comparability of national statistics in the mid-1970s. In 1976, for instance, official national figures overstated the West German unemployment rate by as much as 24 per cent and understated the British rate by 12½ per cent. Since then the deterioration in labour markets has brought some convergence of national and standardised rates. In 1983 the Japanese, Italian and Swedish rates of unemployment, according to national definitions and means of measurement, were the same as the internationally standardised rates for those countries. The national rates for the USA, West Germany, France, Canada and Australia were slightly higher than the standardised rates. Only the UK, of the major OECD countries, remains widely out of line with international practice. Partly as a result of a change in its measurement practice in November 1982, since when only those claiming benefit have been counted as unemployed (see page 23), its national rate of 11.6 per cent in 1983 was equivalent to an internationally standardised rate of 13.1 per cent. In other words, national statistics still understate the UK's unemployment problem relative to other countries by almost 12 per cent.

Within each country the normally lively controversy about the validity of official unemployment statistics has tended to increase in intensity as unemployment has risen. For instance, in Britain official unemployment data (which, as has been seen, underestimate the extent of the problem by international standards) have come in for strong criticism in recent years. This has come both from those who argue that they exaggerate the situation because they include people who are not genuinely seeking work or who are 'unemployable' *and* from those who claim that they understate the number of 'real unemployed' by omitting those who do not register although seeking work. Garside (1980) has carefully reviewed the arguments on both sides.

Those who feel that the statistics, derived from a count of the registered unemployed in individual employment exchange areas on a particular day each month, include persons who ought to be excluded focus on categories such as the short-term unemployed, the unemployable, the disabled, fraudulent claimants and the voluntarily unemployed. As Garside points out (ibid: 72–80), there are problems in trying to exclude any of these categories.

Even if it were agreed that those who were not so much unemployed as between jobs should be excluded how could they be identified? 'In the absence of a method of distinguishing *ex ante* which individuals will be unemployed for a given period of time, . . . revising the aggregate unemployment figures according to a strict and formal definition of frictional unemployment [such as excluding those unemployed for less than four weeks as suggested by the Centre for Policy Studies] could be seriously misleading' (Garside: 75).

The argument for excluding school leavers is even weaker. If they are counted as part of the labour force when they find jobs, they should surely be counted as unemployed if they fail (Hughes 1975: 322).

The superficially attractive case for excluding the 'unemployable' founders on the impossibility of defining the category independently of the state of the labour market. 'It would be foolish to attempt to distinguish a "unemployable" group within the unemployment register if only because so many of them, though out of work at particular times, may well be employed as the pressure of aggregate demand increases . . . The "hard core" of the unemployed is noticeably soft at the edges' (Garside: 77).

Exclusion of the severely handicapped disabled would be possible only if they could be identified separately, which would be as difficult in principle and practice (raising the same problems as the identification of the unemployable) as it would be distasteful.

The call for the exclusion of fraudulent claimants is based on a probable overestimate of their numbers (surveys suggest that they account for less than 3 per cent of those receiving benefit). In any case to claim fraudulently should not necessarily disqualify one from classification as unemployed.

Finally, the attempt to exclude those who are not 'genuinely' seeking work is also problematic. All those who abstain from an active search for a job are not necessarily unavailable for work. Indeed, the returns to active job searching are likely to vary with the trade cycle.

The argument that the count excludes persons who ought to be included is, on the whole, more convincing. Garside identifies seven groups of people who 'by reason of their temporary or tenuous attachment to the labour force create problems of measurement by not registering as unemployed when out of work' (ibid: 84). These include: (a) married women who are not eligible for unemployment benefit; (b) occupational pensioners who do not claim unemployment benefit; (c) persons above normal retirement age who nevertheless seek work to supplement their income; (d) those who are disqualified for one reason or another from claiming unemployment benefit; (e) widows, young entrants to the labour force and the self-employed; (f) short-time employees or those working temporarily at tasks that do not use their skills fully; (g) the 'hidden labour reserve'—those people, mainly married women, who would enter the labour market if appropriate employment opportunities were available. In addition, some professional, semi-professional and skilled workers may not register because they feel either that it is below their dignity or that it would not help them to find a job.

The scale of such non-registration can be estimated by comparing employment exchange registration statistics with census and survey data. In the British case it is estimated by comparison with the census that there was 13 per cent underregistration of males and 67 per cent underregistration of females in March 1971 (Garside: 91).

The extent to which British statisics underestimate actual (internationally-defined) unemployment was increased in November 1982, since when only those claiming benefit have been counted as unemployed. The official estimate is that this makes a difference of between 170,000 and 190,000 to the number counted as unemployed and of about half a percentage point to the unemployment rate (see the Treasury's Economic Progress Report, December 1982). As already emphasised, this takes Britain further away from the international definition according to which, as Garside had commented earlier in a different context, 'it is doubtful . . . whether the receipt of payments to which an individual is entitled is a sufficient basis on which to judge his or her right to be included in the unemployment figures' (ibid: 79).

INTERNATIONALISATION OF THE LABOUR MARKET

While unemployment and under-utilisation of labour have been increasing, the global context in which this has occurred has also been changing. The capitalist world has, in the last few decades, become, in an important sense, a single labour market.

This is partly a matter of the movement of labour across international frontiers. The stock of economically active migrants (i.e. non-citizens of their countries of residence) has been estimated minimally at between 20 million and 22 million in 1980.[11] This is a low figure in relation to the world's labour force but high in relation to that of some labour-importing and some labour-exporting countries, and significant for the evidence it gives of the willingness of employers in high-wage economies to make use, when they need to, of migrant workers from low-wage economies.

Quantitatively, the most important destinations for migrants in search of employment are North America, Western Europe, South America and the Arab region. There are between 5 and 6½ million active foreigners in the United States of whom between 2½ and 4 million (perhaps half of them from Mexico) are 'in an irregular situation'. Western Europe, as Table 1.6 shows, contains at least as many migrant workers as does the US, but the 1980 figure represents a 16 per cent fall from the 1973 peak of 7½ million (which had reflected a phenomenal annual average rate of increase of 14 per cent over the previous fourteen years). Switzerland, where foreigners account for more than 20 per cent of the active population, is still particularly reliant on migrant workers, while about 11 per cent of Portugal's economically active population is in other countries of Western Europe. The number of migrant workers in South America is larger than is generally realised—between 3½ and 4 million, with countries such as Bolivia and Paraguay exporting a huge proportion of their working populations and Argentina and Venezuela the major labour-importers. The most dynamic destination in recent years, however, is the Arab region, where the number of migrant workers in 1980, as Table 1.7 shows, was 2.8 million (90 per cent of them from developing countries) compared with only a few hundred thousand fifteen years earlier. The region contains some of the most migrant-intensive labour markets, such as Kuwait and the United Arab Emirates, with 69 and 85 per cent of non-nationals in their respective workforces in 1975. The picture is completed by the 300,000 or so foreign workers in south Africa, on which Botswana (with a quarter of its national

Table 1.6 Selected Western European Countries: Recorded Number of Migrant Workers in 1980 (in thousands)

	In-migration country									
Out-migration country	*Austria*	*Belgium*	*France*[a]	*Germany (Fed.) Rep.)*	*Luxembourg*	*Netherlands*	*Sweden*	*Switzerland*	*United Kingdom*[b]	*Total*
Algeria	—	3.2	322.7	1.6	—	—	—	—	—	327.5
Finland	—	—	—	3.7	—	—	108.0	—	1.0	112.7
France	—	38.5	—	54.0	8.5	2.0	—	—	14.0	117.2
Greece	—	10.8	3.0	138.4	—	1.2	7.5	—	6.0	166.9
Italy	—	90.5	146.4	324.3	11.2	12.0	—	301.0	73.0	958.4
Morocco	—	37.3	116.1	16.6	—	33.7	—	—	—	203.7
Portugal	—	6.3	430.6	59.9	13.7	4.2	—	—	5.0	519.7
Spain	—	32.0	157.7	89.3	2.3	10.4	—	85.7	17.0	394.4
Tunisia	—	4.7	65.3	—	—	1.1	—	—	—	71.1
Turkey	28.2	23.0	20.6	623.9	—	53.2	—	20.1	4.0	773.0
Yugoslavia	115.3	3.1	32.2	367.0	0.6	6.6	24.0	62.5	5.0	616.2
Other	31.3	83.2	192.4	490.1	15.6	70.2	94.6	237.0	804.0	2,018.4
Total	174.7	332.6	1,487.0	2,168.8	51.9	194.6	234.1	706.3	929.0	6,279.0

Dashes indicate: No migrants recorded or estimated, magnitude less than 500, or not applicable.
[a] October 1980, estimated by INSEE on the basis of its 1980 employment survey, which underestimates by several hundred thousand categories such as small-scale employers, home-based workers and workers living at construction sites.
[b] May-June 1979, estimated by the Department of Employment on the basis of its 1979 labour force survey.
Source: ILO, *World Labour Report* 1, 1984.

Table 1.7 Arab Region: Estimated Number of Migrant Workers in 1980 (actual figures)

	In-migration country										
Out-migration country	*Bahrain*	*Jordan (excl. Palestine)*	*Iraq*	*Kuwait*	*Libyan Arab Jamahiriya*	*Oman*	*Qatar*	*Saudi Arabia*	*United Arab Emirates*	*Yemen*	*Total*
Democratic Yemen	1,125	—	—	9,500	—	120	1,500	65,000	6,600	—	83,845
Egypt	2,800	68,500	100,000	85,000	250,000	6,300	5,750	155,100	18,200	4,000	695,650
India	12,300	500	2,000	45,000	32,000	35,600	11,850	29,700	109,500	2,000	280,450
Iraq	310	—	—	40,000	—	—	—	3,250	1,200	—	44,760
Jordan (incl. Palestine)	1,400	—	7,500	55,000	15,000	2,250	7,800	140,000	19,400	2,000	250,350
Lebanon	300	—	4,500	8,000	5,700	1,500	750	33,200	6,600	500	61,050
Oman	900	—	—	2,000	—	—	1,150	10,000	19,400	—	33,450
Pakistan	26,160	4,000	7,500	34,000	65,000	44,500	20,770	29,700	137,000	3,000	371,630
Somalia	—	—	—	500	5,000	400	—	8,300	5,000	500	19,700
Sudan	900	—	500	5,500	21,000	620	750	55,600	2,100	2,250	89,220
Syrian Arab Republic	150	—	—	35,000	15,000	600	1,000	24,600	5,800	1,000	83,150
Yemen	1,125	—	—	3,000	—	120	1,500	325,000	5,400	—	336,145
Other Arab	—	—	—	300	65,600	120	—	500	—	—	66,520
Other Asian	10,000	1,000	1,500	10,000	27,000	—	4,500	93,500	30,700	300	168,500
Other	10,250	2,000	2,000	45,900	44,200	4,670	22,930	49,800	54,100	1,450	237,300
Total	67,720	76,000	125,500	378,700	545,500	96,800	80,250	1,023,250	411,000	17,000	2,821,720

Dashes indicate: No migrants recorded or estimated, magnitude less than 500, or not applicable.
Note that this table neglects a small number of migrant workers about whom data are practically nonexistent such as Sudanese in Egypt, Syrians in Lebanon, West Africans in the Sudan and Turks in Syria.
Source: ILO, *World Labour Report 1*, 1984.

modern-sector employees working across the border) and Lesotho (with four-fifths) are particularly dependent; and by the 1.3 million or so migrant workers in West Africa, where a long tradition of crossing borders in search of work has been complicated in recent years by Nigeria's oil boom and by political upheavals.

The second aspect of the internationalisation of the labour market in recent decades, perhaps more important, is the fact that industrial production for the world market has begun to be located on an increasing scale in developing countries which previously produced only primary commodities for the world market. The impact of this can be illustrated in various ways. Table 1.8, for instance, shows the very high rates of increase in the volume of exports of manufactured goods achieved by developing countries since 1965.

An alternative illustration is in terms of the share of developing countries in world exports of manufactured goods. This has risen from negligible levels in the 1950s and 1960s to 5 per cent in 1970, just over 6 per cent in 1975, around 8 per cent in 1980 and perhaps 9 per cent in the mid-1980s. The share of developing-country exports in the consumption of a range of selected manufactured goods in industrial countries doubled between 1970 and 1980, as Table 1.9 shows.

These proportions are lower than might be expected from

Table 1.8 Annual Average Rates of Increase in Exports of Manufactured Goods by Developing Countries, 1965–1985 (%)

	1965–73	*1973–80*	*1980–85*[a]
All developing countries	14.9	10.6	8.1
Low-income	6.4	6.9	8.2
Asia	6.6	7.4	8.5
Africa	4.5	0.5	0.9
Middle-income			
Oil importers	18.2	11.5	8.1
Major exporters of m/f	18.6	12.1	8.4
other	15.6	7.1	5.0
Oil exporters	12.7	7.9	7.4

[a]includes projections beyond 1982.
Source: World Bank, *World Development Report*, 1984.

some alarmist talk in industrialised countries about unfair competition from low-wage economies. The extent of their penetration of such markets, shown in Table 1.9, is rightly described by the World Bank as 'trivial' (World Bank 1983: 13). The rate of increase in third-world manufactured exports is, as Table 1.8 shows, slowing down. Moreover, the increase in world market shares is mainly attributable to a relatively small number of countries, particularly the 'Four Little Tigers' (South Korea, Taiwan, Singapore and Hong Kong, responsible for more than half of developing countries' manufactured exports) and Brazil. The trend has almost completely passed by some areas of the developing world, notably low-income Africa. And, although some third-world exporters are moving into more technology-intensive products (for instance, South Korea into heavy engineering, Singapore into precision engineering), the majority of such exports still consists of cheap labour-intensive clothing, footwear and leather products—the only goods, as Table 1.9 shows, to have made major inroads into industrial-country markets.

Nevertheless, it must be recognised that the capacity to export jobs from high-wage to low-wage economies has increased substantially and now affects a wide range of industries. This, along with the capacity of employers in high-wage economies, already discussed, to make use, when they need to, of migrant workers from low-wage economies, means that, in an important sense, the capitalist world can now be regarded as a single labour market. The sense in which this is and is not so has to be carefully defined. Freedom of movement of goods and, even more so, of people is, of course, heavily circumscribed. The world is not a single labour market in the sense that the United States or even the European Economic Community is. But the degree of actual and potential competition between labour in high and low-wage economies and the extent of employers' awareness of the benefits to them of this competition are now such that national labour organisations can no longer plan their strategies on the assumption that each is operating in a separate national labour market (see Chapter Nine for further discussion).

Table 1.9 Share of Developing-Country Exports in the Consumption of Selected Manufactured Goods in Industrial Countries, 1970–80 (%)

	1970	1980
Food	3.5	3.7
Clothing, textiles and footwear	3.1	10.5
Clothing	4.0	16.3
Textiles	2.3	5.4
Footwear	2.6	16.3
Leather products	6.2	17.3
Wood products	1.9	3.6
Paper	0.2	0.5
Chemicals	2.0	3.8
Non metallic minerals	0.3	1.1
Base metals	3.5	4.1
Machinery	0.4	2.1
Cutlery and handtools	0.8	3.3
Metal furniture	0.6	1.6
Radios, televisions, etc.	1.1	6.7
Other	4.0	8.0
Total	1.7	3.4

Source: World Bank, *World Development Report*, 1983.

CONCLUSIONS

As usual the world has changed faster than the economic theories that are supposed to explain it. Theorising about the nature, causes and consequences of unemployment and under-utilisation of labour is still kept largely in two separate compartments—short-run for mature capitalist economies, long-run for underdeveloped economies—and is still usually conducted at a national rather than global level. Adaptations of theory to the new scale and structure of unemployment and under-utilisation of labour in industrialised and developing economies have so far been inadequate. The time is obviously ripe, in the face of such changes, for a rethinking of unemployment theory. Such an effort has to be based, however, on a review and critique of what has gone before. The question to be pursued in the rest of this book is whether, out of the wreckage of the theories of the classicals, neo-classicals, Keynesians, development economists, Marxists and neo-Marxists (reviewed in Chapters Two to Eight), anything can be salvaged which can help chart new directions in a rapidly changing world.

NOTES

1. To be counted as 'not working' one usually has to have worked for less than one hour per day during the reference period.
2. The 'not working' in this instance would have to exclude those who are engaged full-time in unpaid housework, etc. on the grounds that they have no time available to increase their income from paid work.
3. Lipton's 'unemployment' is not that of the international standard definition but approximates, rather, to Sen's income aspect.
4. For a comprehensive review of concepts and measures *see* Standing (1978).
5. *See* Sen (1975: 23–28 and 33–35) for a more elaborate algebraic model from which this result can also be derived.
6. *See* Godfrey (1967) for further discussion of this measurement approach. The method is usually applied to third-world agriculture. *See* Maddison (1983), however, for an analogous approach to the measurement of 'labour slack' in industrialised economies.
7. *See* Sen (1975: 127–131) for a full discussion of Mehra's calculations.
8. It also assumes that labour is homogeneous (i.e. not specific to a certain time of year, month, week or day nor to a certain individual or class of individuals).
9. *See* pp. 125-53 for further discussion.
19. For a fuller discussion of these issues as they relate to the US and Britain, *see* Hughes and Perlman (1984: 1–24).
11. This is a minimum estimate, which excludes: the stock of non-immigrant workers in the US; active foreigners in Australia, Canada and New Zealand; irregular and undocumented workers in Western Europe and other countries. In the words of the ILO World Labour Report (1984: 101), 'whether the global stock of migrant workers is nearer 25 than 30 million must remain a matter of speculation'.

2 Classical Theories of Surplus Population

Ironically the economists of the eighteenth and nineteenth centuries seem in many ways better equipped to analyse the global unemployment of the nineteen eighties than many of those alive today. This is so in two important respects. In the first place, the classical economists were *political* economists, who put social institutions and social relations at the centre of their analysis. 'For the classical economists, and especially for Marx, the study of Political Economy and the analysis of exchange-value necessarily started from those socio-economic conditions that shaped the class relations of society' (Dobb 1973: 31). This meant also that, at least implicitly, they had a theory of the state; the interests and actions of government were endogenous to their analysis, not something standing outside it. Secondly, they were concerned with the long-period questions of growth and development, and so their analysis of the causes of unemployment was essentially long-period, bound up with the relationship betwen the available labour force and an economy's productive capacity. Whatever the verdict on individual theorists, in at least these two respects the classical approach looks potentially relevant to the present-day employment problems not only of underdeveloped economies (to which its relevance has long been recognised, see Chapter Five) but also of industrialised economies.

As far as the short period is concerned, most[1] classical economists accepted Say's law that supply creates its own demand. Indeed, John Stuart Mill (1848, ch. xiv,, para 2) provides the clearest statement of the doctrine:

> What constitutes the means of payment for commodities is simply commodities. Each person's means of paying for the productions of other people consist of those which he himself possesses. All sellers are inevitably, and by the meaning of the word buyers. Could we suddenly double the productive powers of the country, we should double the supply

> of commodities in every market; but we should, by the same stroke, double the purchasing power. Everybody would bring a double demand as well as supply; everybody would be able to buy twice as much, because everyone would have twice as much to offer in exchange.

Thus unemployment due to a deficiency of effective demand was impossible.

ADAM SMITH (1723–1790)

Adam Smith put forward a 'subsistence wage' theory of the supply of labour and a 'wage fund' theory of the demand for labour. On the supply side, 'every species of animals naturally multiplies in proportion to the means of their subsistence, and no species can ever multiply beyond it' (Smith 1776: 182). Thus there is a strong connection between the demand for labour and its supply. If the reward of labour is 'liberal', this encourages an increase in population and hence labour supply; if multiplication is excessive, the wage falls and so does the rate of increase of labour supply (probably through an increase in child mortality). 'The demand for men, like that for any other commodity necessarily regulates the production of men; quickens it when it goes on too slowly, and stops it when it it advances too fast' (*ibid*: 183). The demand for labour depends on 'the funds which are destined for the payment of wages', which are of two kinds: 'first, the revenue which is over and above what is necessary for the maintenance; and secondly, the stock which is over and above what is necessary for the employment of their masters' (*ibid*: 171).

Thus, since the rate of change in the demand for labour depends on the rate at which a nation's wealth and therefore its surplus revenue and surplus stock are changing and since labour supply responds with an inevitable lag to changes on the demand side, 'scarcity of employment' is quite possible in the long period. Smith illustrates this by distinguishing between countries with increasing, stationary and declining national wealth. His prime example of the first category is North America, where population doubles in twenty or twenty-five years but 'the demand for labourers, the funds destined for maintaining them, increase, it seems, still faster than they can find labourers to employ' (1776: 173). In a stationary state, on the other hand:

> . . . the funds destined for the payment of wages, the revenue and stock of its inhabitants, may be of the greatest extent; but if they have continued for several centuries of the same or very nearly of the same extent, the number of labourers employed every year could easily supply, and even more than supply, the number wanted the following year. There could seldom be any scarcity of hands, nor could the masters be obliged to bid against one another in order to get them. The hands, on the contrary, could in this case, naturally multiply beyond their employment. There would be a constant scarcity of employment, and the labourers would be obliged to bid against one another in order to get it. If in such a country the wages of labour had ever been more than sufficient to maintain such a labourer, and to enable him to bring up a family, the competition of the labourers, and the interest of the masters would soon reduce them to this lowest rate which is consistent with common humanity' (*ibid.*: 174).

China is Smith's example of a country in such a stationary state, with wages having fallen until labour could be fully absorbed, even at a bare subsistence level.

> Marco Polo, who visited more than five hundred years ago, describes its cultivation, undustry and populousness, almost in the same terms in which they are described by travellers in the present times . . . The accounts of all travellers, inconsistent in many other respects, agree in the low wages of labour, and in the difficulty which a labourer finds in bringing up a family in China . . . The poverty of the lower ranks of people in China far surpasses that of the most beggarly nations in Europe . . . Marriage is encouraged in China, not by the profitableness of children, but by the liberty of destroying them . . . China, however, though it may perhaps stand still, does not seem to go backwards . . . The lowest class of labourers, therefore, notwithstanding their scanty subsistence, must some way or another make shift to continue their race so far as to keep up their usual numbers (*ibid.*: 174–5).

Should such stagnation give way to decline, however, with 'the funds destined for the maintenance of labour . . . sensibly decaying', the situation would be far worse.

> Every year the demand for servants and labourers would, in all the different classes of employments, be less than it had been the year before. Many who had been bred in the superior classes, not being able to find employment in their own business, would be glad to seek it in the lowest. The lowest class being not only overstocked with its own workmen, but with the

overflowings of all the other classes, the competition for employment would be so great in it, as to reduce the wages of labour to the most miserable and scanty subsistence of the labourer. Many would not be able to find employment even upon these terms, but woud either starve, or be driven to seek a subsistence either by begging or by the perpetration perhaps of the greatest enormities. *Want, famine and mortality would immediately prevail in that class and from then extend themselves to all the superior classes, until the number of inhabitants in the country was reduced*[2] to what could easily be maintained by the revenue and stock which remained in it, and which had escaped either the tyranny or calamity which had destroyed the rest. This perhaps is nearly the present state of Bengal and of some other of the English settlements in the East Indies' (*ibid.*: 175–6).

The long-run tendency, then, is towards a dynamic equilibrium in which the wage is such as to match exactly the rate of change of labour supply to the rate of change of demand for labour. This is consistent with any of the three states described by Smith—progressive (North American), stationary (Chinese) or declining (Bengali). Unemployment is a disequilibrium phenomenon in this model but one which could persist for a long time.

The mechanism of Smith's theory is brutal but his vision is not inherently gloomy. At least by implication his emphasis on the role of accumulation and growth suggests that it is in principle possible for a country to move from a declining to a stationary to a progressive state, with beneficial consequences for the demand for labourers, whatever its population/land ratio.

THOMAS MALTHUS (1766–1834)

Malthus, in contrast, closes all doors to hope by elevating what was for Smith a particular case to the status of an eternal law. Taking as unchallengeable postulates the necessity of food and of passion between the sexes, he points to the 'constant tendency' of population 'to increase beyond the means of subsistence' (Malthus 1826: 3). A review of the evidence from a wide range of societies leads him to pronounce 'that population, when unchecked goes on doubling itself every twenty-five years, or increases in geometrical ratio' (*ibid.*: 4). On the other hand, 'considering the present average state of the earth, the means of subsistence, under circumstances the most favourable to human industry, could not possibly be made to increase faster than in an arithmetical ratio' (*ibid.*: 6). The produce of the earth 'may increase for ever and be greater than any assignable quantity; yet still the power of population being in every period so much superior, the increase of the human species can only be kept down to the level of the means of subsistence by the constant operation of the strong law of necessity, acting as a check upon the greater power' (*ibid.*: 7). In the absence of moral restraint or of 'promiscuous intercourse, unnatural passions, violations of the marriage bed, and improper arts to conceal the consequences of irregular connexions, . . . preventive checks that clearly come under the head of vice' (*ibid.*: 9) the ultimate check is provided by shortage of food.

> As, by that law of our nature which makes food necessary to the life of man, population can never actually increase beyond the lowest nourishment capable of supporting it, a strong check on population, from the difficulty of acquiring food, must be constantly in operation. This difficulty must fall somewhere, and must necessarily be severely felt in some or other of the various forms of misery, or the fear of misery, by a large portion of mankind (*ibid.* p.3).

Malthus' emphasis on the difficulties of expanding food supplies leads him to question the extent to which an increase in Smith's national wealth would contribute to a real wage increase or to the maintenance of additional labour. Accumulation, he suggests (*ibid.*: 415–18), by increasing the nominal price of labour, would lead to a proportional rise in food prices, a tendency which would be offset only very slowly by the attraction of additional capital into agriculture and only in exceptional circumstances by the possibility of importing sufficient food. Thus an attempt by China to move out of its stationary state would not necessarily be to the advantage of its labouring classes.

> At present the country appears to be over-peopled compared with what its stock can employ, and no labour is spared in the production of food. An immense capital could not be employed in China in preparing manufactures for foreign trade without altering this state of things, and taking off some

> labourers from agriculture, which might have a tendency to diminish the produce of the country. Allowing, however, that this would be made up, and, indeed, more than made up, by the beneficial effects of improved skill and economy of labour in the cultivation of the poorest lands, yet, as the quantity of subsistence could be but little increased the demand for manufactures, which would raise the price of labour, would necessarily be followed by a proportionate rise in the price of provisions, and the labourer would be able to command but little more food than before. The country would, however, obviously be advancing in wealth; the exchangeable value of the annual produce of its land and labour would be annually augumented; yet the real funds for the maintenance of labour would be nearly stationary . . . it must be allowed then, that the funds for the maintenance of labour do not *necessarily* increase with the increase of wealth, and very *rarely* increase in *proportion* to it (*ibid.*: 418–19).

Thus for Malthus the prospect is one of constant alternation between Smithian stationary and declining states, with little likelihood of any, even temporary, periods of labour scarcity—a miserable vision indeed.

DAVID RICARDO (1772–1823)

Ricardo was marginally more hopeful than Malthus, taking over the substance of his surplus population theory[3] but allowing for the possibility of wages exceeding the bare minimum of subsistence and placing more emphasis on the accumulation of capital as 'the means of employing labour' (1821: 55).

On the supply side of the labour market he assumes an infinitely elastic supply of labour at what he calls the 'natural price' of labour, defined as 'that price which is necessary to enable the labourers, one with another, to subsist and to perpetuate their race, without either increase or diminution' (*ibid.*: 52). The natural price of labour thus depends on its cost of production, that is, on 'the price of the food, necessaries, and conveniences required for the support of the labourer and his family'. The tendency of the market price of labour to conform to its natural long-run price, however, does not mean that wages can never rise over the long period.

> It is not to be understood that the natural price of labour, estimated even in food and necessaries, is absolutely fixed and constant. It varies at different

times in the same country, and very materially differs in different countries. It essentially depends on the habits and customs of the people. . . Many of the conveniences now enjoyed in an English cottage would have been thought luxuries at an earlier period of our history (*ibid.*: 54–55).

On the demand side Ricardo's crucial assumption is of diminishing returns in agriculture, which implies downward-sloping and therefore separate average and marginal productivity-of-labour curves, as in Kaldor's neat diagrammatic summary of the Ricardian analysis in Figure 2.1. Quantities of corn (representing all agricultural produce) are measured along the *Y*-axis and quantities of labour along the *X*-axis. PA_p is the average productivity of labour curve and PM_p the marginal productivity of labour curve.[4] Since an unlimited supply of labour is available at the wage OW, the

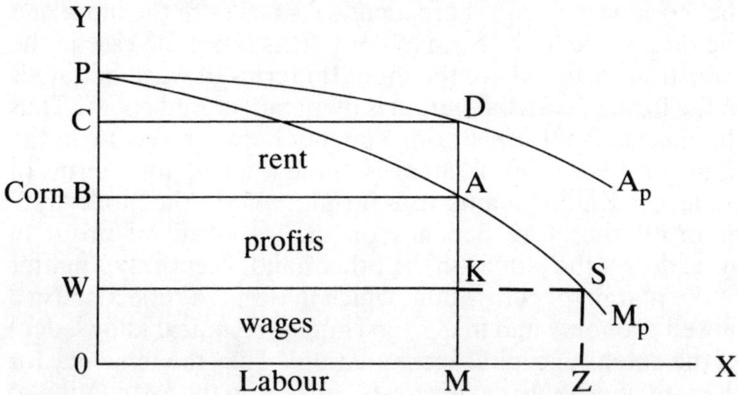

Figure 2.1: The Agricultural Sector in Ricardo's Model
Source: Kaldor (1955)

number of labourers employed depends on the size of the wages fund available; in this case it is OWKM, enough to employ OM workers. This means that the total output of corn is OCDM. Since rent is the difference between the product of labour on marginal land and the product of average land (represented in Figure 2.1 by BCDA) profits (out of which accumulation is financed) are determined as a residual, WBAK in this case. Increases in the wages fund and therefore in employment and output progressively squeeze profits between wages and rising rent until ultimately (when OZ workers are employed in Figure 2.1) they disappear altogether. The Ricardian stationary state is reached when accumulation and growth cease because 'profits are so low as not to afford (the capitalists) an adequate compensation for their trouble, and the risk which they must necessarily encounter in employing their capital productively' (*ibid.*: 73). The tendency of profits to fall can be arrested only by technical progress, which shifts the average and marginal productivity curves to the right.

The introduction of a second (industrial) sector does not affect the results of the analysis. In equilibrium the money rate of profit earned on capital must be the same in agriculture and in industry; otherwise capital would move between sectors. In the agricultural sector the money rate of profit and the 'corn' rate of profit are identical since both the input and the output are in the form of corn. This is not the case in the industrial sector where the input (in terms of wage outlay) is in the form of corn but output is of manufactured goods. Thus the mechanism for restoring equality between sectors in the money rate of profit is changes in the inter-sectoral terms of trade. As Kaldor summarises it (*ibid.*: 355), 'the money rate of profit therefore depends on the corn-rate of profit in agriculture, the latter, on the other hand, is entirely a matter of the margin of cultivation, which in turn is a reflection (in a closed economy and in a given state of technical knowledge) of the extent of capital accumulation'. Thus the tendency for the rate of profit to decline rests entirely on the assumption of diminishing returns in agriculture.

Whether or not unemployment emerges at any point in this process depends on the relationship between the rate of increase of population and of labour supply, on the one hand, and that of the wages fund on the other. Here, unlike Malthus, Ricardo distinguishes between different countries or different stages of society. 'When there is an abundance of fertile land . . . accumulation is often so rapid that labourers cannot be supplied with the same rapidity as capital,' in which case 'the demand for labour would increase still faster than the supply'. However, 'in proportion as these countries become populous, and land of a worse quality is taken into cultivation, the tendency to an increase of capital diminishes'. Soon 'population increases faster than the funds required for its support. Every exertion of industry, unless accompanied by a diminished rate of increase in the population, will add to the evil, for production cannot keep pace with it. With a population pressing against the means of subsistence, the only remedies are either a reduction of people or a more rapid accumulation of capital'. But in countries 'where all the fertile land is already cultivated, the latter remedy is neither very practicable nor very desirable, because its effect would be, if pushed very far, to render all classes equally poor' (*ibid.*: 56).

In short, in countries with an abundance of fertile land, accumulation *could* relieve the pressure of population against the means of subsistence and of employment, but in countries where all the fertile land was already cultivated the harsh Malthusian logic would apply and a reduction in the number of people would be the only remedy. 'It is a truth which admits not a doubt that the comforts and well-being of the poor cannot be permanently secured without some regard on their part, or some effort on the part of the legislature, to regulate the increase of their numbers, and to render less frequent among them early and improvident marriages' (*ibid.*: 61).

KARL MARX (1818–1883)

The British classical economists discussed so far were interested in *absolute* surplus population and saw endogenous variations in birth and death rates as the mechanism through which the supply of labour adjusts to changes on the demand side. They also tended to emphasis the pressure of population against the means of subsistence rather than against the means of employment. Marx focuses more directly on the labour market, with emphasis on *relative* surplus population pressing against the means of *employment*. Indeed, he pours scorn on the 'beautiful law which pretends to make the action of capital dependent on the absolute variation of the population'. According to this 'dogma of the economists', as he describes it:

wages rise in consequence of accumulation of capital. The higher wages stimulate the working population to more rapid multiplication, and this goes on until the labour market becomes too full, and therefore capital, relatively to the supply of labour, becomes insufficient. Wages fall, and now we have the reverse of the medal. The working population is little by little decimated as the result of the fall in wages, so that capital is again in excess relatively to them, or, as others explain it, falling wages and the corresponding increase in the exploitation of the labourer again accelerates accumulation, whilst at the same time, the lower wages hold the increase of the working-class in check. Then comes again the time when the supply of labour is less than the demand, wages rise, and so on. A beautiful mode of motion this for developed capitalist production! Before, in consequence of the rise of wages, any positive increase of the population really fit for work could occur, the time would have been passed again and again, during which the industrial campaign must have been carried through, the battle fought and won (Marx 1867 I, xxv.3: 597).

He is particularly opposed to Malthus' attempt to posit surplus population as an eternal law rather than a condition specific to bourgeois society:

The labouring population . . . produces, along with the accumulation of capital produced by it, the means by which it itself is made relatively superfluous, is turned into a relative surplus population; and it does this to an always increasing extent. This is a law of population peculiar to the capitalist mode of production; and in fact every special historic mode of production has its own special laws of population, historically valid within its limits alone. An abstract law of population exists for plants and animals only; and only in so far as man has not interfered with them (*ibid.*: 591–2).

Relative surplus population, according to Marx, emerges from the process of accumulation and the associated progressive qualitative change in the composition of capital (or, in terms more familiar to development economists, increasing capital-intensity):

Increasing accumulation and centralisation becomes a source of new changes in the composition of capital, of a more accelerated diminution of its variable, as compared with its constant constituent. This accelerated relative diminution of the variable constituent, that goes along with the accelerated increase of the total capital, and moves more rapidly than this increase, takes the inverse form at the other pole, of an apparently absolute increase of the labouring population, an increase always moving more rapidly than that of the variable capital or the means of employment. But in fact, it is capitalistic accumulation itself that constantly produces, and produces in the direct ratio of its own energy and extent, a relatively redundant population of labourers, i.e. a population of greater extent than suffices for the average needs of the self-expansion of capital, and therefore a surplus-population (*ibid.*: 590).

At the same time as emerging from the process of accumulation and technical change this surplus population is functional to further accumulation:

But if a surplus labouring population is a necessary product of accumulation or of the wealth on a capitalist basis, this surplus-population becomes, conversely, the lever of capitalistic accumulation, nay, a condition of existence of the capitalist mode of production. It forms a disposable industrial reserve army, that belongs to capital quite as absolutely as if the latter had bred it at its own cost (*ibid.*: 592).

The functionality of the reserve army is two-fold. On the one hand it is literally in reserve, ready for action in expansionary phases of the cycle:

With accumulation, and the development of the productiveness of labour that accompanies it, the power of sudden expansion of capital grows also. . . The mass of social wealth, overflowing with the advance of accumulation and transformable into additional capital, thrusts itself frantically into old branches of production, whose market suddenly expands, or into newly formed branches, such as railways, etc., the need for which grows out of the development of the old ones. In all such cases, there must be the possibility of throwing great masses of men suddenly on the decisive points without injury to the scale of production in other spheres. Over-population supplies these masses. The course characteristic of modern industry, viz., a decennial cycle (interrupted by smaller oscillations), of periods of average activity, production at high pressure, crisis and stagnation, depends on the constant formation, the greater or less absorption, and the re-formation of the industrial reserve army or surplus-population . . . The whole form of the movement of modern industry depends, therefore, upon the constant transformation of a part of the labouring population into unemployed or half-employed hands (*ibid.*: 593–3).

Its second function is in the process of wage determination and of productivity increase. Wages are seen as being constrained[5] not, as in the Ricardian/Malthusian model, by variations in the absolute number of the working population, 'but by the varying proportions in which the working class is divided into active and reserve army, by the increase or diminution in the relative amount of the surplus-population, by the extent to which it is now absorbed, now set free' (*ibid.*: 559).

Productivity increases arise from the intensification of labour use:

> The over-work of the employed part of the working-class swells the ranks of the reserve, while conversely the greater pressure that the latter by its competition exerts on the former forces these to submit to overwork and to subjugation under the dictates of capital. The condemnation of one part of the working-class to enforced idleness by the overwork of the other part, and the converse, becomes a means of enriching the individual capitalists, and accelerates at the same time the production of the industrial reserve army on a scale corresponding with the advance of social accumulation (*ibid.*: 595–6).

In short:

> . . . the industrial reserve army, during the periods of stagnation and average prosperity, weighs down the active labour-army; during the periods of over-production and paroxysm, it holds its pretensions in check. Relative surplus-population is therefore the pivot on which the law of demand and supply of labour works. It confines the field of action of this law within the limits absolutely convenient to the activity of exploitation and to the domination of capital (*ibid.*: 598).

The relative surplus population, according to Marx, takes various forms. First is the *floating* form, in 'the centres of modern industry—factories, manufactures, ironworks, mines. &c'—where 'the labourers are sometimes repelled, sometimes attracted again in greater masses, the number of those employed increasing on the whole, although in a constantly decreasing proportion to the scale of production' (*ibid.*: 600). Marx emphasises employers' preference for youthful labourers and the short average duration of life of the factory worker.

The second form of relative surplus population is *latent*, consisting of 'part of the agricultural population constantly on the point of passing over into an urban or manufacturing proletariat, and on the look-out for circumstances favourable to this transformation' (*ibid.*: 601). The extent of this latent surplus population 'becomes evident only when its channels of outlet open to exceptional width. The agricultural labourer is therefore reduced to the minimum of wages, and always stands with one foot already in the swamp of pauperism' (*ibid.*: 602).

The third, *stagnant* category of surplus population is part of the active labour army, but with extremely irregular employment. With 'conditions of life . . . below the average normal level of the working class . . . it is characterised by maximum of working-time and minimum of wages' (*ibid.*: 602). Its typical form is that of 'domestic industry'. It recruits new members especially from 'those decaying branches of industry, where handicraft is yielding to manufacture, manufacture to machinery' but is at the same time a 'self-reproducing and self-perpetuating element of the working class'. This category 'furnishes capital an inexhaustible reservoir of disposable labour-power'.

Finally, there are the 'dangerous' classes—the vagabonds, criminals and prostitutes—and 'the lowest sediment of the relative surplus—population (which) . . . dwells in the sphere of *pauperism*' (*ibid.*: 602). There are three categories of paupers: those able to work; orphans and pauper children, speedily enrolled into the active labour army in times of great prosperity; and:

> the demoralised and ragged, and those unable to work, chiefly people who succumb to the incapacity for adaptation, due to the division of labour; people who have passed the normal age of the labourer; the victims of industry, whose number increases with the increase of dangerous machinery, of mines, chemical works, &c, the mutilated, the sickly, the widows, &c. Pauperism is the hospital of the active labour-army and the dead weight of the industrial reserve army . . . [It] forms a condition of capitalist production and of the capitalist development of wealth (*ibid.*: 603).

Marx's theory of relative surplus population and the reserve army is, as has already emerged, partly cyclical in nature. He sees the course of modern industry as 'a decennial cycle (interrupted by smaller oscillations), of periods of average activity, production at high pressure, crisis and stagnation' (*ibid.*: 593). But superimposed on crisis and deepening it is the long-term tendency of the rate of profit to fall. The basis of this tendency is not the classical law of diminishing returns in agriculture (which Marx rejects) but his assumption of a tendency for the ratio of constant-to-variable (i.e. fixed-to-circulating) capital to increase. In a passage which finds an echo in more recent analyses of industrialisation in developing countries with rising capital-intensity (see page 145), he states that:

> the gradual growth of constant capital in relation to variable capital must necessarily lead to a gradual fall in the general rate of profit, so long as the . . . intensity of exploitation of labour by capital remain the same. . . It is a law of capitalist production that its development is attended by a relative decrease of variable in relation to constant capital, and consequently to the total capital set in motion. This is just another way of saying that owing to the distinctive methods of production developing in the capitalist system the same number of labourers, i.e., the same quantity of labour power set in motion by a variable capital of a given value, operate, work up and productively consume in the same time span an ever increasing quantity of means of labour, machinery and fixed capital of all sorts, raw and auxiliary materials—and consequently a constant capital of an ever increasing value. This continued relative decrease of the variable capital *vis-à-vis* the constant, and consequently the total capital, is identical with the progressively higher organic composition of the social capital in its average. It is likewise just another expression for the progressive development of the social productivity of labour (Marx, 1867, iii: 212).

As Robinson has pointed out (Robinson 1937: 75-82) this analysis is flawed. An increase in the productivity of labour will not necessarily lead to a fall in the rate of profit as long as we assume, as Marx does, that the supply price of labour remains unchanged. Moreover, the 'counteracting influences', which Marx recognises to exist and, indeed, discusses at some length (*ibid.*: 323-240), are fairly powerful. They include increasing the intensity of exploitation through lengthening the working day; the depression of wages below the value of labour power; foreign trade; and the cheapening of elements of constant capital. The last counteracting influence is particularly subversive of the analysis. 'A rate of technical transformation (through capital saving technology) can always be posited which would resolve the problem—generating a mass of surplus value sufficient to generate the normal rate of profit on the mass of capital employed' (Bienefeld *et al.*, 1977: 433).

An alternative analysis of the tendency towards cyclical crisis, espoused by some Marxists (particularly Luxemburg), is underconsumptionist. Marx hints at but never develops such an analysis. For instance, he points out that:

> the condition of direct exploitation, and those of realising it, are not identical. They diverge not only in place and time but also logically. The first are only limited by the productive power of society, the latter by the proportional relation of the various branches of production and the consumer power of society. . . The market must, therefore, be continually extended. . . But the more productiveness develops, the more it finds itself at variance with the narrow basis on which the conditions of consumption rest. It is no contradiction at all on this self contradictory basis that there should be an excess of capital simultaneously with a growing surplus of population (*ibid.*: 244–5).

Marx has several tentative theories of cyclical crisis of which this underconsumptionism is only one. But he certainly rejects Say's Law, even though, as will be discussed in the next section, he distances himself from Malthus' short-period theory of unemployment and its bizarre policy implications. The underconsumptionist analysis also seems consistent with what can be observed in the real world.

> As productivity increases it tends to increase surplus value and profit and thus to solve the profit problem created by the rising capital intensity of production; but at the same time it creates a problem of markets, in that at any given level of demand a smaller quantity of labour time is now required to meet consumption demands. If one solves the market problem by allowing wages to rise, then one negates the beneficial effect of the productivity increase on profits. Hence solving one problem exacerbates the other. This explains why the crisis, when it occurs, is never a crisis of inadequate production but always an 'upside down' crisis of inadequate markets for mountains of products which lie idle ('realisation crisis') or of men and machines forced to be idle because profitable investment opportunities cannot be identified—('valorisation crisis'). It is for this reason also that such crises are always reflected in intense battles for export markets which lead eventually to protectionism and sometimes to war (Bienefeld *et al.*, *op. cit.*: 433).

Whatever the causes of the crisis, Marx argues convincingly that it is a necessary part of the way that capitalism works. By devaluing the existing capital stock it serves to restore the possibility of capital accumulation. He describes 'the periodical depreciation of existing capital' as 'one of the means immanent in capitalist production to check the fall of the rate of profit and hasten accumulation of capital value through formation of new capital' (*ibid.*: 249). Also the existence of relative surplus population in all its forms is crucial to the system's powers of recovery.

MALTHUS' SHORT-PERIOD THEORY OF UNEMPLOYMENT

As has already been emphasised, the classical economists' analysis of surplus population was essentially long-run in nature. As far as the short-run was concerned, Say's law, that supply creates its own demand, was assumed to apply. The most notable exception (apart from Marx) was Malthus who in his later years developed a short-period theory of unemployment due to deficiency of effective demand. Its basis was a vigorous dismissal of Say's law:

> It has been thought by some very able writers, that although there may easily be a glut of particular commodities, there cannot possibly be a glut of commodities in general; because, according to their view of the subject, commodities being always exchanged for commodities, one half will furnish a market for the other half, and production being thus the sole source of demand, an excess in the supply of one article merely proves a deficiency in the supply of some other, and a general excess is impossible. M. Say, in his distinguished work on political economy, has indeed gone so far as to state that the consumption of a commodity by taking it out of the market diminishes demand, and the production of a commodity proportionably increases it. *This doctrine, however, to the extent in which it has been applied, appears to me to be utterly unfounded, and completely to contradict the great principles which regulate supply and demand.*[6] It is by no means true, as a matter of fact, that commodities are always exchanged for commodities. The great mass of commodities is exchanged directly for labour, either productive or unproductive; and it is quite obvious that this mass of commodities, compared with the labour with which it is to be exchanged, may fall in value from a glut just as any one commodity falls in value from an excess of supply, compared either with labour or money (Malthus 1820: 353–4).

Thus, according to Malthus, it is quite possible for the rate of accumulation to be too high, in the sense of leading to the production of goods for which there was no demand:

> It is undoubtedly possible by parsimony to devote at once a much larger share than usual of the produce of any country to the maintenance of productive labour; and it is quite true that the labourers so employed are consumers. . . But . . . the consumption and demand occasioned by the persons employed in productive labour can never alone furnish a motive to the accumulation and employment of capital; and with regard to the capitalists themselves, together with the landlords and other rich persons, they have, by the supposition, agreed to be parsimonious and by depriving themselves of their usual conveniences and luxuries to save from their revenue and add to their capital. Under these circumstances, I would ask, how it is possible to suppose that the increased quantity of commodities, obtained by the increased number of productive labourers should find purchasers, without such a fall in price as would probably sink their value below the costs of production, or, at least, very greatly diminish both the power and the will to save (*ibid.*: 352–3).

In other words, the incentive to invest may be inadequate to ensure full employment of a given labour force.

This leads Malthus to suggest that 'it is absolutely necessary that a country with great powers of production should possess a body of unproductive consumers' (*ibid.*: 463). Capitalists would not normally behave in this way since 'the great object of their lives is to save a fortune' (*ibid.*: 465). Landlords are more promising:

> but if the powers of production among capitalists are considerable, the consumption of the landlords, in addition to that of the capitalists themselves and of their workmen, may still be insufficient to keep up and increase the exchangeable value of the whole produce, that is to make the increase of quantity more than counterbalance the fall of the price. And if this be so, the capitalists cannot continue the same habits of saving. They must either consume more, or produce less (*ibid.*: 466).

As might be expected, this underconsumption theory did not meet with the approval of other classical economists. Ricardo's comments on it were particularly exasperated:

> A body of unproductive labourers are just as necessary and as useful with a view to future production, as a fire which should consume in the manufacturer's warehouse the goods which those unproductive labourers would otherwise consume. . . In what way can a man's consuming my produce, without making me any return whatever, enable me to make a

fortune? I should think my fortune would be more likely to be made, if the consumer of my produce returned me an equivalent value. . . I cannot express in language so strong as I feel it my astonishment at the various propositions advanced in this section (Ricardo 1820: 421–3).

Ricardo (*ibid.*: 303–18) points to an inconsistency between this new theory and Malthus' long-run theory of population (see pp.34-6), according to which saving and investment could not result in any general deficiency of effective demand. Such 'parsimony' would not diminish the wants of consumers generally but would transfer them, together with the power to consume, to another set of consumers, i.e. to the labourers. If wages were to rise, as suggested by the effective demand theory, this would result in an increase in population. Thus the check to accumulation caused by labour scarcity, would be only temporary: 'profits would be low because wages would be high, and would only continue so until population increased and labour again fell.' Meanwhile, 'the condition of the labourer would then be most happy, for what can be more prosperous than the condition of him who has a commodity to sell for which there is an almost unlimited demand, while the supply is limited, and increases at a relatively slow rate' (*ibid.*: 303).

Marx contented himself, in *Capital*, with poking gentle fun at Malthus' new theory:[7]

In order to charm out of his bosom the awful conflict between the desire for enjoyment and the chase after riches, Malthus, about the year 1820, advocated a division of labour, which assigns to the capitalist actually engaged in production, the business of accumulating and to the other sharers in surplus-value, to the landlords, the place-men,the beneficed clergy, &c., the business of spending. It is of the highest importance, he says, to keep separate the passion for expenditure and the passion for accumulation (Marx, 1867: 558).

In the knowledge that Keynes saluted Malthus as 'the first of the Cambridge economists', modern Marxists have attacked his short-period theory more vigorously. For instance, Meek recognises its ingenuity in combining 'both a warning against the over-rapid development of capitalism, and an apology for the continued existence under capitalism of people like the landlords and their 'unproductive' associates who did nothing except consume' (Meek 1971: 14). He points out that it did not become popular in Malthus' own lifetime (most of his contemporaries were convinced by Ricardo's critique) but that 'today, as an important constituent part of Keynesian economic doctrine, a modified variant of the Malthusian theory of effective demand has been made to play a role just as reactionary as that which Malthus intended the original theory to play' (*ibid.*: 15). Keynesian theory will be discussed in the next chapter.

CONCLUSIONS

Apart from Malthus' effective demand theory, just discussed, the classical theories were all long-period, with emphasis on accumulation of capital as the source of the demand for labour. In this respect, and in their incorporation of social and political factors, they have much to offer to the analysis of current global employment problems, as emphasised in the introduction to this chapter. Development economists have certainly borrowed a great deal from classical theory—particularly the emphasis on growing capital-intensity generating unemployment, subsistence wage levels and different savings functions for different classes (see Chapter Five).

Perhaps the most striking aspect of this review, however, is the extent to which Marx's theory seems to be an advance on those of his predecessors—more subtle and more plausible empirically. In particular, Marx's focus on *relative* rather than *absolute* surplus population as the means of restoring an unlimited supply of labour at the long-run supply price looks more convincing. In this respect his jibe at the 'dogma' of the British classical economists, whereby labour market equilibrium is restored by variations in population growth rates, rings true and is worth repeating: 'Before, in consequence of the rise of wages, any positive increase of the population really fit for work could occur, the time would have been passed again and again, during which the industrial campaign must have been carried through, the battle fought and won' (Marx 1867: I, 597). How much more realistic to posit the maintenance of an excess supply of *workers* by capitalists, independent of the population growth rate.

Significantly, only part of Marx's reserve army would be captured by modern definitions of unemployment. The members of his *floating* surplus population (see p. 42) would be regarded as unemployed in the senses both of 'not working' and 'seeking work' (or, in Sen's terms, both of being deprived of income as a result of not working and of recognising themselves as unemployed—see page 9). His *latent* and *stagnant* categories, however, would not be defined as unemployed in either of these senses, though receiving an extremely low average income. Hence the observation of low rates of open unemployment over fairly long periods of time in mature capitalist economies does not refute Marx's relative surplus population theory. As for Sen's production aspect of labour under-utilisation (see p. 10), Marx's analysis is somewhat ambiguous on this point. He emphasises, as has been seen, the *functionality* (even the vital necessity) of the reserve army to the operation of capitalist industry. Under a different system, members of the surplus population could presumably be redeployed without loss of output but *capitalist* industry would run into serious trouble if they ceased to perform their reserve army function. These issues will be raised for further discussion in later chapters.

NOTES

1. One exception was Malthus who, in his later phase, put forward an effective-demand theory of short-period unemployment and based on it a plea for more 'unproductive consumption' on the part of landlords and capitalists (*see* p. 46). Marx, while deriding this Malthusian policy implication, also rejects Say's Law (*see* p. 45). Even Mill, in his *Essays on Some Unsettled Questions*, does express doubts about it.
2. Our emphasis.
3. Although rejecting his later short-period effective-demand theory of unemployment (*see* p. 46).
4. These are not the normal labour–productivity curves of neo-classical analysis which assume a given total quantity of fixed capital. These 'labour-plus-capital–productivity' curves assume fixed coefficients as

between fixed capital and labour, and variable coefficients as between labour and land. Thus fixed capital accumulation would not in itself shift the curves to the right, whereas technical progress would.

5. But not determined. Unlike the British classical economists (apart from Ricardo), Marx emphasised the role of class struggle in the determination of wages.
6. Our emphasis.
7. He criticises it at greater length in *Theories of Surplus Value* (*see* Meek, 1953: 171–89).

3 Neoclassical and Keynesian Theories of Unemployment in a Mature Capitalist Economy

Towards the end of the nineteenth century, economics took what many would now regard as a regrettable turning, into a *cul-de-sac* from which so far it has been unable to escape. The classical concern with political economy, growth and development and with the long period question of the relationship between the available labour force and an economy's productive capacity was abandoned in favour of a narrowly economistic preoccupation with static efficiency and a view of employment as essentially non-problematic. Even when in the nineteen thirties Keynes successfully challenged this view his concern was still with the short-period question of the determinants of utilisation of existing capacity. When (from the late 1960s onwards) Keynesian prescriptions appeared no longer to fit the facts the theoretical clock was turned back, but to the early twentieth rather than to the nineteenth century. This chapter briefly traces the swing from neoclassicism to Keynesianism and back again and its implications for the debate about the causes of unemployment.

EARLY NEOCLASSICALS

Although Keynes, in his assault on his opponents, lumped together as 'classical' economists all those who accepted Say's law, it is more useful for our purposes to draw a line between the classical economics of accumulation and growth and the marginalist, 'neoclassical' economics of static efficiency. The turning point came in the 1870s, with the publication of the major works of Menger, Jevons and Walras. After that,

> economists typically posited some given supply of productive factors determined independently by elements outside the purview of analysis.

The essence of the economic problem was to search for the conditions under which given productive services were allocated with optimal results among competing uses, optimal in the sense of maximising consumers' satisfactions. This ruled out consideration of the effects of increases in the quantity and quality of resources and the dynamic expansion of wants, effects that the classical economists had regarded as the *sine qua non* of rising economic welfare. For the first time, economics truly became the science that studies the relationship between *given* ends and *given* scarce means that have alternative uses. The classical theory of economic development was replaced by the concept of general equilibrium within an essentially static framework (Blaug 1968: 273).

Although neoclassical economists moved, thus, away from the classicals' interest in the long-period questions of accumulation and growth (as well as from their emphasis on *political* economy), they retained their faith in Say's law. Indeed, the following statement of the law in an early work by Marshall, was later quoted by Keynes as typical of the neoclassical[1] position:

The whole of a man's income is expended in the purchase of services and of commodities. It is indeed commonly said that a man spends some portion of his income and saves another. But it is a familiar economic axiom that a man purchases labour and commodities with that portion of his income which he saves just as much as he does when he seeks to obtain present enjoyment from the services and commodities which he purchases. He is said to save when he causes the labour and the commodities which he purchases to be devoted to the production of wealth from which he expects to derive the means of enjoyment in the future (Marshall 1879: 34)

In search, some would argue, of a straw man, Keynes later picked on Pigou's *Theory of Unemployment* as 'the only detailed account of the classical theory of employment which exists' (Keynes 1936: 7). Pigou's conclusion was that,

with perfectly free competition among workpeople and labour perfectly mobile, . . . there will always be at work a strong tendency for wage-rates to be so related to demand that everybody is employed. Hence, in stable conditions everyone will actually be employed. The implication is that such unemployment as exists at any time is due wholly to the fact that changes in demand conditions are continually taking place and that frictional resistances prevent the appropriate wage adjustments from being made instantaneously (Pigou 1933: 252).

This conclusion echoes that of Marshall, who had earlier

pointed to the 'natural tendency of trade unions to press for a rise in standard money wages during inflations of credit'. He urged that industry be

> more quick to consent to some relaxation of a high standard of money wages when the crest of a wave of high prices, to which it was adapted, had passed away. Such adjustments are full of difficulty: but progress towards them might be hastened if there were a more general and clear appreciation of the fact that high wages, gained by means that hinder production in any branch of industry, necessarily increase unemployment in other branches. For, indeed, the only effective remedy for unemployment is a continuous adjustment of means to ends' (Marshall 1920: 590–1).[2]

Thus the neoclassical position can be summarised as attributing unemployment to interferences with the free and flexible working of the perfectly competitive labour market, such as trade unions, minimum wage legislation and unemployment benefit. In the absence of such 'imperfections', the economy would quickly move to an equilibrium in which there was no involuntary unemployment. Thus any unemployment is regarded as essentially voluntary in that work available at a perfectly-competitive-market-clearing wage is rejected.

The real-world policy implication of the neoclassical position in the nineteen thirtees was, of course, a cut in wages. A cut in *money* wages, it was assumed, would be reflected in a cut in *real* wages, on which ultimately the level of employment depends.

The 'groundwork' of the neoclassical argument about the consequences of wage cuts is wickedly caricatured by Keynes, as follows:

> In any given industry we have a demand schedule for the product relating the quantities which can be sold to the prices asked; we have a series of supply schedules relating the prices which will be asked for the sale of different quantities on various bases of cost; and these schedules between them lead up to a further schedule which, on the assumption that other costs are unchanged (except as a result of the change in output), gives us the demand schedule for labour in the industry relating the quantity of employment to different levels of wages, the shape of the curve at any point furnishing the elasticity of demand for labour. This conception is then transferred without substantial modification to industry as a whole; and it is supposed, by a parity of reasoning, that we have a demand schedule for

> labour in industry as a whole relating the quantity of employment to different levels of wages. It is held that it makes no material difference to this argument whether it is in terms of money-wages or real wages. If we are thinking in terms of money-wages, we must, of course, correct for changes in the value of money; but this leaves the general tendency of the argument unchanged, since prices certainly do not change in exact proportion to changes in money-wages (Keynes 1936: 258).

This simplified neoclassical model can easily be shown not to work. Quite simply, the assumption made in the partial-equilibrium analysis of a tiny sub-sector of the labour market, that a fall in money wages will not affect the demand for the product and its price, cannot be transferred to an analysis of a whole economy, since wage-earners are also consumers. If direct effects alone are taken into account, it is impossible to escape from the conclusion that money wage cuts must lead to a fall in prices in the same proportion and thus to no increase in the demand for labour. Figure 3.1 illustrates this point. In the bottom diagram MPL is the demand curve for labour, drawn with an elasticity greater than one in order to be as favourable as possible to the effects of a wage cut. Thus an initial cut in the money-wage from w_o to w_1 leads to an increase in wage income as employment increases from ON_o to ON_1, since $O\frac{w_1}{p}BN_1$ is greater than $O\frac{w_o}{p}AN_o$. If the direct effect stopped here we would have to concede the possibility of an increase in consumer demand (and thus in demand for labour) following a wage cut. However, we also have to take into account the effect on production (y) shown in the top diagram. An increase in employment from ON_0 to ON_1 would lead to an increase in production from Oy_o to Oy_1. But Oy_1 would only have been preferred to Oy_o by profit maximising employers if it had involved an increase in profits. Now, even if wage-earners spend the whole of their increment in income on consumption (i.e. their marginal propensity to consume is equal to one), profit-earners are unlikely to do so. So the increase in supply resulting from the wage cut is likely to exceed the increase in demand. In short, even if a cut in wages leads to an increase in wage income (i.e. the demand for labour has an elasticity greater than one) *and* wage-earners devote all of their extra income to consumption,

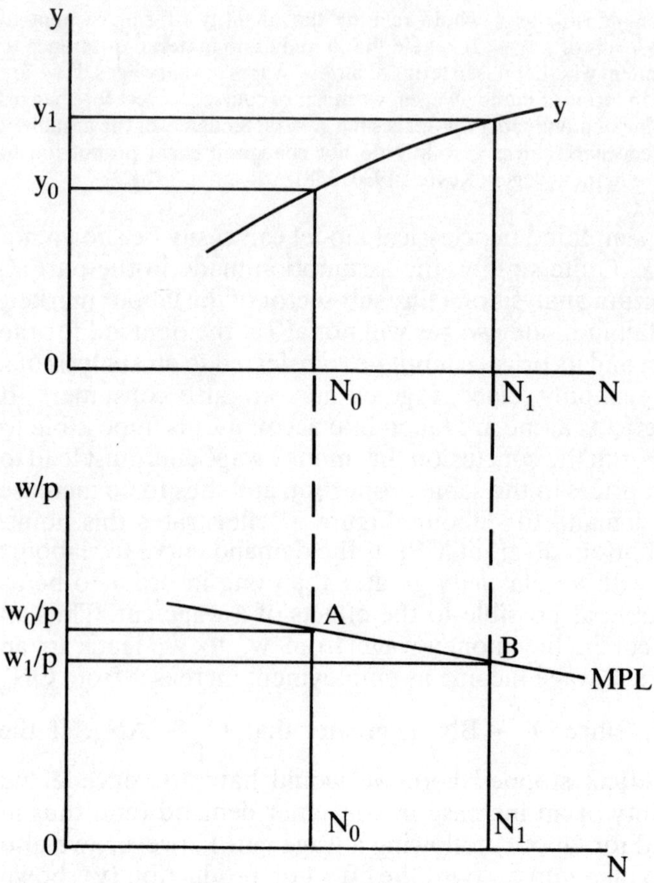

Figure 3.1: Direct Effects of a Wage Cut
Source: Ackley (1961)

prices can only be prevented from falling proportionately by another special assumption—that profit recipients also consume the whole of their resulting increase in income. Analogously, if the initial fall in real wages is the result not of a cut in money wage but of an increase in prices, analysis of the direct effects alone again points to the conclusion that the fall in real wage will not be sustainable. Prices will have to return to their former level if the resulting increase in output is to be sold.

So the neoclassical claim that wage cuts will cure unemployment must rest on the indirect effects of such cuts. However, few neoclassicals, apart perhaps from Pigou in his *Theory of Unemployment* (which Keynes, as we have seen, disingenuously picked as 'the only detailed account of the classical theory of employment which exists') would have been so crude as to rest their case on the direct effects alone. Most would have emphasised the indirect effects or 'roundabout repercussions' as Keynes called them (Keynes 1936: 257). Indeed, Pigou himself later identified one of the most important of these—the real-balance effect (Pigou 1941). This is based on the standard neoclassical assumption of diminishing marginal utility, which applies to a consumer's stock of wealth as well as to consumption. A fall in prices following a money wage cut will increase the total real value of the public's stock of wealth through its effect on that part of it (such as government bonds and money itself) which has a fixed money value. This will diminish the public's desire to add to its stock of wealth and so stimulate consumption and the derived demand for labour.

Other indirect effects include the effect of wage and price falls on the demand for exports and on the real net tax burden in a situation where income taxes are progressive and transfer payments are fixed in money terms. Both of these should give some stimulus to the demand for labour, although extension of the export-demand argument beyond the case of a single country soon runs into the fallacy of composition; all the countries in the world cannot export their unemployment to each other (for further discussion see Chapter Nine).

KEYNES

Keynes' great challenge to his predecessors is his claim to demolish Say's Law:

> that supply creates its own demand—meaning by this in some significant but not clearly defined sense that the whole of the costs of production must necessarily be spent in the aggregate, directly or indirectly, on purchasing the product (and) . . . that any individual act of abstaining from consumption necessarily leads to, and amounts to the same thing, as,

> causing the labour and commodities thus released from supplying consumption to be invested in the production of capital wealth (Keynes 1936: 18-19).

He regards this doctrine as underlying 'the whole classical theory, which would collapse without it', even though among his contemporaries it might be expressed implicitly rather than explicitly. Of the true classical economists he exempts Malthus from his strictures. Noting that 'in the later phase of Malthus the notion of insufficiency of effective demand takes a definite place—as a scientific explanation of unemployment' (*ibid.*: 362), he calls him 'the first of the Cambridge economists' (Keynes 1936: 144) and exclaims, 'if only Malthus, instead of Ricardo, had been the parent stem from which nineteenth-century economics proceeded, what a much wiser and richer place the world would be today!' (*ibid.*: 120).

In his view, those who believed in Say's law were

> deceived by an optical illusion, which makes two essentially different activities appear to be the same. [Those who use it] are fallaciously supposing that there is a nexus which unites decisions to abstain from present consumption with decisions to provide for future consumption; whereas the motives which determine the latter are not linked in any simple way with the motives which determine the former (1936: 21).

Once this link is broken there is no reason at all why general equilibrium between demand and supply in an economy should coincide with full utilisation of capacity. Thus in the usual simple Keynesian income detemination diagram (Figure 3.2) the *equilibrium* level of income (Y_e), at which withdrawals (saving (S), imports (M) and taxation (T)) are equal to injections (investment (I), exports (X) and government expenditure (G)), may be lower than full-employment income (Y_f).

One of the problems for a discussion of Keynes' employment theory is that it was loosely and obscurely expressed. Indeed, it seems likely that even Keynes himself was not clear in his own mind about some of its finer points (Leijonhufvud 1968: 102). This has given enormous scope for disputes over its interpretation, and for changes in fashion as to the prevailing view of 'what Keynes really meant'.

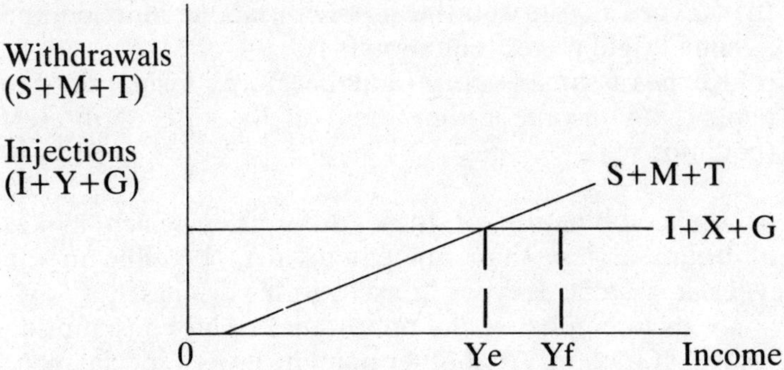

Figure 3.2: Income Equilibrium at Less than Full Employment

In textbook versions of the 1950s and 1960s the differences between the Keynesian and neoclassical models were usually reduced to a few equations. For instance, the 1961 edition of Ackley's widely used macroeconomics textbook put forward a seven-equation version of each of the two models, as follows:

	Neoclassical	*Keynesian*
(1)	$M = lPy$	$M = lPy + L(r)$
(2)	$y = y(N)$	$y = y(N)$
(3)	$dy/dN = W/P$	$dy/dN = W/P$
(4)	$N = N(W/P)$	$W = W_o$
(5)	$s = s(r)$	$s = s(y)$
(6)	$i = i(r)$	$i = i(r)$
(7)	$s = i$	$s = i$

Where M is the quantity of money,
l is the transactions demand for money expressed as a fraction of the money value of transactions for the period,
P is the price level,
y is output,
L is the speculative demand for money,
N is employment,
W is money wage rate,
s is real saving,
r is the rate of interest,
i is real investment.

The only differences between the two models are these:

(a) Keynes added the speculative demand for money, a function of the rate of interest, to the transactions demand (equation (1)).

(b) Keynes suppressed the supply of labour function and assumed rigid wages (equation (4)).
(c) Keynes assumed saving (and therefore consumption) to depend on income rather than on the rate of interest (equation (5)).

It is the combination of these differences which makes equilibrium at less than full employment possible in the Keynesian system. Keynes himself, in his dismissal of Say's law, seems to emphasise the importance of his consumption and saving function. At another point he gives a special place to the speculative demand for money:

> Unemployment develops . . . because people want the moon; men cannot be employed when the object of desire (i.e. money) is something which cannot be produced and the demand for which cannot be readily choked off. There is no remedy but to persuade the public that cheese is practically the same thing and to have a green cheese factory (i.e. a central bank) under public control (*ibid.*: 235).

What he wants to avoid is the charge that wage rigidity is his crucial assumption, since this does not differentiate him sufficiently from the neoclassicals who not only recognised that rigid wages could cause unemployment but regarded them as the only cause.

In fact, when set down in this form, the Keynesian model is not as far away from the neoclassical as his caricature of his opponents' position seems to imply. For instance, as we have seen (page 57), on the neoclassical analysis a fall in money wages, via at least its indirect effects, would tend to lead to some increase in employment. How different is this version of the Keynesian model in this respect? It must be admitted that the possibility of a fall in money wages leading to an increase in employment cannot be ruled out. As Keynes puts it, 'the consequences of a change in money-wages are complicated' (Keynes 1936: 257). Thus a wage cut will increase employment, output and income initially (equation (2)). Consumption will increase as a function of income (equation (5)), but investment must also increase if the extra output is to be sold. This can only happen at a lower rate of interest (equation (6)). Given the quantity of money, this requires a reduction in transactions demand for money and thus a reduction in the price level to offset the increase in income (equation (1)). However, the fall in prices will be at a lower rate than the fall in money wages. Thus, *in principle*, a money wage cut could lead to an increase in employment, even on Keynesian assumptions, through its effect in lowering the transactions demand for money, lowering interest rates and stimulating investment. However, in practice, investment and/or the demand for money may be insufficiently interest-rate-elastic to allow such an adjustment—even if a real balance effect (absent from Keynes' model) were added to the analysis.

The properly agnostic conclusion of a Keynesian analysis of the effects of wage changes is given by Robinson:

> Any change in money wages will set up a number of complicated repercussions, which may lead to a change in employment, in one direction or another, to some extent, but . . . a change in money wages is not likely to lead to any great change in employment in either direction (Robinson 1937: 41).

Thus Keynes' politically important and analytically influential rejection of wage cuts is based not on the rejection of the logical possibility that they could, under certain circumstances, lead to an increase in employment but on the view that this effect would be slow and circuitous and, under other circumstances, perverse. He rejects them also because, except in a highly authoritarian society, a flexible-wage policy would not work. 'One can imagine it in operation in Italy, Germany or Russia, but not in France, the United States or Great Britain' (*ibid.*: 269).

Kalecki, who, it is now generally agreed (see Klein 1975; Robinson and Wilkinson 1977), anticipated Keynes' theory of aggregate demand deficiency, went further than him in many respects[3]. Kalecki's analysis is long-period with emphasis on the need to expand productive capacity proportionately to full employment output. Moreover, his capitalist economy is one of oligopolistic rather than perfect competition in which profit-earners have a higher propensity to save than wage-earners and in which the struggle between employees and employers over the distribution of income between wages and profits is central. The role of unemployment in this system is to maintain discipline in the factories and to restrain demands for wage increases and improvements in conditions of work. In this way the claims of labour for a higher real wage are held back to a level compatible with the profit demands of oligopolists. Perhaps the most important difference from Keynes is Kalecki's 'political-economy' approach, with the state as an endogenous element in the model rather than a neutral recipient of economists' advice. This makes Kalecki (1943) pessimistic about the prospects of achieving lasting full employment under capitalism. The second world war, he recognises, changed the consciousness of workers about the tolerability of unemployment and led business leaders to concede that 'something must be done in the slump'. But their opposition to the *maintenance* of full employment, he suggests, was unaffected by the war. The pressure of rentier and, particularly, big business interests—'as a rule influential in government departments—would most probably induce the government to return to the orthodox policy of cutting down the budget deficit' (Kalecki 1943: 428). The resulting regime he calls the 'political business cycle'—'an artificial restoration of the position as it existed in nineteenth-century capitalism. Full employment would be reached only at the top of the boom, but slumps would be relatively mild and short lived' (*ibid.*: 429).

Compatible with the Kalecki model, although developed without reference to it, are the segmented-labour-market theories, which explain the fact that workers of equal efficiency do not receive equal wages by segmentation on the demand side of the labour market. In the most influential version of the theory, this is seen as being divided into two sectors, primary and secondary, with distinct characteristics. 'The primary market offers jobs which possess several of the following traits: high wages, good working conditions, employment stability and job security, equity and due process in the administration of work rules, and chances for advancement. The secondary market has jobs which, relative to those in the primary sector, are decidedly less attractive. They tend to involve low wages, poor working conditions, considerable variability in employment, harsh and often arbitary discipline, and little opportunity to advance. The poor are confined to the secondary labour market' (Piore 1971). Within, the primary sector an 'internal labour market' (Doeringer and Piore 1971) operates; most jobs within the firm are filled internally by upgrading workers along established promotion ladders. Within the secondary sector employment prospects for a large number of urban workers in menial jobs are little affected by schooling, training and other factors affecting productivity; promotion ladders are non-existent; and a 'vicious circle of instability' operates, whereby employers organise jobs in such a way that worker instability (itself a response to lack of opportunity for improving wages of status) does not significantly reduce efficiency. Thus certain types of jobs are characterised as inherently unstable, independent of cyclical fluctuations in activity, thereby ensuring a pool of unemployed in which 'excluded' disadvantaged groups (defined by ethnicity, citizenship, age, sex, income level or whatever) are disproportionately represented and which is topped up at least as fast as it is tapped.

Conclusions based on simple, comparative–static versions of the Keynesian model have tended to be reinforced in recent years by more sophisticated, disequilibrium approaches. Clower (1965) emphasises that the key contribution of Keynes, in contrast to previous economists who were essentially analysing barter economies, was to spell out the implications of monetisation. Households wanting to purchase goods must normally first exchange their labour services for money before they can exchange the money for goods. This introduces the possibility of disequilibrium, with households, unable to find purchasers for their labour, unable therefore to carry through their expenditure plans. In the absence of a Walrasian auctioneer (who would have ensured instantaneous adjustment of prices to the new equilibrium before trading took place) 'false trading' will occur at disequilibrium prices. Since traders will be unable to sell all they want at these prices, further 'deviation-amplifying' effects will set in, as producers further curtail their demand for labour, and so on.

As Leijonhufvud (1968), following Clower, puts it, the

'revolutionary' element in the *General Theory* was this reversal of the Marshallian ranking of price- and quantity-adjustment speeds: 'Keynes' predecessors had not attempted a comparably ambitious systematic investigation of the dynamic behaviour of an interdependent macrosystem characterised by relatively inflexible prices and, consequently, by quantity (income) adjustments' (p. 53). Thus the emergence of involuntary unemployment[4] does *not* depend on the existence of monopolistic restraints on the movement of prices and wages, in spite of the fact that 'many "Keynesians" appear to agree that Keynesian economics would not be very relevant to a truly competitive economy' (Leijonhufvud 1968: 107). Even in the absence of such imperfections, in a complex modern economy in which:

> few prices and almost no wage rates are made to, or allowed to, 'clear' their respective markets; knowledge and foresight by participants in most of these markets are notably imperfect; given modern technology, investment decisions committing vast resources for decades ahead must be made on the basis of precarious information and hunches; contagious moods of optimism or pessimism can sweep financial and other markets: participants in most markets form expectations which, much of the time, are surely not 'rational' in the special sense of that term' (Ackley 1975: 419);

full employment equilibrium is only likely be achieved and maintained by accident.

The new disequilibrium approach to Keynesian macroeconomics has, as might be expected, inspired many micro-economists to try to provide it with choice–theoretic underpinnings. Among the most influential are those (for example Baily 1974; Gordon 1974; Azaridis 1975) who have suggested that labour market transactions can be viewed as implicit contracts between risk averse employees and less risk averse employers. In such contracts employers are seen as 'insuring' their employees by paying them real wages which fluctuate less than they would otherwise do; in return, employers are compensated by premia in the form of lower average wages which workers are implicitly willing to pay for such insurance. This analysis yields a prediction of stickiness in real wages and hence of layoffs and persistent, disequilibrium unemployment as aggregate demand falls.

However, the logic of this conclusion is in dispute (Parkin 1980; Akerlof and Miyazaki 1980) and asymmetric information between firms and workers has to be introduced (Grossman and Hart 1980) to generate both sticky wages and excessive layoffs when times are bad. Most would agree with Nickell (1982b: 5) that 'a good deal of work remains to be done on the theoretical foundations of the disequilibrium model.'

Although interpretations of 'what Keynes really meant' were, during the late 1960s, becoming more subtle and disturbing, Keynesian demand management policy continued to be based on the simplest of the textbook versions of the model. Thus, in the situation described by Figure 3.2, where households are wanting to save more than is compatible with full employment income, Y_f, all that government has to do is to organise, through fiscal and/or monetary policy, an increase in investment (I) and/or government expenditure (G) sufficient to raise the I+X+G schedule until it intersects the S+M+T schedule at Y_f. This is what Robinson and Wilkinson (1977: 6) call 'bastard Keynesianism', according to which it is possible artificially to restore Say's Law. In this way what Keynes intended as a diagnosis of a defect inherent in capitalism becomes 'a defence of *laissez-faire*, provided that just the one blemish of excessive saving was going to be removed' (*ibid.*: 7).

KEYNESIAN AND NEOCLASSICAL GROWTH MODELS

In essence, as emphasised at the beginning of this chapter, both the neoclassical and Keynesian approaches are static and short-period—the neoclassicals concerned with general equilibrium within a static framework and the Keynesians with the determinants of utilisation of existing capacity.[5] There have, however, been attempts to 'dynamise' both approaches, in the form of the growth models which have proliferated in recent decades.

The first of these, building directly on Keynes' *General Theory* was that of Harrod (1939). He defines the 'warranted rate of growth' of an economy as 'that rate of growth which, if it occurs, will leave all parties satisfied that they have produced neither more nor less than the right amount. Or, to state the matter otherwise, it will put them into a frame of mind which will cause them to give such orders as will maintain the same rate of growth' (*ibid.*: 45). The 'fundamental equation' is

$$G_w = s/\acute{K}$$

where G_w is the warranted rate of growth, s is the proportion of income saved and $\acute{K}$ is the capital–output ratio or 'the value of capital goods required for the production of a unit increment of output'.

This equation defines an equilibrium growth path but one which is highly unstable—or 'knife-edge'. 'A departure from equilibrium, instead of being self-righting, will be self-aggravating' (*ibid.*: 53). For instance, if there is a departure from the warranted rate of growth such that the actual growth rate, G, exceeds the warranted rate, then the actual capital–output ratio will be below what is required. New orders for stocks and equipment will result, leading to a further increase in output. So G will move further away from G_w in an upward direction and the further it diverges, the greater the stimulus to expansion. Similarly if G falls below G_w, a downward spiral will set in, as firms' replacement demand for capital declines.

Unemployment is brought into the analysis by the introduction of the 'natural rate of growth' (G_n) defined as the 'maximum rate of growth allowed by the increase of population, accumulation of capital, technological improvement and the work/leisure preference schedule' (*ibid.*: 61). There is no inherent tendency for G_w and G_n to coincide. If the warranted rate exceeds the natural rate, actual growth at the warranted rate will not be sustainable and the economy will topple off its knife-edge equilibrium path into depression and cyclical unemployment. If the natural rate exceeds the warranted rate, equilibrium growth can be maintained, but with a chronic unemployment problem of the type confronting an underdeveloped economy with a capital shortage even in boom times (see Chapter Five).

A model developed independently by Domar at around the same time was so similar to that of Harrod that it is now usual to talk of the Harrod–Domar model. Domar points out that, 'because investment in the Keynesian system is merely an instrument for generating income, the system does not take into account the extremely essential, elementary and well known fact that investment also increases productive capacity' (Domar 1946: 67). From this recognition of the *dual* character of the investment process Domar derives the equilibrium rate of growth of investment, $\propto\sigma$, where $\propto$ is the marginal propensity to save and σ is the productivity of investment (the inverse of $\acute{K}$ in Harrod's formula). This produces an emphasis on a slightly different aspect of the Harrod Knife-edge growth path. 'In a private capitalist society where it cannot be readily changed, a higher level of income and employment at any given time can be achieved only through increased investment. But investment, as an employment-creating instrument, is a mixed blessing because of its σ effect. The economy finds itself in a serious dilemma: if sufficient investment is not forthcoming today, unemployment will be here today. But if enough is invested today, still more will be needed tomorrow . . . As far as unemployment is concerned, investment is at the same time a cure for the disease and the cause of even greater ills in the future' (Domar 1957: 101).

The fixed-proportions assumptions of the Harrod–Domar model, and the pessimistic conclusions that they generate about the capacity of a capitalist economy to maintain full employment over a long period, attracted predictable criticisms from neoclassical economists. Solow (1956) and Swan (1956) point out that the prediction of knife-edge instability rests crucially on the assumption that K in Harrod's fundamental equation is constant:

> There is no possibility of substituting labour for capital in production. If this assumption is abandoned, the knife-edge notion of unstable balance seems to go with it. Indeed it is hardly surprising that such a gross rigidity in one part of the system should entail lack of flexibility in another (Solow 1956: 162).

Under neoclassical variable-proportions assumptions if the

warranted growth rate exceeded the natural rate the ensuing labour shortage would make labour more expensive relative to capital and induce labour-saving changes in techniques. This would raise the capital-output ratio and so reduce G_w until it coincided with G_n. If, on the other hand, G_w were lower than G_n, the resulting unemployment would depress the cost of labour relative to that of capital and a shift towards more labour-intensive techniques would take place. The resulting fall in the capital output ratio would raise G_w until it coincided with G_n.

As Sen (1970: 21) comments, 'not a little of the attraction of this model lies in its beautiful simplicity, and this was undoubtedly a major step in the history of growth theory'. However, he also points to several unsolved problems with the model, including: the need for a special assumption about the nature of technological progress (i.e. that it is 'Harrod-neutral'), if steady growth is to be assured; the need for flexibility of factor prices; the absence of an investment function and the consequent failure to assign a major role to entrepreneurial expectations about the future (once an independent investment function is introduced, the instability problem quickly reappears); the problem of aggregating heterogenous producer goods into a scalar value of capital; and the assumption that technological progress is completely exogenous (Sen 1970: 21–28). There are also potential problems with the length of time that adjustment would take.

The Harrod–Domar and the Solow–Swan models were only the beginning of a vast output of growth models,[6] most of them with a family resemblance to one or other of their fixed proportions or variable proportions forerunners. For those interested in the analysis of unemployment the problem with this literature is not merely that it is unsettled (which is true of most economics) but also that it has remained at an extremely abstract and esoteric level. As Sen comments rather gently, 'its link with public policy is often very remote' (*ibid.*: 9).

THE PHILLIPS CURVE: COLLAPSE AND RESURRECTION

The only constraint on the operation of 'bastard Keynesian' demand management policy was the trade off between unemployment and price inflation. This was usually summarised in a 'Phillips Curve', named after the economist who brought it to the world's attention. Phillips argued, on the basis of data for the UK between 1861 and 1957, that:

> the rate of change of money wage rates can be explained by the level of unemployment and the rate of change of unemployment, except in or immediately after those years in which there is a sufficiently rapid rise in import prices to offset the tendency for increasing productivity to reduce the cost of living. Ignoring years in which import prices rise rapidly enough to initiate a wage–price spiral, which seem to occur very rarely except as a result of war, and assuming an increase in productivity of 2 per cent per year, it seems from the relation fitted to the data that if aggregate demand were kept at a value which would maintain a stable level of product prices the associated level of unemployment would be a little under 2½ per cent. If, as is sometimes recommended, demand were kept at a value which would maintain stable wage rates the associated level of unemployment would be about 5½ per cent (Phillips 1958: 255–6).

The original Phillips curve, as shown in Figure 3.3 related the unemployment rate and the rate of change in money wage rates for the period 1861–1913. After 1913 Phillips found the relationship to be somewhat looser but of the same general shape, hence his conclusion, quoted above. The important implication for demand management policy was that near full employment was compatible if not with zero at least with tolerably low rates of wage and price inflation.

Some early attempts to explain the Phillips relationship were consistent with a broadly Keynesian/Kaleckian approach. This was the case, for instance, with cost–push theories of inflation (for example Dicks–Mireaux 1961), which hypothesised that the market power and pushfulness of trade unions, and hence the rate of change of wages (and prices), would tend to vary inversely with the rate of unemployment. Even Lipsey's attempt to provide an explanation which did not resort to assumptions of less than perfect competition (Lipsey 1960) was at a macroeconomic

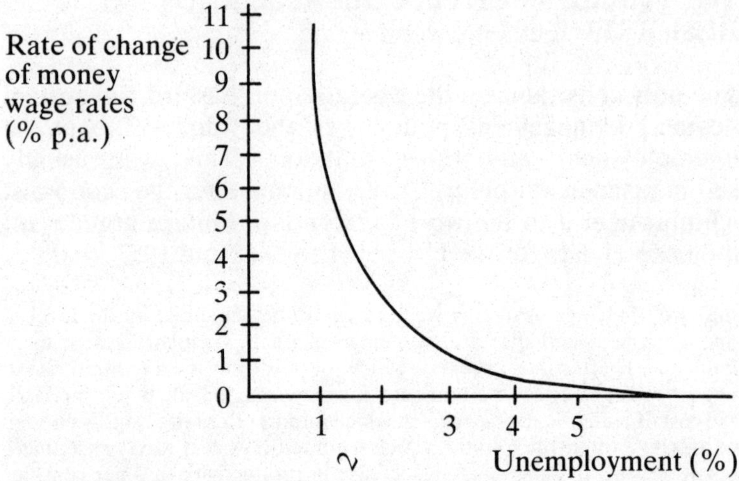

Figure 3.3: Phillips Curve for the UK, 1881–1913
Source: Phillips (1958)

level (and has indeed been criticised for having 'no choice or price theoretic content' (Parkin 1980: 285)). Lipsey assumed that wages (and hence prices) would rise as a result of excess demand in the labour market, at a rate which would increase as the extent of that excess demand increased. This was made consistent with the Phillips curve by the assertion that the labour market was in equilibrium not when unemployment was zero but when the number of unemployed was matched by the number of vacancies. This might be seen as a statement of the Keynesian 'inflationary gap' theory in a (somewhat arbitrarily) special form.

It was not long, however, before choice–theoretic economists began to explore the micro-foundations of the Phillips curve in ways which were aimed at preserving their assumption that involuntary unemployment was impossible. For instance, some (Phelps 1970; Holt 1970) assume product and labour markets perfect in every respect except for the unavailability, to both workers and employers, of free and complete information about the labour market. This gives rise to 'search unemployment', as workers turn down or leave jobs in favour of the possibility of getting something better paid (equalisation of wages for a given category being hindered by the imperfection of information) and as employers delay hiring in order to advertise or otherwise improve their knowledge of the market. Given the additional assumption that the unit cost of an employer's search activity increases over time the temptation grows to raise the wage rate as an alternative to searching. Other employers will tend to follow suit and wage increases will be passed on in the form of price increases. These assumptions yield an inverse, non-linear relationship of the Phillips kind between unemployment rates and the rate of change of wages and prices, since the lower the rate of unemployment, the higher the vacancy rate and the greater the effectiveness for employers of increasing wages relative to searching as a means of obtaining workers—and vice versa. And search unemployment is 'frictional' rather than involuntary in the Keynesian sense.

During the late 1960s and the 1970s the relationship posited by Phillips between the rate of change of wages and the rate of unemployment seemed to be breaking down. If a curve existed it seemed to be shifting outwards, so that, from year to year, a given unemployment rate came to be associated with an ever higher inflation rate. This gave impetus to neoclassical criticisms of the 'Keynesian' assumptions supposedly underlying the Phillps curve. For instance, Friedman (1975) describes Phillips' analysis as seemingly 'very persuasive and obvious, yet . . . utterly fallacious', because his vertical axis refers to the *nominal* wage rate rather than to the *real* wage rate. This says Friedman, is because Phillips accepts the Keynesian assumption that changes in anticipated nominal wages are equal to changes in anticipated real wages. Friedman rejects this assumption and suggests that the vertical axis of the diagram should be relabelled 'rate of change in nominal wages *less* anticipated rate of change in prices'. Thus instead of the implicit Phillips equation, $w=f(U)$ (where w is the rate of change of nominal wages and U is the unemployment rate), we have

$$w=f(U)+p^e$$

(where p^e is the expected rate of price change). This means that there is a whole family of Phillips curves, one for every expected rate of price change. For instance, Figure 3.4 shows what would happen, on this analysis, if an initial expectation of price stability were disturbed.

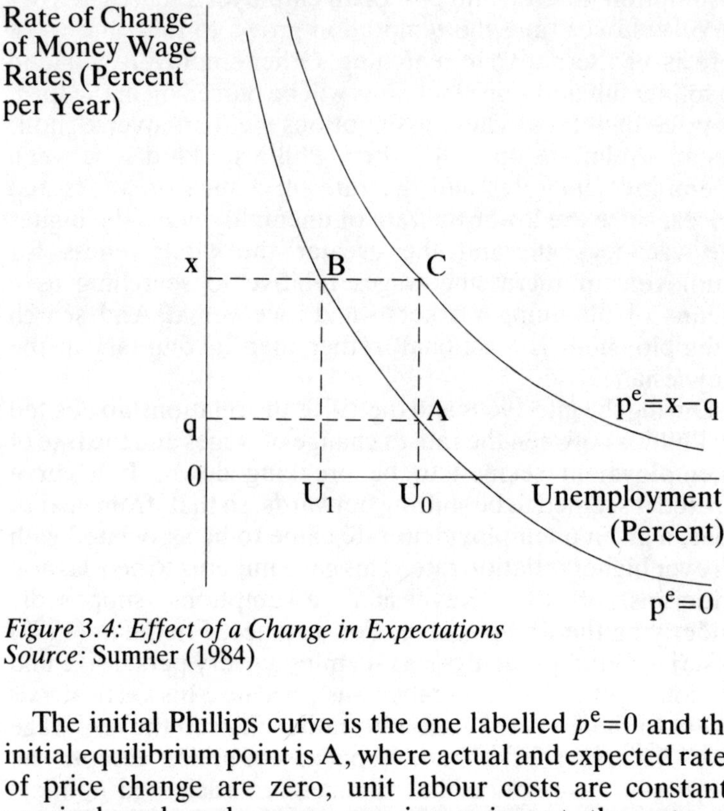

Figure 3.4: Effect of a Change in Expectations
Source: Sumner (1984)

The initial Phillips curve is the one labelled $p^e = 0$ and the initial equilibrium point is A, where actual and expected rates of price change are zero, unit labour costs are constant, nominal and real wages are increasing at the rate of productivity growth (0q) and the unemployment rate is OU_0. Suppose now that an expansion in demand reduces the unemployment rate to OU_1, and increases the rate of wage inflation to 0x, moving the economy along the curve to point B. Since wages are now rising faster than productivity, prices will begin to rise also, at $x-q$ per cent per year. The $p^e = 0$ Phillips curve is, thus, no longer valid. As expectations adjust to the new level of price inflation the curve will shift upwards, until full adjustment of expectations has taken place (shown by the new curve labelled $p^e = x - q$ in Figure 3.4). However, this is not yet a stable situation. If the unemployment rate remained below OU_0 wages would increase at more than 0x per cent per year and the price inflation rate would continue to increase. As the *expected* inflation rate changed accordingly the Phillips curve would continue to shift outwards. Full equilibrium will not be restored on the $p^e = x - q$ curve until the unemployment rate returns to OU_0, at which the actual and anticipated rates of prices change are equal; point C illustrates such a situation of full equilibrium.

OU_0 in this diagram is the so-called *natural rate of unemployment*, the rate at which expectations are consistent with experience, so that there is neither upward nor downward pressure on the rate of inflation. More awkwardly but less tendentiously, it can be called the non-accelerating-inflation rate of unemployment (NAIRU). If the stable inflation rate consistent with the NAIRU is considered to be too high it can be reduced by allowing an increase in the unemployment rate, which reduces the rate of wage inflation and sets the whole process going in the opposite direction. Friedman, thus, denies that it is possible in the long run (the time necessary for the change in expectations to work its way through) for there to be a trade-off between inflation and unemployment. In the long run, in other words, the Phillips curve is *vertical*, equivalent in Figure 3.4 to the line U_0 AC.

THE NATURAL RATE OF UNEMPLOYMENT AND ITS DETERMINANTS

Economists have devoted a great deal of energy and ingenuity to testing this expectations-augmented Phillips curve hypothesis, by assuming either that expectations are determined (usually adaptively) by experience or that expectations will be 'rational', at least in the sense that systematic errors will be avoided.[7] Their results vary widely. Adaptive-expectations approaches do seem to be helpful in describing a long-term breakdown in money illusion and a sudden shift upwards of the curve in the seventies, although they have less to offer to an understanding of *why* this 'gear shift' took place. Nevertheless a new conventional wisdom seems to have emerged from all this econometric work—that there *is* such a thing as a NAIRU or natural rate of unemployment. As one contributor to this literature has put it, there 'is now much less disagreement about the empirical nature of the interaction of real income and inflation: there is a short-run trade off between inflation and unemployment and it does seem to vanish in the long run' (Laidler 1981: 25).

In an earlier paper (1977) Laidler had suggested that the natural rate hypothesis, if accepted, would undermine the whole intellectual basis of the post-war, Keynesian, 'demand management' approach to employment policy. This is going too far. At any moment actual unemployment may presumably have a natural element but also an element (super-natural?) which *is* amenable to reduction by expanding aggregate demand. For instance, in Figure 3.4, any unemployment rate above OU_0 per cent is reducible by these means. Thus the extent to which the demand-management approach is undermined will depend on how high the natural rate is assumed to be; a natural rate of, say, 2 per cent is much less undermining than one of 10 per cent.

In practice, estimates of the size of the natural rate tend to depend on the methodology used. In general models based on adaptive expectations generate lower natural rates than those based on rational expectations. For instance, Sumner and Ward (1983), using an expectations augmented model which allows for a break in expectations after 1970, estimate the natural rate in the UK during the 1970s at around 4 per cent. On the other hand, Minford (1983), who implausibly assumes rational expectations throughout the period, puts it at over 4 per cent in 1975 and at 7¼ per cent and still rising by 1979; in fact the assumption of rational expectations ensures that the actual and natural rates keep close together.

Whatever the disagreement about the absolute and relative size of the natural rate of unemployment in any economy the new consensus that it exists means that theoretical attention is focused primarily on its determinants, which are assumed to be found in 'the structure of the "real" side of the economy—the institutions of the labour market, etc.' (Laidler 1975: 24). There are broadly two types of analysis of these determinants, with differing implications for policy. One approach emphasises mismatches of various kinds between the jobs that are available and the unemployed job-seekers, resulting in what is usually called structural unemployment. The other regards all unemployment as voluntary in the sense that it is attributable to a refusal to accept work at a wage that employers are willing to offer.

The two most important types of mismatch usually identified as giving rise to structural unemployment[8] are those involving skills and geography. Mismatch of skills exists if vacancies exist but an unemployed person is not qualified to fill any of them. A decline in relative important of unskilled jobs is often cited as a cause of rising unemployment, particularly in industrialised economies among the young. But, as Standing (1983: 140) points out, the average level of skill in jobs described as 'skilled' may well have declined, with the spread of automation making it easier to acquire the requisite skill through on-the-job training. Geographical mismatch, due to immobility between regions, is less disputable, although there are empirical problems in defining the regions relevant to such analysis, and most industrial countries appear to have experienced a long-term reduction in regional differences in unemployment rates (Standing 1983: 143).

The problem with this analysis of unemployment in terms of mismatch lies in the lack of evidence as to its scale and nature. Thus the costly, fashionable programmes to improve 'labour market flexibility' through 'active manpower policies', such as training and retraining for the unemployed, relocation assistance schemes and special subsidies to improve the relative employment prospects of target groups, which are based on a faith in the importance of structural unemployment, are to a large extent leaps in the dark. As Standing points out (1983: 150) this is potentially dangerous: 'if the unemployment is not "structural" the emphasis given to these policies may breed resentment and cynicism about their inefficiency among both those for whom they are designed and those responsible for implementing them'.

The second approach to the analysis of the determinants of the natural rate, which regards all unemployment as voluntary, bears a superficial resemblance to the segmented-labour-markets approach (see page 62) but differs in its emphasis on the supply side rather than the demand side of the labour market. For instance Hall (1975) posits a rigid wage sector (the government) and a flexible wage sector (the rest of the economy). The widening gap between wages in the two sectors as aggregate demand falls increases the pay off to job search. As a result job-seekers prefer to remain voluntarily unemployed for longer periods in the hope of finding a more highly paid rigid-sector job.

In Minford's 'new classical' model (Minford 1983), on the other hand, the two sectors are the union and non-union sectors. In the union sector the mark-up over the non-union wage is determined by the trades unions' monopoly power in interaction with technology and demand conditions. A worker does not have to search for knowledge of the going wage in the unregulated, non-union sector. He/she compares this going rate, in a standard optimising manner, net of tax and expenses, with net out-of-work benefits, on the one hand, and with expected future net real non-union wages, on the other. The union wage does not affect his/her work decision, since it is assumed that his/her chances of getting a union job are not affected by taking a non-union job. Thus 'the people who are "on the margin" of supply in the labour market are in the non-union sector (in "unprotected jobs"), typically on low wages and in unattractive jobs. Hence the importance in labour supply of the replacement ratio (i.e. the ratio of benefits out of work to net in-work income) for low income households, for these are the ones most likely to withdraw into unemployment and swell the statistics under additional downward pressure on wages' (*ibid.*: 11).

As can be seen, we are now in the world of 'saloon-bar economics', the equivalent of 'the story about the friend of the wife's brother who knows of someone working as a coach driver during the summer and wintering in the Bahamas on his unemployment pay' (Nickell 1979: 34). Indeed, Minford virtually admits as much: 'to those accustomed to the ways of prosperous Southern areas of the country, such ideas may seem unfamiliar, even outrageous; but it has to be said that they are part of the everyday gossip and "casual empiricism" of an area such as Liverpool' (*ibid.*: 12).

Minford is not the only economist to suggest that an increase in the ratio of benefits to income-in-employment either raises the rate of flow into unemployment by making individuals more willing to give up their jobs or increases the length of unemployment spells by enabling individuals to be more choosey about the jobs they will accept (e.g. see Maki and Spindler 1975; Cubbin and Foley 1977; Taylor 1977). Some have even applied this explanation to the experience of inter-war Britain. While conceding that 'the sharp increases in unemployment in 1921 and 1930–31 were mostly the result of monetary and other shocks to aggregate demand', Benjamin and Kochin argue that:

> however, the late twenties and thirties were characterised by high and rising real income, and the high unemployment of those times was the consequence almost solely of the dole. The army of the unemployed standing watch in Britain at the publication of the General Theory was largely a volunteer army (Benjamin and Kochin 1979: 474).

The policy implications of such an approach are: to cut unemployment benefit and make it proportional to wages (and hence remove the floor under wages in the unregulated sector); to tighten up procedures for allowing benefit; to raise tax thresholds to improve incentives to work; and to reduce substantially the power of the trade unions (cf. Minford: 4–8). This yearning for wage flexibility echoes uncannily the pre-Keynesian analysis of such economists as Pigou, quoted at the beginning of this chapter (page 53). The wheel has turned full circle. It is as if Keynes had never lived.

If there are dangers in the 'mismatch' approach to the analysis of the determinants of the natural rate of unemployment, there are even greater dangers in this 'new classical' approach, for several reasons.

First, the designation of unemployment as 'voluntary', which underlies this analysis and policy prescription, seems deliberately mischievous. As Nickell comments (1982: 4) 'in some sense it is clear that more or less all unemployment if voluntary for, by offering to dig gardens, wash cars and so on *at a low enough wage*, almost any unemployed individual could find work. However, this does not seem to me to be a very sensible use of the word voluntary, particularly if the wage mentioned above is less than that required to keep body and soul together'.[9] Nickell reasonably proposes confining the use of the term voluntary unemployment to cases in which readily available work at the ruling level of wages is rejected. This is not a trivial point, since it effects the urgency with which employment problems are tackled.

Secondly, as long as an economy's demand curve for labour as a function of the real wage is downward sloping (as in the bottom half of Figure 3.1), a fall in the real wage results, by definition, in an increase in employment. However, wage flexibility means in the first instance money wage flexibility and the original Keynesian case for at least agnosticism about the repercussions of a fall in money wages (discussed above, pp. 54-7), does not seem to have been effectively refuted at a theoretical level. Keynes' worries about the authoritarian preconditions for an effective flexible wage policy still look highly relevant also.

A third cause for concern is the scarcity of empirical backing for these tough new theories on which policy is being based in many industrialised economies. On the demand side there is some evidence, at least at a sectoral level, of a (limited) impact of real wage increases on employment and of trade unions on real wages (Nickell 1982b). On the supply side, however, while Minford feels sufficiently confident about his results to suggest that a '10 per cent rise in real (unemployment) benefits would, at current unemployment levels, raise unemployment (in Britain) by nearly 0.75 million' (*ibid.*: 20), other research suggests a much smaller impact. Nickell comments in a letter to *The Guardian* newspaper (July 14, 1983) on Minford's results that 'we must not allow the welfare of unemployed individuals to be jeopardised because credence is given to certain unusually large estimates of the impact of benefits on unemployment, which arise simply because of problems with the underlying analysis'.

Finally, it is important to note that the variable which such theories attempt to explain is usually the rate or level of open unemployment. As we saw in chapter One (pp. 5-12), this has different meanings in different places, at different times for different groups but is generally defined to consist of those who are both 'not working' and 'seeking work' and is only one form of underutilisation of labour. To repeat Sen's helpful terminology (Sen 1975), such underutilisation has three aspects: an *income* aspect, in that those who are doing less work than they are capable of are deprived of income as a result; a *production* aspect, in that under-utilisation of labour results in a loss of output; and a *recognition* aspect, in that those who are not engaged in what they and others recognise as worthwhile jobs may not regard themselves as being employed and will certainly be seeking work. As Sen points out, the standard definition of unemployment is extremely restrictive, including only those who qualify *both* under the income *and* under the recognition criteria.

It seems likely that, even at its most successful, the approach can only hope to explain why a given level of under-utilisation of labour takes one form rather than another. Thus if unemployment benefit of all kinds in Britain were abolished altogether open unemployment (on current definitions!) would fall to zero. Under-utilization of labour in all three of Sen's aspects would not disappear however. It would merely take a different form—work of extremely low productivity—just as it does in developing countries without social security systems.

CONCLUSIONS

If this chapter gives an impression of disarray in theorising about the causes of unemployment in a mature capitalist economy it is not misleading. However, it is important to be clear about what has and what has not been discredited by recent events and their interpretation. The collapse of the Phillips curve relationship between the rate of change of money wage rates and the unemployment rate, and its subsequent resurrection in an expectations augmented form, has *not* discredited Keynesian analysis of the causes of unemployment. As Robinson and Wilkinson (1977: 7) point out, Keynes would not have been surprised by the upsurge in price inflation following a long run of high employment and high profits: he 'foresaw that it would be a difficult political problem to prevent free wage bargaining from generating inflation in conditions of continuous high employment'. His (and Kalecki's) demolition of Say's law and diagnosis thereby of a defect inherent in capitalism still stand. At any moment at least part of unemployment in any economy is likely to be due to deficiency in aggregate demand. What *has* been discredited is what Robinson and Wilkinson call the 'bastard Keynesian' doctrine that the failure of Say's law is a minor blemish that can be cured by the application of simple demand management policies. Whether or not the 'natural rate' hypothesis is accepted in its entirety, there is clearly a ceiling on employment compatible with non-accelerating inflation, in economies with free wage bargaining, which is well short of full employment.

There is a dire shortage of *policy relevant* theory to deal with this situation. The natural rate theorists can only offer us either complacency (since all the unemployed are voluntarily so) or elusive 'mismatches'. Some Keynesians might derive a role for incomes policies from the Phillips curve saga, but the record of such policies over the past thirty years is not encouraging (see Sumner 1984 for a summary of the literature). It is difficult to escape the conclusion that successful management of full employment capitalism would entail extending the involvement of trade unions beyond tinkering with the process of wage determination (Robinson and Wilkinson 1977: 10).

NOTES

1. Keynes called it the classical position.
2. That Marshall had *some* doubts is shown by the fact that, after quoting with approval Mill's summary of Say's Law, he remarked (1920, p. 591, reproduced from 1879, III: 1.4): 'but though men have the power to purchase they may not choose to use it.' However, he made it clear in a footnote (p. 593) that he was not one of those 'hasty writers' who alleged that a remedy for depression is to be got 'by a study of consumption'.
3. *See* Kalecki (1943, 1944, 1945, 1965, 1971) and, for an excellent exposition, Sawyer (1982).

4. Keynes' formal definition of involuntary unemployment is tortuous: 'Men are involuntarily unemployed if, in the event of a small rise in the price of wage-goods relatively to the money-wage, both the aggregate supply of labour willing to work for the current money-wage and the aggregate demand for it at that wage would be greater than the existing volume of employment' (Keynes 1936: 15). His less formal statement, that 'the population generally is seldom doing as much work as it would like to do on the basis of the current wages . . . More labour would, as a rule, be forthcoming at the existing money-wage if it were demanded' (*ibid.* p. 7), is a clearer explanation of what is involved. *See* Kahn 1976 for a further discussion.
5. Some might regard this characterisation as unfair to both approaches, since neoclassicals nowadays emphasise the supply side and are interested in what determines an economy's capacity, and Keynes emphasised the role of expectations in the determination of equlibrium. But the policy recommendations of both schools still derive from simple theoretical frameworks that are essentially static.
6. For surveys of the literature *see* Sen (1970), Dobb (1973: 225–40).
7. *See* Sumner (1984) for a comprehensive review of this literature.
8. *See* Standing (1983) for a full discussion.
9. Cf. also the conclusion of a recent review by Standing of the 'notion of voluntary unemployment': 'The assertion that many of those counted as jobless and wanting work are in fact voluntarily unemployed, whether in low-income urbanising countries or in relatively affluent industrialised countries, has not been substantiated' (Standing 1981: 576).

4 Neoclassical Theories of Unemployment in Underdeveloped Economies

While neoclassical analysis is, essentially, as has been seen, based on the concept of general equilibrium within a static framework this has not prevented economists from claiming that many of its tools are adequate to deal with the problems of development and underdevelopment. For instance, Bauer and Yamey recognise the irrelevance of much of this general equilibrium analysis, which regards as given 'the principal long-term determinants of income and wealth, such as the factors underlying the growth of capital, the size of population, the attitude towards work, saving and risk-bearing, the quality of entrepreneurship and the extent of markets' (Bauer and Yamey 1957: 10). Nevertheless they claim that:

> some of the basic tools and concepts of economics apply widely to underdeveloped countries. This is true, for instance, of the basic elements of supply and demand analysis. Similarly, the theory of inflation, the concepts of substitution at the margin, and of the complementary or competitive relationship between factors of production, are equally enlightening whether used to elucidate events or circumstances in advanced or in under-developed countries' (*ibid.*: 8).

Lal goes even further and suggests that:

> paradoxically, with its neglect of the adjustment process between two equilibria (at least in its most readily usable 'comparative statics' form) and its emphasis on the flexibility of the prices of both commodities and factors of production, neo-classical economics is likely to be more applicable to developing than to developed countries. For, unlike in richer countries, economic agents in poor ones will have few 'reserves' to fall back upon and will thus have to adjust speedily to a change in their economic environment by swiftly altering the terms on which they are willing to exchange economic commodities (Lal 1983: 107).

'ARTIFICIAL' FACTOR PRICES

As far as the causes of unemployment are concerned, such economists, as might be expected, seek explanations in various types of government intervention or imperfection. The author of perhaps the most succinct statement of the neoclassical position on unemployment in underdeveloped economies (Ranis 1971) has attributed the problem to the failure of governments of developing countries to allow 'the changing factor endowment of society to be 'heard' over time' by 'permitting a closer relationship between the market prices of the factors of production and their equilibrium levels' (*ibid.*: 144). In Ranis' view initial import substitution policies usually combine overvalued exchange rates, low interest rates, internal terms of trade favourable to industry and high wages. Such protective devices are difficult to dismantle and artificially induce capital and import intensity. For instance, low interest rates mean that credit is rationed rather than allocated by price and a capital-intensive bias is imparted to choice of technology or output; private savings are also discouraged. Overvaluation of the exchange rate encourages imports of capital goods and discourages use of domestic labour-intensive inputs. Turning the terms of trade against agriculture by keeping food artificially cheap bestows windfall profits on protected industry.

Ranis is more cautious about wages—'a horse of a somewhat different colour'—but suggests that 'any continuing increase in real wages as a consequence of union and/or government pressure via minimum wage legislation is bound to be highly unfavourable to the maximum utilisation of the relatively abundant unskilled labour supply along the economy's production functions' (*ibid.*: 145). On the supply side, the growing gap in real wages between the agricultural and industrial sectors is blamed for a rate of rural-urban migration which is higher than the rate of growth or urban job opportunities. This analysis is regarded as valid, whatever the social system—whether 'a society has determined, in its own wisdom, to follow either a socialist, a capitalist or a mixed economy path' (*ibid.*: 147).

DEMAND FOR LABOUR: VARIABILITY OF FACTOR PROPORTIONS

As has already been emphasised, a crucial assumption of this position is that possibilities exist for substituting labour for capital. Ideally production functions will be such that isoquants (or equal-product curves) will have the shape shown in Figure 4.1. The isoquant shows all the combinations of labour and capital which, in given technical conditions, will produce a given output. For it to have the convex shape shown it is necessary to make two assumptions: (1) that the marginal rate of substitution of one factor for the other will always diminish along the curve—i.e. the more labour is being used the less capital it will be possible to give up in exchange for a further unit of labour if product is to be kept constant, and vice versa; (2) that it will diminish smoothly and continuously.

The importance of the shape of the isoquant is illustrated if we introduce a price line, showing the combinations of labour and capital it is possible to use, given total outlay and factor prices, as in Figure 4.2. Initially, given price line AC, OL

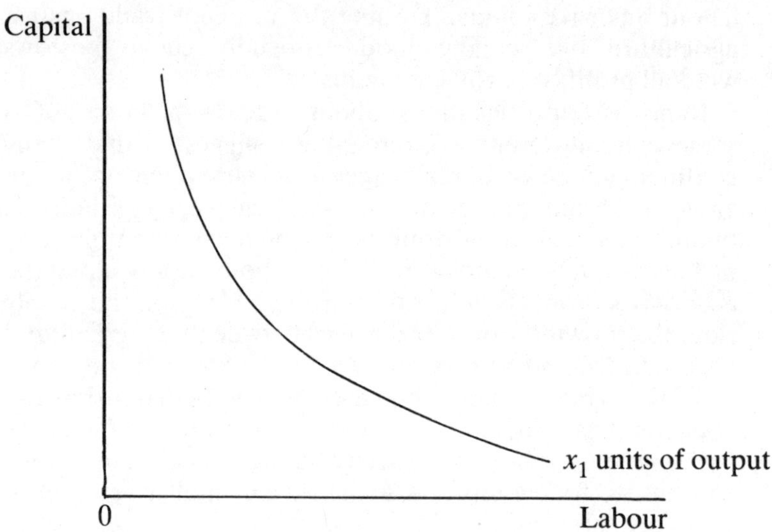

Figure 4.1: A Convex Isoquant

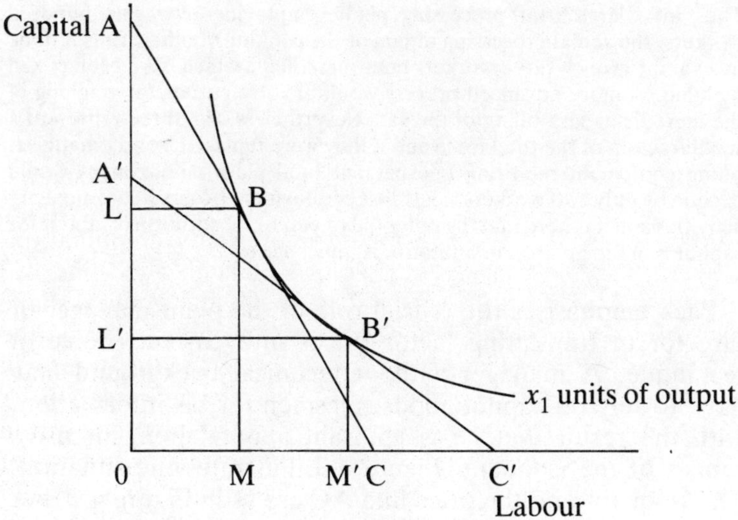

Figure 4.2: The Effect of a Fall in Wages

units of capital are used in combination with OM units of labour to produce x_1 units of output. Should labour become cheaper relative to capital (signified by the change in slope of the price line to that of A′C′) it would be possible to produce the same output with less capital (OL′) and more labour (OM′). indeed the shape of the isoquant ensures that quite small changes in factor-price ratios can be reflected in changes in factor combinations. Neoclassical analysis rests on the assumption either that isoquants are generally of this shape or that, even if there is only one way of producing a given commodity, it is still possible to vary the output mix in ways which reflect changing factor endowments and price ratios.

In this respect Pack (1979) has pointed out that the absence of substitution possibilities in the central processing operation of a manufacturing plant would not necessarily imply a similar absence in the other four basic processes—material receiving, material handling, packaging and storage of the final product. On the basis of research in Kenya, he suggests that in most plants a relatively small percentage of the labour force is involved in the actual processing operation.

Thus in a large fruit processing plant, employing over one hundred workers, the actual processing of jam or the cooking of other fruits is done in a vat into which three workers pour ingredients which have been mixed by hand. A more advanced process would involve automatic weighing of the ingredients and filling of the vat. Nevertheless, the three represent a small fraction of the total force and if they were replaced by automatic vat filling equipment requiring one person, total plant employment would decline by only two workers. . . . Most employment occurs in the auxiliary activities and it is here that the potential payoff to substitution of labour for capital is of the greatest quantitative significance (*ibid.*: 24).

Pack emphasises the crucial role of the plant manager or director in translating factor prices into correct choice of technique. A manager without technical background may have to rely on capital goods salesmen for his information, with the result that he is ignorant about labour-intensive ranges of the isoquant. Figure 4.3 illustrates the situation. The isoquant and the price line AC are as in Figure 4.2, but management is unaware of the existence of the dashed part of the curve beyond point B. Thus factor combination B is chosen, a more costly combination than the optimum D,

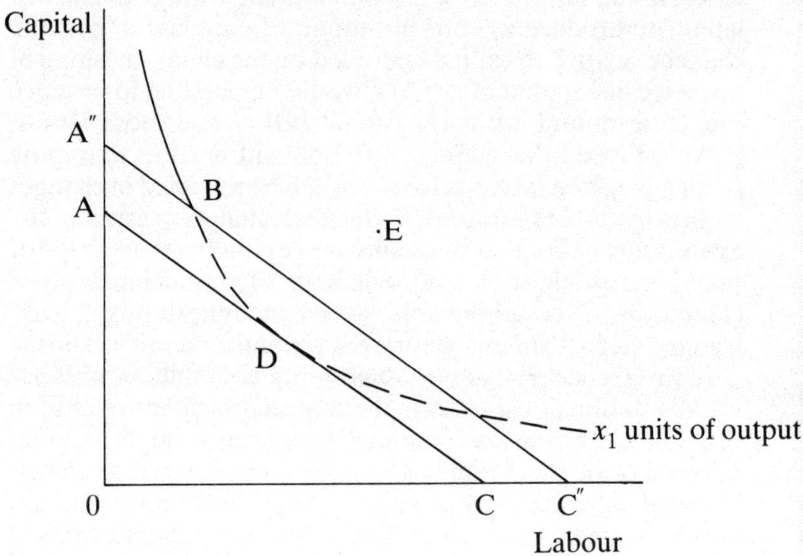

Figure 4.3: The Effect of Managerial Ignorance

signified by the fact that it is on a higher price line, A″C″. If all firms in the economy were similarly afflicted managerial ignorance might be regarded as an obstacle to the achievement of full employment. For instance, if Figure 4.3 is now taken to represent the economy as a whole, factor endowment E with existing isoquants (parallel to that shown and similarly unextended), implies substantial unemployment. However, if isoquants were extended full employment would be possible and at a high level of output since E is on a higher curve than B.

Other obstacles to a smooth response to factor price changes, emphasised by Pack in another paper (Pack 1976), are the limited flexibility of existing equipment, meaning that changes in technique are most easily made when new production decisions are taken; and the limited incentive to adjust factor proportions in high-profit, protected industries. The former, the implications of which have been explored in several 'putty-clay' (as opposed to 'putty-putty') models, is a more serious challenge to the pure neoclassical analysis than the latter which is merely taken as a sign of the need to close avenues to increased profitability other than improved productive efficiency (for example, bargaining with government for higher nominal protection or for larger quotas on critical inputs).

A more sophisticated analysis of factor price distortions is that of McKinnon (1973) who suggests that fragmentation of the economy in general and the capital markets in particular 'contributes significantly to underemployment in some areas and overinvestment in others' (*op.cit.*: 33). Fragmentation is defined as the situation in which 'firms and households are so isolated that they face different effective prices for land, labour, capital and produced commodities and do not have access to the same technologies' (*op.cit.*: 5). He attributes contemporary fragmentation largely to the usual government interventions—import tariffs and restrictions, licensing, industrial taxes and subsidies etc. The main focus is on the capital market, the unification of which is held to be necessary to eliminate other forms of fragmentation. Indeed, he defines 'economic development' as 'the reduction of the great dispersion in social rates of return to existing and new investments under domestic entrepreneurial control' (*op.cit.*: 9).

McKinnon uses the term 'entrepreneurs' to describe individuals who provide labour, make technical decisions, consume, save and invest. The scope for intertemporal decision making, within which each entrepreneur maximises his utility, is limited by: (1) his endowment of owned deployable capital; (2) his own peculiar productive or investment opportunity; and (3) his market opportunities for external lending or borrowing outside his own enterprise (*op.cit.*: 10). Entrepreneurs with (1) may lack (2) and be unattracted by the rates available under (3); others with (2) may lack (1) and (3). In addition the indivisibility of investments associated with the adoption of markedly improved technologies makes self-finance of the whole of such an investment impossible for a small entrepreneur.

Yet public policies to circumvent the capital market (tariff protection for infant industries, import licences and the associated financial leverage, corruption and monopoly privilege, the cheapening of capital goods, the turning of the terms of trade against agriculture, some types of land reform and reliance on foreign direct investment and commercial credits) induce a bias towards self-finance. For instance, raising output prices through tariffs or other subsidies enriches the holder of a production opportunity and increases the (reinvestible) cash flow from it. Self-finance, McKinnon argues (*op.cit.*: 31), can contribute to unemployment by inducing forms of overinvestment. For instance a Pakistani or Indian farmer who has successfully increased his cash flow by investing in new seeds and fertilisers may have no alternative, in the absence of high-yielding assets outside his own enterprise, to the purchase of a tractor as his next investment. And excess capacity in urban industry may also reflect the reinvestment of internal cash flow in low-priority uses.

The efficient diffusion of modern technology, according to McKinnon's paradoxical argument, will result not from the provision of cheap external finance to small-scale industry and agriculture but from *raising* rates of interest, 'so as to induce some entrepreneurs to disinvest from inferior processes to permit lending for investments in improved technology and increased scale in other enterprises' (*op.cit.*: 15). At the same time high rates of interest on financial assets are seen as a means of preventing *premature* self-financed modernisation or mechanisation. 'The well-off Pakistani farmer might open a new savings account rather than buy a new tractor. The industrialist might reduce his investment in his own plant capacity or inventories used as an inflation hedge, in order to acquire commercial claims on other firms at higher real rates of return' (*op.cit.*: 32).

Whether or not production functions are such that factor combinations are highly responsive to changes in factor price ratios, there is also the question of the extent to which factor prices are in fact 'artificial' and to which liberating market forces would result in changes in such prices. There is no doubt about the artificiality of the price of capital, in the sense that monetary authorities in developing countries keep interest rates in the organised banking system at below market equilibrium levels. McKinnon cites numerous examples of regimes of 'financial repression', including Chile in the late 1950s and Brazil in the mid-1960s, wherein:

> bank credit remains a financial appendage of certain enclaves: exclusively licensed import activities, specialised large-scale mineral exports, highly protected manufacturing, large international corporations, and various government agencies, such as coffee marketing boards or publicly controlled utilities. Even ordinary government deficits on current account frequently pre-empt the limited lending resources of the deposit banks. Financing of the rest of the economy must be met from the meagre resources of moneylenders, pawnbrokers and cooperatives (*op.cit.*: 68).

The equilibrium rate for lending by the organised banking system to rural and other small-scale borrowers would have to be substantial to be profitable (McKinnon, writing in the early seventies estimates a need for *real* rates of between 15 and 25 per cent), although they would still undercut traditional lenders.

In the case of wages, on the other hand, it is by no means obvious that 'high' levels in industrial sectors are always entirely due to 'union and/or government pressure via minimum wage legislation' (Ranis: *op.cit.*: 145). There are several good reasons, consistent with neoclassical analysis,[1] why wages may be higher in the larger-scale, more capital-intensive sectors of an economy even in a perfect labour market. Part of the differential may be due to the costs of moving and the higher cost of living near such sectors, part to differences between jobs in net psychic benefits. More subtly, there may be a positive relationship between wages and productivity. This may be a matter of high-wage employers being able to select more effective workers for a given task; or to obtain greater 'commitment' from their workers, with lower turnover and absenteeism; or to enjoy higher productivity due to the better health and nutritional standard of their workers. In any of these cases it would pay employers to offer higher wages than would be necessary to attract the minimum number of workers required. There is some evidence from Africa (Sabot 1978) that large manufacturing employers have done exactly this, increasing wages in order to shift from a high turnover, target-worker to a low-turnover, committed labour force. In such a case even a perfect labour market would not clear.

PROTECTION AS A RESTRAINT ON THE DEMAND FOR LABOUR

In addition to the capital-intensive bias allegedly imparted by factor price distortions to choice of technique and/or output mix, neoclassical economists also emphasise the restraint imposed on the rate of growth of output and employment by regimes of heavy protection and currency overvaluation.

For instance, the ILO/UNDP team (led by Ranis) which reported in 1974 on the employment problems of the Philippines points to various biases in its protected industrial structure in addition to that towards capital-intensity: towards import substitution at the finishing stages in a wide range of consumer goods; against exports of manufactures and capital goods production, which have to pay more for their inputs without receiving any benefit through higher prices for their outputs; towards large-scale enterprise; and towards regional concentration in manufacturing (ILO, 1974: 109-10).

The bias against exports of manufactured goods and capital goods production, as a result of protection of import-substituting industries, is usually analysed in terms of 'effective protection'. Thus Little, Scitovsky and Scott (1970) define the nominal rate of protection of an industry as the percentage by which the prices of the goods produced domestically can exceed what they would have to be if imports were unrestricted. If tariffs are the only form of protection and if the full potential of the protection offered is realised, this nominal rate corresponds to the *ad valorem* rate of duty on the product. The effective rate, on the other hand, is the percentage by which import restrictions both on competing products and on inputs enable *value added* by the industry to exceed what it would be in their absence.

The distinction between the nominal and effective protection rate can be summarised in an equation:

$$Z_j = \left(t_j - \sum_{i=1}^{n} a_{ij} t_i\right) / \left(1 - \sum_{i=1}^{n} a_{ij}\right)$$

where Z_j is the effective rate or protection of industry j; t_j is the nominal rate of protection of industry j; t_i is the nominal rate of protection of input *i*; and a_{ij} is what the share of input *i* in the cost of production of industry j would be in the absence of protection. From this it can be seen that the effective rate of protection of an industry will be the greater, the greater its own nominal rate and the smaller the nominal rates of its supplying industries, and the greater the percentage of total cost which is accounted for by inputs from other industries.

To this analysis of protection is added that of overvaluation of the currency, which works in the opposite direction to protection and thus may stimulate demands for more protection. Power (1972: 14) defines the net effective protection rate (N) as:

$$N = (1+Z)(1-U) - 1$$

where U is the percentage undervaluation of foreign exchange (in relation to the exchange rate that would balance the international payments account in the absence of protection). Thus net effective protection can be below effective and nominal protection if foreign exchange is significantly undervalued (i.e. the domestic currency is significantly overvalued); and undervaluation of foreign exchange, both cause and consequence of protection, will be the greater, the lower are elasticities of supply of and demand for exports.

The bias against manufactured exports in a system of protection can, then, be seen to be two-fold. They often suffer from negative effective protection, in that there are tariffs on their inputs, while import-substituting industries with high rates of effective protection (and thus with the internal terms of trade in their favour) are able to bid resources away from them. In addition, the undervaluation of foreign exchange means that *net* effective protection of these activities will be negative to an even greater extent. Similarly, the bias against capital goods production results from low nominal and negative effective protection (they are often importable duty-free) and from undervaluation of foreign exchange, which together mean that machinery can be imported at less than free trade prices. Both these biases are assumed to result in a level of employment lower than would otherwise be the case. The cheapness of imported capital goods encourages choice of capital-intensive techniques. And the absence of a domestic capital goods sector implies higher effective protection for industry as a whole.

Another way of presenting neoclassical analysis of the effects of protection is in terms of the relative rates of return to investment in import-substituting and exporting industry and hence on rates of growth of output and employment. Figure 4.4 illustrates the suggestion of the ILO team that protection has raised the rate of return to investment in import substitution in the Philippines above the minimum required as an inducement to investors. This brings rapid growth in investment and output for a while but only up to the point, K_1 in Figure 4.4, where the capital stock is large enough to supply the whole of the domestic market and imports are eliminated. Further expansion pushes the rate of return down (as prices are forced down or excess capacity develops) from the with-protection level of 30 per cent to the minimum 15 per cent required, when capital stock reaches OK_2. From this point onwards growth in demand (signified by the arrows in Figure 4.4) is the only source of inducement to investors. The team claims that this is a schematic summary of the sequence actually followed by the Philippines between 1948 and 1972 (*ibid.*: 110–2).

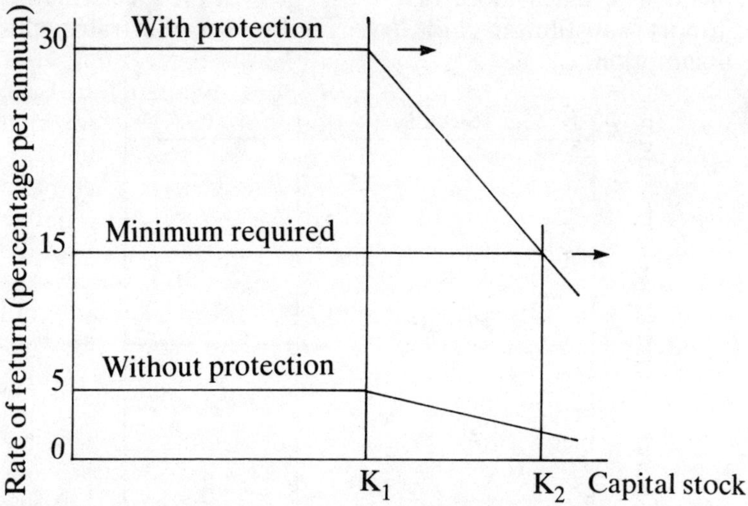

Figure 4.4: Returns to Investment in Import Substitution
Source: ILO (1974: 111)

Protection and tax holidays for import-substituting industry, it is also claimed, mean that social profitability is much lower than private profitability. Tariffs, quota restrictions and bans on imports push up prices paid by consumers for a given quantity of goods; production is stimulated to some extent by direct tax concessions and/or subsidised credit; and production replaces imports on which high duties would have been levied. So part of the investor's return is a transfer of income to him from consumers or from the government.

Unprotected industries, on the other hand, particularly those producing for export, pay taxes on some of their inputs (such as imported fuel) as well as direct taxes and often export taxes, while almost the whole value of their output represents a net benefit to society. Thus, in contrast to protected industry, social profitability is in their case higher than private profitability. This conclusion is reinforced if, as is claimed to be the case in the Philippines, the unprotected industries are more labour-intensive than the protected industries. Moreover, the export manufacturing sector is assumed to be faced with much more favourable growth prospects than is import substituting industry. Figure 4.5 illustrates this assumption.

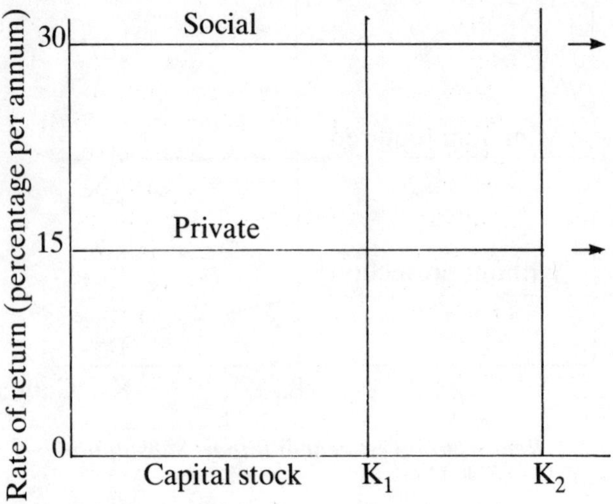

Figure 4.5: Returns to Investment in Exporting
Source: ILO (1974: 111)

Both social and private rates of return, in contrast to the import-substituting case shown in Figure 4.4, are assumed to be independent of the rate at which capital accumulates. So, as the capital stock in the sector grows from OK_1 to OK_2, rates of return do not fall. This is equivalent to an assumption of infinite world elasticity of demand for a country's exports. The excess of social over private rate of return implies that some of the benefits accrue to workers (through higher wage incomes) and to the government (through higher taxes) and not to the private investor, while most or all of the initial sacrifice of consumption required to finance the investment is made by the private investor. However the private rate of return has to be high enough to be an inducement to the investor. Examples of the types of industry thought likely to meet these conditions in the Philippines at that time are the 'highly labour intensive' cases of garments, shoes, furniture, handicrafts, electronics and tourism. It is assumed that growth of such industries could be fast enough to mop up the country's labour surplus and inaugurate an era of rising real wages (*ibid.*: 114-116).

The neoclassical analysis of the evils of protected import-substituting industrialisation is undoubtedly powerful and, with the backing of the International Monetary fund and the World Bank, has swept all before it in policy circles (e.g. World Bank 1981). In its more subtle forms (e.g. Power 1972) it does not deny the validity of traditional analyses of market failures, such as the infant industry and external economies arguments, though it maintains that tariffs and quotas are not the best way to deal with these. There is still a tendency among many neoclassical economists, however, to proceed as if future factor supplies were given, rather than the consequence of current decisions about resource allocation, and to plan in terms of static rather than dynamic comparative advantage.

There is also a tendency to understate the stringency of the conditions for a successful devaluation, not only in the traditional terms of elasticities of demand and supply but also in terms of the capacity to prevent it from being eroded by inflation. As Lewis has pointed out, 'there are countries which can devalue effectively, as shown by a considerable change in their balance of payments. There are also other countries which cannot devalue effectively because they lack the necessary discipline to keep money costs under control in the face of increased prices of imports' (Lewis 1972: 235). Recent African experience has underlined this point; in four countries which have pursued a relatively active exchange rate policy between 1977 and 1982, in response to World Bank and IMF pressure, 'quite large depreciations in nominal effective rates have still left the real effective rate either appreciated or only slightly devalued' (World Bank 1983: 9).

Moreover, the assumptions about growth prospects for third-world manufactured exports and about their social profitability underlying Figure 4.5 look decidedly shaky.[2] Markets for such exports are growing only slowly. The *World Development Report 1984* (World Bank 1984) implicitly predicts slower growth in industrialised economies in the rest of the 1980s than in the 1970s (see Chapter Nine, for further discussion). This would not be critical, as far as manufactured exports are concerned, as long as access to industrialised-economy markets remained open. As Lal points out, 'by replacing increasingly uncompetitive, import-competing goods in developed country markets, developing countries can expand their manufactured exports even though total incomes, and therefore aggregate demand for manufactures, are stagnant in developed countries' (Lal 1983: 36). But such growth as is likely to occur in industrialised economies is expected to be relatively jobless, offering no relief to existing massive unemployment there. This means not only that markets for primary products are going to be growing even more slowly than usual (due to slow growth), but also that the protectionist mood in industrialised countries is likely to be reinforced and competition in third markets for manufactured goods to be increased.

The dangers of the drift towards protectionism are recognised nowadays by neoclassical economists. For instance, Lal emphasises that 'the growing resistance of the North to . . . desirable shifts in industrial structure . . . poses a danger to the ability of poor countries to develop in line with their own comparative advantage' (Lal *op.cit.*: 37). This means that, even for a single relatively small economy such as the Philippines, the assumption of infinite elasticity of world demand for its manufactured exports embodied in Figure 4.5 looks highly dubious. And, of course, if *all* the developing economies currently in receipt of neoclassical advice to become aggressively outward-looking in their industrialisation policies actually followed it, the fallacy of composition would come into play with disastrous consequences. A simulation exercise mounted by Cline shows that generalisation of the export-led growth model of Hong Kong, South Korea, Singapore and Taiwan across all developing countries would result in untenable market penetration into industrial countries. Such a generalisation

> would require LDC exports of manufactures to rise seven-fold, implying a surge in their share of industrial country manufactured imports from approximately one-sixth to approximately three-fifths. Using an LDC import penetration ratio of 15% as a threshold beyond which protective response would be expected, fully four-fifths of the industrial country markets for manufactured exports from LDCs would be vulnerable to probable protective action in the face of the flood of LDC exports caused by general adoption of the East Asian export model (Cline 1982: 88).

As for social profitability, this is affected by the cheap (often young female) labour basis of much of this type of industrialisation, the tax and other concessions offered to foreign investors[3] and the often heavy government investment in infrastructure. Poor market conditions and prospects intensify competition for investors between exporting countries, often expressed in a 'concessions auction' to the further detriment of social profitability. Moreover, such competition, for markets and capital, requires that labour be kept weak. For instance, Little emphasises the importance of 'free labour markets' to the strategy and instances Sincapore, where

> the unions were very strong, and were also communist-dominated. There was great labour unrest in the early sixties. Prime Minister Lee Kuan Yew then successfully rode the tiger! Very comprehensive labour and union legislation was enacted in the late sixties. Employment conditions that were previously in the sphere of collective bargaining are now controlled by law, and the government has wide powers to settle strikes (which require a secret ballot) (Little 1981: 44).

There are echoes here of Keynes' remarks about the authoritarian preconditions for flexible-wage policy in the thirties: 'one can imagine it in operation in Italy, Germany or Russia, but not in France, the United States or Great Britain' (Keynes 1936: 269).

THE COSTS AND BENEFITS OF EXPORTING WORKERS

In addition to the bias against exports of manufactured goods resulting from regimes of protection and factor prioce distortion there is also seen to be a bias against the export of workers. An overvalued currency and 'too high' domestic wage rates make it difficult for a country's workers to compete in the labour markets of labour-shortage economies. Getting prices right woud help to improve such competitiveness. As in the case of manufactured exports there may be a tendency for neoclassical economists to exaggerate the market prospects and overstate the net social benefits likely to be obtained from the process of exporting workers.

From an internationalist viewpoint the process is, virtually by definition, beneficial. For instance, Johnson (1968) starts with the assumption that the international circulation of human capital is a beneficial process, since it reflects the free choices of the individuals who choose to migrate, and the presumption that any argument to the contrary needs very careful scrutiny. Since it can be assumed that there is a private gain to the migrant Johnson would have to be convinced that the net social loss is greater than this private gain before he would agree that migration is undesirable. However, the assumption underlying this internationalist view is that the policy objective is to maximise world welfare, without regard to the geographical location of the beneficiaries. Perhaps unfortunately, this is not the actual policy objective of national governments.

A slight modification of this position is to assume that the national objective is to maximise the nation's income per head, including in the nation those who have emigrated as well as those who have remained at home. This implies that emigration is to be welcomed as long as (a) the emigrant improves his/her income and (b) his/her departure does not reduce the income per head of those left behind. Again (a) is assumed to be the case where migration is voluntary and those remaining behind are judged to suffer 'only under rather rare circumstances' (Grubel and Scott 1966). But again the underlying assumption does not correspond to the objectives of most national planners.

When the nation is more narrowly defined as those residing within national boundaries, the usual neoclassical procedure is to analyse the issues within a cost/benefit or rate of return framework. For instance, Hadley (1977) uses the following formulae to define the benefits and costs of the export of workers from Egypt. Benefit is defined as:

$$B = \sum_{i=1}^{n} \frac{(m+t_E)(Y_{Ai}) + F_i}{(1+r)^i}$$

where Y_A is the after-tax income of migrants in the labour-importing country;
m is the proportion of income remitted to Egypt;
t is the proportion of income taxed by Egypt;
F is the foreign exchange transfers in return for labour exports;
n is the expected period of migration in years; and
r is the discount rate.

Cost is defined as:

$$C = M - S + \sum_{i=1}^{n} \frac{Y_{E_i} + E_i}{(1+r)^i}$$

where M is the direct costs of migration;
S is any subsidy payments made by the labour-importing country;
Y_E is the before-tax income that the emigrant would have earned if (s)he had remained in Egypt; and
E is forgone externalities in Egypt.

These are particularly narrow definitions, with benefit defined entirely in terms of the remittances, tax receipts and transfers received during the period that the migrant remains abroad and cost entirely in terms of the costs incurred by the Egyptian economy during the period of migration. This is almost guaranteed to yield an internal rate of return that compares favourably with that on alternative investments—particularly if Y_E can be assumed to be close to zero (for example, if emigration is from unemployment or low-productivity employment in a labour-surplus economy), *E* to be negligible and *m* to be high. A more comprehensive and dynamic approach would take into account indirect effects on the benefit as well as the cost side and would analyse the repercussions of migration over whatever period they took to work themselves out.

In practice, in an economy like Egypt, the indirect effects of exporting workers are likely to be so important as to cast doubt on the validity of a partial-equilibrium tool such as cost/benefit or rate-of-return analysis. Remittances are spectacular (around $27,000 million in total in 1980 and, in the case of Egypt, equivalent to 60 per cent of export earnings) but often in the form of consumer goods rather than money; and money remittances tend to be spent predominantly on consumer goods (usually with a high import content), housing, land and schooling. Clearly the lucky recipients benefit, but indirect effects may be negative. Appreciation of the exchange rate may affect the competitiveness of manufactured exports and the profitability of primary products. Land and other prices may rise and the demonstration effect of remittances may be strong. In the areas where a high proportion of the labour force is abroad this may come to be seen as the only route to higher incomes and spectacular consumption patterns, with a debilitating effect on the local economy.

As another indirect effect, returned migrants might be expected to be an important source of skills to galvanise the rural and industrial economies to which they return. The extent to which this happens varies widely but in general experience has been disappointing. For instance, Piore reports of migrants into the United States that they 'have not been a significant source of industrial skills' for their home economies.

> The most skilled of the migrant workers are reluctant to return home. Those who do return often turn out to have acquired little in the way of industrial skills and are, in any case, loath to enter in their home country the kinds of industries and occupations in which they worked abroad (Piore 1979).

They also contribute further to the demonstration effect which their remittances have already generated.

The proportion of income remitted (*m* in the benefit equation) will be high in the early stages of migration from one country to another (when migrants are predominantly single adult males) but tends to fall over time as migrants are joined by or acquire dependents. Hence, there may be a coincidence of interest between host-country and source-country governments, which both (for different reasons) prefer temporary, unaccompanied migration—in conflict with the preferences of many of the migrants themselves.

If migrants are relatively skilled, rather than unskilled surplus labour, the direct cost of their absence (Y_E in the cost equation) may be higher than is generally assumed. A fairly high proportion of migrants has some skills. For instance, 62 per cent of foreign workers entering France between 1964 and 1978 were classified as skilled or semi-sklled (Ecevit and Zachariah 1978: 34) and the comparable figure for Saudi Arabia in 1975 was 46 per cent (*ibid.*: 37). Even when unskilled, a high proportion of migrants may be young males with key roles in the division of labour within the village economy; considerable reorganisation of work may be necessary to avoid a fall in output as a consequence of emigration.

Thus, if it is left to the free play of market forces, the strategy of exporting workers is likely to have a higher cost and to yield a smaller benefit in the short or medium term than a glance at the huge reserves of surplus labour available, the staggering figures on remittances and the apparent process of skill acquisition would suggest. In the longer run its impact on the productive capacity and rate of growth of the labour-exporting economy (as opposed to the consumption of some groups within that economy) may be minimal or even negative, tying the economy into chronic dependence on labour export rather than laying the basis for eventual growth towards full employment.

However, the stakes are too high to be rejected out of hand. There is a structured and centrally organised approach to exporting workers, pioneered by South Korea and much imitated by others including the Philippines (with the slogan, the Philippines Overseas Employment Development Board 'delivers Filipino workers anywhere in the world') and even China. In the Korean version this involves construction and engineering contracts, using Korean contractors, materials, equipment and labour teams, thus maximising foreign exchange earnings in addition to workers' remittances. In the Chinese version unskilled workers are employed by Italian corporations which pay a fee direct to the Chinese government (F in the benefit equation) which in turn pays the workers. Without going as far as this governments of most labour-exporting countries now have schemes to encourage the channelling of at least some of the foreign exchange remittances into official hands. Such schemes, if efficiently devised and implemented, can go a long way towards making exporting workers a nationally profitable business at least for as long as excess demand persists in the labour-importing countries (see Chapter Nine, page 228).

In the end the impact of exporting labour on the source economy may depend primarily on the context from which such exports are being made. Emigrants' remittances and acquired skills will not, in themselves, dynamise a stagnant economy but a well-managed migration policy, with remittances effectively channelled into productive investment, might well be a useful part of a *planned* strategy for growth of output and employment.

LABOUR SUPPLY: INTERNAL MIGRATION AND URBAN UNEMPLOYMENT

On the labour supply side there is the same emphasis on the impact of 'too high' wages and an abundance of choice-theoretic models of rural-urban migration and urban unemployment. Bauer, for instance, describes the way in which 'the operation of formal or informal minimum wage controls above the equilibrium level for the type of labour involved' leads to the growth of urban unemployment.

> the attraction of being employed at these wages, together with the need to be available for employment when required, results in the formation of pools of unemployed or intermittently employed labour. This situation, which is unrelated to population pressure or growth, is observable in the urban labour markets of many LDCs (Bauer 1981: 52).

This approach, with its obvious family resemblance to the search models applied to mature capitalist economies (see page 70), has been set out more formally by Harris and Todaro (Harris and Todaro 1970; Todaro 1976). In contemplating rural–urban migration, Todaro argues:

> members of the labour force, both actual and potential, compare the discounted value of their expected net income streams for a given time horizon in the urban sector (i.e. the difference between returns and costs of migration) with the discounted value of expected net rural incomes (assumed to be determined by labour's average rural productivity) and migrate if the former exceeds the latter (Todaro, 1976: 41).

As a schematic depiction of an individual's thought processes, dealing with a migrant's *subjective* expectations, this is irrefutable. To be useful, therefore, it has to be translated into a testable macroeconomic migration function. Todaro (1976: 46) suggests the following version:

$$m = F(E_U/U_L, Y_U/Y_R, Z)$$

where m is the migration rate in relation to the rural labour force; E_U is the level of modern sector employment; U_L is the urban labour force; Y_U is the urban wage; Y_R is the rural average product; and Z is other factors, such as distance, personal contacts, urban amenities, etc.

In other words, the migration rate is held to depend primarily on the probability that an urban labourer can successfully find a modern sector job and on the urban–rural income differential; but also on 'other factors' which 'exert some influence on the migrant's perception of the relative "costs" and "benefits" of origin and destination areas' (*ibid.*: 46).

Put in this way, a distinctive feature of the model emerges: the dependence of supply upon demand and the consequent prediction 'that there is no inherent tendency for rural workers . . . to continue to pour into urban areas at such a pace that the unemployment rate becomes ever more serious merely because the wage paid to those fortunate enough to possess a job in the modern sector is higher than that received by the typical rural workers' (Todaro, 1968: 389). The policy implication of this is that there is no point in trying to increase urban employment opportunities since 'an increase in employment is accompanied by an increase in unemployment'[4] (Frank, 1968: 266). The implication for research, according to Todaro (1976: 75), is that 'a more scrupulous and detailed estimation of income and employment elasticities of migration for different countries at different points in time' is a 'major priority . . . From the policy point of view a knowledge of such migration elasticities would go a very long way towards improving the empirical base from which effective wage, employment and income policies designed to induce a socially more efficient spatial allocation of human resources can be formulated'.

While accepting the core of the Harris–Todaro model—the intersectoral wage gap and the labour supply function based on expected rather than actual incomes—neoclassical economists have lost no time in refining its details. For instance, if 'other factors' in the above macro-economic migration function are ignored, a condition of zero-migration equilibrium can be derived from it as follows:

$$\frac{E_U}{U_L} Y_U = Y_R$$

and the equilibrium employment rate is then

$$\frac{E_U}{U_L} = \frac{Y_R}{Y_U}$$

This gives rise to some problems. For instance, Fields (1975) points out that, as incomes per head in urban areas are anywhere from two to eight times as high as in rural areas, this would predict unemployment rates of between 50 and 88 per cent. Yet the highest urban unemployment rate observed in seventeen developing countries is 20 per cent (Turnham, 1971: 57). Fields' answer to this discrepancy is to replace the implicit Harris–Todaro assumption that 'persons living in rural areas have no chance whatever of finding urban jobs' with the assumption that agricultural workers have some chance of obtaining urban employment. This yields an equilibrium employment rate, E_U/U_L, greater than the ratio of rural to urban wages, Y_R/Y_U. Thus 'there is a lower equilibrium unemployment rate in general than would be predicted by the Harris–Todaro model; and the greater the relative chance of rural workers finding urban jobs, the greater the discrepancy between the general result and the Harris–Todaro result' (Fields, 1975: 171).

Fields extends the model in various other ways. The introduction, of a third sector, which he calls the 'murky sector', seen as a better base for a job search than rural employment and not much worse for this purpose than open unemployment, further reduces the equilibrium unemployment rate. The additional assumption that employers use educational attainment as a criterion for hiring and select the better educated in preference to those with less education reduces the rate even further. This is because, 'when an educated worker is hired, he fills a position which some greater number of uneducated workers had been seeking'. For example, in the equilibrium employment equation above, if Y_R/Y_U for uneducated workers is 1/3, the equilibrium employment rate for such workers, E_U/U_L, is also 1/3. 'For each educated worker who is hired preferentially, there is one less urban job available to uneducated workers, and in equilibrium there would be three fewer job seekers' (*ibid.*: 177). However if the urban probability embodied in the model is the probability of *being hired* for an urban job rather than the probability of currently being in employment (as the use of the proxy E_U/U_L implies) this considerably increases the sensitivity of the urban unemployment level and rate to additions to the number of modern-sector jobs.

A further refinement explored by Harris and Sabot (1982) is that of relaxing the assumption that workers have perfect knowledge of labour market conditions, which 'converts unemployment from a queueing phenomenon to one in which workers engage in job search as a means of improving their information and hence their own prospects' (*ibid.* : 70). Unlike search models previously applied to industrial economies (see page 70), Harris and Sabot assume that the distribution of offers facing any searcher is *not* independent of other searchers. This produces the result that the duration of search is likely to be longer (and hence average levels of unemployment for a given labour force are likely to be higher) the greater the dispersion of wage offers and the higher the initial level of unemployment. They analyse non-homogeneous labour markets in a similar way—for instance, explaining the generally higher levels of open unemployment for relatively well-educated groups by the fact that the more educated are likely to face a much wider dispersion of potential offers; it will pay them, therefore, to invest more time in search since the potential returns to further search are much higher. The relation between unemployment and migration becomes more complicated than in the Harris–Todaro model, since unemployment is determined not only by the excess of job-seekers over vacancies but also by the search behaviour of participants in the labour market. In the Harris–Sabot model, even if total job vacancies exceed the number of searchers, urban unemployment arising from search behaviour is still likely, since many job offers at low wages will be refused. However, migration is still endogeneously determined and likely to vary inversely with the rate of urban unemployment.

The 'search' explanation of the tendency towards high rates of unemployment among educated people in some developing countries had earlier been elaborated by Blaug, who describes educated unemployment in India as a 'revolving queue: it is not that some are permanently employed and others are permanently unemployed, but rather that large numbers are made to wait years before finding a first job' (Blaug. 1973: 207). Over time earnings differentials between the more educated and the less educated have narrowed, in line with the predictions of neoclassical theory, as employers have upgraded their hiring standards in the face of an excess supply of applicants. But the narrowing has never been fast enough to clear the market or even to reduce the rate of educated unemployment. Factors slowing down the process of adjustment to unemployment and in particular the rate at which the unemployed reduce their 'reservation price', in Blaug's view, include: strong taboos about changing jobs to enhance one's prospects, which necessitate care in choosing one's first job; the poor organisation of the labour market which makes searching for work a full-time occupation; and the possibility of relying almost indefinitely on support from one's extended family.

Blaug's explanation of the Indian case reflects the neoclassical analysis of the (private or social) decision to invest in education in terms of rate of return, based on the formula:

$$\sum_{t=a}^{t=z} \frac{E_t - C_t}{(1+r)^t} = 0$$

where r is the internal rate of return;
E is the excess of annual earnings[5] of those educated to this level over those educated to the previous level;
C is the costs of education to this level;[6]
t=a is the year of entry to the labour force;
t=z is the year of retirement from the labour force.

In the case of India Blaug emphasizes that the private rate of return (the value of r that makes the left-hand side of the equation equal to zero) on matriculate qualifications and degrees, even in arts subjects and even taking into account the likelihood of a long period of unemployment was still (at the end of the 1960s) high enough to make additional education a good investment for individuals. The apparent preference for non-technical courses on the part of students is explained by the fact that admissions to technical courses have been restricted while those to non-technical courses have not.

The social rate of return, in his view, is another matter. Indian education is heavily subsidised, with three quarters of total educational expenditure coming from government funds. In secondary and higher education institutions fees are set below costs and scholarship finance is made available to some students. At the same time the government recovers little of the extra earnings of the better educated through direct taxation. As a result, social rates of return on educational investment are below private rates of return and social rates of return to secondary and general higher education are well below those to primary and middle school education[7] (Blaug, 1973: 208).

Thus the emergence and persistence of educated unemployment are explained by a combination of factors favouring a lengthy job search and of government subsidies to education. Manpower planning explanations which emphasise a mismatch between the types of skills being produced by the education and training system and those required in the economy are generally rejected by neoclassical economists, who assume very high elasticities of substitution between skilled persons and very high elasticities of demand for different skills (cf. Blaug, 1970: 216). So are explanations in terms of the unwillingness of educated people to get their hands dirty, with their implication that attitudes can be changed by changes in school curricula and syllabi. Most of them would agree, in this respect, with Foster's view that

> the vocational aspirations of children and the occupations which they enter are almost exclusively determined by factors which lie outside the schools. Indeed, in terms of the actual opportunities open to them, the students' perceptions are remarkably realistic. It follows, therefore, that no amount of formal technical, vocational or agricultural instruction alone is going to check the movement from the rural areas, reduce the volume of unemployment, or indeed necessarily have any effect on the rate of economic development (Foster: 1966).

These choice–theoretic models of the supply side of the

labour market nicely illustrate the limitations of neoclassical explanations of unemployment in economies undergoing rapid structural change. Although there may be doubts about some of the assumptions of some versions (for instance, are the more educated always likely to face a wider dispersion of wage offers and is the convenience of full-time job search always enough to offset fears of employers' preference for recruits who are already employed?), in general they have undoubted intuitive appeal as characterisations of decisions by individuals at a single point in time. It is when the attempt is made to use an aggregation of those decisions as the base for building a theory of macrochanges *over time* that they run into trouble. It is no accident, for instance, that even the simplest of these models, the original Harris–Todaro version, has never been adequately tested as a theory of the determination of the rate of rural–urban migration over time.[8] This is partly because of the intrinsic difficulties of generating time–series data on migration. More fundamentally, however, even if such data were available, rapid structural change would pose a virtually insurmountable problem for an aggregated theory of this kind.

If it is the case (as is suggested in Chapter Six, page 156) that different rural class/income categories, ever-changing in their composition, respond to different aspects of the urban class/income structure which is itself changing, Todaro's call for more research on migration elasticities (see page 104) looks misguided. To put it in the terminology of elementary economic analysis, if we have a function relating the aggregate migration rate to the expected average income differential, in conditions of rapid structural change not only are shifts in the curve likely to be massively more important than movements along it, but also the slope of the curve is likely to change unpredictably over time as the distribution between categories underlying any given average income changes. Even in terms of data collection time alone, the search for a migration function which is sufficiently disaggregated to handle *both* structural changes *and* response to the expected income differential, in a way that would yield elasticities stable enough for policy putposes, looks likely to be unprofitable.

Thus neo-classical supply-side theorems are likely to be useful, if at all, only in explaining *patterns* of migration and unemployment. Why, say, is the unemployment rate higher in Nairobi than in Mombasa? Why is it higher among secondary school leavers than among primary school leavers? These are the kinds of questions which such theorems can handle. They are likely to be much less successful in explaining why the unemployment rate in a particular city is higher in 1984 than it was in 1972.

CONCLUSIONS

The neoclassical prescription of 'getting factor prices right' as a cure for unemployment is based, as has been seen, on specific assumptions; on the demand side, about such things as the nature of production functions and of factor market imperfections, growth prospects for third-world manufactured exports and their social profitability; and, on the supply side, about individuals' responses to expected income differentials.

Its framework of analysis, also in less as in more industrialised economies, is essentially static. Thus, in Figure 4.2, on the demand side, it is concerned with moving along a given isoquant by changing factor prices rather than with shifting to a higher-output isoquant; and, on the supply side, it is concerned with moving along a given migration curve rather than with shifting it. On the determinants of the growth and structural change which shift the curves it has little to say. Some neoclassical economists admit as much; for instance, Lal concedes that 'it is true . . . that [neoclassical] economic theory is unable to offer a rigorous account of the *process of development, the so-called dynamic aspects*' (*op.cit.*: 106).[9]

Moreover, as in industrialised economies, most neoclassical theorists implicitly recognise only one form of labour underutilisation—open unemployment. They are particularly scathing about the concept of surplus labour in agriculture, implying productivity of zero at the margin. Perhaps the best known attack on the concept is that of Schultz, who derides the visiting agricultural expert who 'sees

. . . many workers in agriculture producing unbelievably little when they work, and many of them appear to be idle much of the time. The belief that he is seeing even more excess labour in agriculture than he knows exists, for example, in the United States is highly plausible to him' (Schultz, 1964: 59). In Schultz's view:

the tap root of this doctrine [of labour of zero value] has been a set of bad statistical estimates that emerged from playing the game of treating agricultural production as if it could be organised to employ all agricultural workers ten hours a day the year round (Sundays and holidays off, of course), or of taking the combination of factors of production and the higher labour outputs that had been achieved in a technically more advanced country and applying this mix of factors to the poor agricultural country (*ibid.*: 58).

He quotes approvingly Viner's judgement that 'it is impossible to conceive of a farm of any kind on which, other factors of production being held constant in quantity, and even in form as well, it would not be possible, by known methods, to obtain some addition to the crop by using additional labour in more careful selection and planting of the seed, more intensive weeding, cultivation, thinning and mulching, more painstaking harvesting, gleaning and cleaning of the crop (Viner, 1957: 347).

Other neoclassical economists share Schultz's and Viner's scepticism about surplus labour. Two questions which cause them particular difficulties are: how can the possibility of zero marginal productivity of labour by reconciled with the presumption of positive marginal disutility of effort? And why would employers take on additional workers once marginal product had fallen below the wage?

The first worry is based on a misunderstanding of what the concept of surplus labour involves. For instance, Lal appears to think that he is challenging the concept when he maintains that for third-world labourers 'as for workers in the developed world the cost of 'sweat' rises the harder and longer they have to work. No less than their Western counterparts, they are unlikely to be in 'surplus' in any meaningful economic sense' (*op.cit.*: 105). But, as Sen has pointed out (see pages 16-20), a 'zero-marginal-product' surplus of workers is easily reconcilable with positive marginal disutility of effort as long as only a slight relaxation of the *ceteris paribus* assumption is allowed.

As for the second question raised by neoclassical economists, concerning the conflict between the employment of workers with marginal productivity below their wage and normal profit-maximising assumptions, this is answerable in a number of ways. The most ingenious reconciliation is that of Leibenstein (1957: ch. 6) who posits a wage–productivity relationship similar to that discussed in pages 89-90. In a situation where the level of nutrition and thus of productivity varied directly with the wage it might be to the benefit of landowners' profits to pay a wage above the competitive level, especially where that level was tending towards zero. Lewis (1954) seeks an answer in differences in motivation on the part of employers in the subsistence sector: 'the code of ethical behaviour so shapes itself that it becomes good form for each person to offer as much employment as he can. The line between employees and dependents is very thinly drawn. Social prestige requires people to have servants, and the grand seigneur may have to keep a whole army of retainers who are really little more than a burden upon his purse'. But the simplest answer is Nurkse's, namely (1953: 33) that the analysis was not intended to be applied to wage labour but to 'family employment in peasant communities'. In this cast the purpose of production is not profit or surplus maximisation but maximisation of, or achievement of a given level of, output, and it makes sense to take on extra workers as long as they are either adding to output or reducing the number of man-hours per worker required to produce a given level of output.

At any rate the concentration on open unemployment allows a somewhat complacent view to be taken of the employment problems of the third world. In the extreme case, if all unemployment were of the search variety then, as Berry and Sabot put it (1978: 1220), 'the unemployed would in fact be self-employed in information collection, and under certain conditions such labour would be optimally allocated'. Though many neoclassical economists would not go as far as that, they do tend to suggest that the welfare costs of unemployment are reduced by intra-family transfers and by the availability of flexible-income sectors as employers of last resort. Berry and Sabot report research results suggesting that 'the pool of unemployed comprises predominantly non-heads of household, the young and married women who do not bear economic responsibility for others and who have a high degree of access to transfer payments from parents of husbands . . . Most of the unemployed are educated, which places their parents in the top half or third of the income distribution . . . Being without work is a luxury only a small proportion of the labour force can afford for longer than several months at a time' (*op.cit.*: 1221).

This may be true, but open unemployment represents only a small part of the underutilisation of labour that occurs in a developing economy—in Sen's terms (pages 6-9) the tiny overlap between the income and recognition aspects. The large number of those who are not working but also not, in terms of the census definition, seeking work and of those who are seeking work but 'working' is excluded, as is any consideration of the production aspect of under-utilisation of labour.

NOTES

1. *See* Berry and Sabot (1978: 1207) for a guide to the relevant literature.
2. For further discussion *see* Chapter 8.
3. Foreign investment or a link with a foreign buying group is usually a precondition of breaking into the markets of industrialised countries.
4. A special assumption that average rural production does not rise as a result of migration is needed for this policy implication to follow.
5. Before-tax earnings for a social-rate-of-return calculation; after-tax earnings for a private-rate-of-return calculation.
6. For a social-rate-of-return calculation costs would include: current operating costs; capital repayments on the plant; interest on the capital; and forgone output. For a private-rate-of-return calculation costs would include: fees; additional maintenance costs and forgone income.
7. Similar findings have been reported in other countries. For instance Psacharopoulos (1973) summarises rate-of-return results from twenty-two developing countries as follows:

Level of education:	*Primary*	*Secondary*	*Higher*
Private rate of return	29	19	24
Social rate of return	27	16	13

The use of earnings differentials as a measure of *social* (as opposed to private) benefit raises several conceptual problems, including those arising from the fact that: all employers are not profit maximisers (eg the civil service and other parts of the public sector); even in profit-maximising sectors all labour markets are not perfectly competitive; more educated workers often 'bump' less educated workers out of given occupations, etc. In addition, there is the practical problem (for both private and social rate of return calculations) of isolating the contribution of *education* (as opposed to intelligence, class background etc) to earnings differentials. *See* Chapter Six, page 151, for discussion of the screening hypothesis, which disputes the impact of schooling on productivity and income.

8. Barnum and Sabot (1977), in their study of Tanzania, described by Todaro as 'the first really comprehensive and significant test' of his hypothesis, are the only economists so far to have attempted to bring time into the analysis. *See* Godfrey (1979) for a critique of their ingenious but ultimately unconvincing approach.
9. 'But', he continues, 'neither have the [development economists] succeeded in supplying an alternative theoretical framework for studying and influencing the dynamic processes. The arguments for *dirigisme* based on so-called 'dynamic aspects' usually turn out to be either incoherent or merely handwaving.' The truth or otherwise of this accusation will be considered in the next three chapters.

5 Pioneering Development Economics: Surplus Labour as an Opportunity

Most of the economists who write about development are not 'development economists' in the sense in which the title is used in this chapter. They are, rather, neoclassical economists who happen to work on developing countries, and their work, in so far as it relates to employment, has been reviewed in the previous chapter. In this and the next two chapters the title of development economist is reserved for those who are most likely to raise the blood pressure of neoclassical economists such as Lal. Three elements of their approach, as he combatively describes them, are as follows:

> The major one is the belief that the price mechanism, or the working of a market economy, needs to be supplanted (and not merely supplemented) by various forms of direct government control, both national and international, to promote economic development. A complementary element is the belief that the traditional concern of orthodox micro-economics with the allocation of given (though changing) resources is at best of minor importance in the design of public policies . . . The third element is the belief that the classical 19th century liberal case for free trade is invalid for developing countries, and thus government restriction of international trade and payments is necessary for development (Lal 1983: 5).

Lal's summary is unfair in its emphasis on the necessary extent of government intervention (he calls development economics the 'Dirigiste Dogma'). But the development economists discussed in this and the next chapter certainly regard structural change as being much more important in the process of development than response to price (and hence are often called 'structuralists') and often work with fixed-proportions models or with models in which price is not an important variable. While rejecting the comparative-advantage theory of gains from trade, some of them revert explicitly to the classical approach towards analysis of growth and development. Others are influenced by Leontief, Tinbergen and the Soviet planners. It is not surprising that their diagnosis of the nature and causes of surplus labour in underdeveloped countries is very different from that of the neoclassicals. This chapter and the next concentrate on the development-economics theories which regard shortage of *capital* as the constraint on the growth of output and employment. In Chapter 7 those theories which emphasise constraints on the *demand* side are reviewed.

THE GAINS FROM PROTECTION: REWRITING COMPARATIVE ADVANTAGE

Both sets of development economists share a sceptical view of the law of comparative costs as it affects a labour-surplus primary producing economy. Even from the world point of view, Lewis (1954) points out that the principle of comparative advantage is often misinterpreted in the case of countries which have surplus labour, since it uses comparisons based on money wages which do not in such cases reflect the real cost of labour. If the marginal productivity of workers in food production in a labour-surplus country is zero, the social cost of labour to the non-food sector is also zero—which means that world output would be higher if a labour-surplus economy (such as India, Egypt and Jamaica) lived by exporting manufactures and importing food and a land-surplus economy (such as the USA and Argentina) were a net exporter of agricultural products.

From the national point of view development economists argue for protection of import-substituting industry in primary-producing economies on the grounds that the gains from free international trade between an industrialised and a primary-producing economy are unfairly distributed and that it is inimical to aims other than maximisation of current output.

The unequal distribution of gains from international trade was argued strongly during the 1950s and 1960s by the United Nations Economic Commission for Latin America (particularly by Prebisch 1959) and by Singer (1950). The argument has six main bases. The first is Engels' law, that the demand of the industrialised central economies for imports of agricultural raw materials, foodstuffs and tropical beverages has an income elasticity of less than one. Secondly, it is claimed that there are additional factors holding back the growth of the centre's demand for such primary products, including measures to protect agriculture at the centre, technological advance enabling a more efficient use of raw materials and an increasing use of synthetic substitutes. Thirdly, the periphery's demand for imports from the centre is judged to have an income elasticity greater than one. These three conditions taken together, given equal rates of increase in productivity at centre and at periphery, produce the result of a deterioration in the periphery's international terms of trade, as prices of primary products come under downward pressure and those of goods produced at and exported from the centre remain steady.

The process is accentuated by the fourth assumed condition —that the centre's demand for primary products has a price elasticity of less than one, which means that an increase in output of a given per cent will lead to a fall in price of a greater per cent and so to a fall in revenue. Fifthly, aggravation comes also from peculiarities in supply elasticities of primary products, alleged to be positive for price increases but zero for price falls, leading to an increase in supply over time.

The sixth and final unfavourable effect on the periphery's terms of trade comes from the tendency towards 'unequal exchange'[1], reflecting the different effects of productivity increases at the centre and at the periphery. These derive from the differing degrees of competition assumed to exist in their product and labour markets. At the centre both labour and export product markets are non-competitive. Therefore, a productivity increase at the centre results not in a fall in price but, due to union pressures in the labour market, in a rise in wages. Even if the increase in wages is smaller than the increase in productivity, the monopolistic structure of the product market prevents a price fall. At the periphery, in contrast, both labour and export product markets are competitive. An unlimited supply of labour to the export sector prevents wages from rising when productivity increases, and competitive conditions in the product market, along with the nature of the demand curve, ensure a fall in price. The two independent originators of the theory describe the resulting process as follows. 'While the centres kept the whole benefit of the technical development of their industries, the peripheral countries transferred to them a share of the fruits of their own technical progress' (Prebisch 1959). And 'technical progress in manufacturing industries showed in a rise in incomes, while technical progress in the production of food and raw materials in underdeveloped countries showed in a fall in prices' (Singer 1950).

The other aims[2] besides current output maximisation emphasised by development economists are growth (or output maximisation at some future date), avoidance of fluctuations and avoidance of risk. Concern with growth means, to begin with, that it may be justified to give temporary tariff protection to an infant industry, which is initially uneconomic but which will eventually become competitive when it reaps the benefits of internal economies of scale and 'learning by doing'. It means, secondly, that the external effects of industrialisation must be taken into account. Singer, for instance, maintains that specialisation along the lines of static comparative advantage has denied under-developed countries the indirect benefits of manufacturing industries as 'growing points for increased technical knowledge, urban education, and the dynamism and resilience that goes with urban civilisation, as well as the direct Marshallian external economies' (*op.cit.*). Others argue that 'dynamic external economies' justify intervention in favour of investments that are not privately profitable at current market prices. These dynamic external economies (discussed in detail in Chapter Seven, pages 168-70) are defined as those 'received by an industry from cost reductions or demand increases in other sectors' (Chenery: 1955). They imply that a group of investments may be profitable only if undertaken *together*, because of the reductions in cost and increases in demand accruing to each other as their output rises.

In general, concern with growth rather than current output maximisation means that classical trade theory's assumption of a given supply of factors is called into question. *Future* factor supplies are not given but are a consequence of current resource allocation, and planning for current resource allocation must take this consequence into account. Thus dynamic rather than static comparative advantage is the relevant criterion. Economies can set out to 'rewrite' their comparative advantage as the experience of Japan has shown.

Additional (less important) reasons for breaking away from specialisation according to the principle of comparative advantage may be a desire to avoid fluctuations in price and income and the risks of too narrow a specialisation. Given the price inelasticity of demand for primary products, variations on the supply side, combined with variations in demand, are likely to lead to a greater degree of instability in volume and price of such exports than is the case for manufactured exports.

Employment fits into this analysis in so far as the faster growth of output that is assumed to result from rewriting an economy's comparative advantage is expected to result in a faster growth of employment also. The process of growth of output and employment through structural change is assumed to be constrained by capital; thus, the rate of saving becomes the crucial variable. As Lewis puts it, 'the central problem in the theory of economic development is to understand the process by which a community which was previously saving and investing 4 or 5 per cent of its national income or less converts itself into an economy where voluntary saving is running at about 12 to 15 per cent of national income or more' (Lewis 1954: 416).

CAPITAL CONSTRAINT AND FIXED PROPORTIONS ASSUMPTIONS

In search of an engine of growth of output and employment, the development economists covered by this chapter turn the Harrod–Domar model on its head and use its central equation (see page 66) for a quite different purpose from that for which it was intended—to derive the rate of growth implied by a given saving rate rather than to address the question of whether a steady equilibrium growth path is possible. In doing so, they take over its anti-neoclassical assumptions of fixed capital-output, savings/output and capital/labour ratios.

The classic use of the formula is that recommended to planners by the United Nations (UN ECAFE: 1959). As in the original model,

$$\frac{\Delta Y}{} = \frac{s}{k}$$

where Y is output, s is the rate of saving, and k is the incremental capital/output ratio.

Planners are advised to estimate s and k, then substitute the resulting values in the formula to derive the feasible growth rate. Thus, if the rate of saving is 6 per cent and the incremental capital/output ratio 4, the feasible growth rate (i.e. that which equates saving and investment) is 1½ per cent.[3] Alternatively the formula can be used to derive the implications of a growth rate target. For instance, a target of 3½ per cent, given k, implies a need to raise the rate of saving to 14 per cent. The emphasis on capital as the constraint on growth is overwhelming:

> If any one scarce factor associated with underdevelopment should be singled out, it would be capital. The final goal of development programming is, therefore, to find the best way of breaking the vicious circle between capital shortage and underdevelopment and to design the most efficient and optimum rate of capital accumulation . . . Capital may very well be regarded as the core process by which all other aspects of growth are made possible (UN ECAFE: 1959).

Needless to say, this is a long way from Harrod's original Keynesian growth model, which gave central place to the inducement to invest rather than to capital shortage.

The assumption of fixed factor proportions, at the opposite extreme from the variability assumed by neoclassicals (see page 84), is illustrated in Figure 5.1. As described by Eckaus (1955: 355–6), this represents the single case of one good, two factors and one process, where, irrespective of relative factor prices, points a, b, c, etc. are the combinations of factors

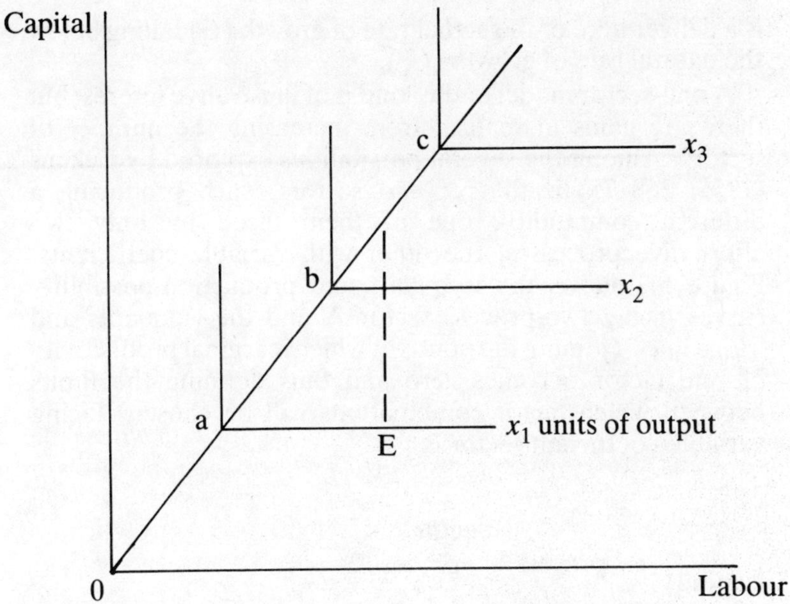

Figure 5.1: Fixed Factor Proportions: the Single-sector Case
Source: Eckaus (1955)

which will be used to produce output and the slope of the straight line joining these points (the production possibility curve) is equal to the constant capital/labour ratio. Only when the factors of production are actually available in proportions equal to the fixed capital/labour ratio does the possibility exist that both can simultaneously be fully utilised. If the actual factor endowment is off the line 0abc, for example at point E, there must inevitably be some unemployment which cannot be alleviated by any increase in aggregate demand. Labour is, in effect, a redundant factor, and only by increasing capital stock by the amount of the dashed line can this unemployment be eliminated. The growth process embodied in the Harrod–Domar formula will, of course, move the economy up the line 0abc towards this point but, if the labour force is not constant, the outcome will be determined by the relative rates of growth of labour force and capital stock. In terms of our earlier discussion (Chapter Three, page 65) there is a danger here of the actual rate of growth (G) falling below the natural rate of growth (G_n).

A one-sector model of this kind is of illustrative interest but there are gains in realism from increasing the number of sectors. Among the several possibilities explored by Eckaus (1955: 368–75) is that of two sectors, each producing a different commodity, one of them faced by only two alternative processes, the other with variable coefficients. Figure 5.2 shows the isoquants and production-possibility curves facing two-process sector A and the isoquants and 'ridge lines' (joining the points at which marginal productivity of one factor becomes zero and thus defining the limits between which factor combinations will be chosen) facing variable-coefficient sector B.

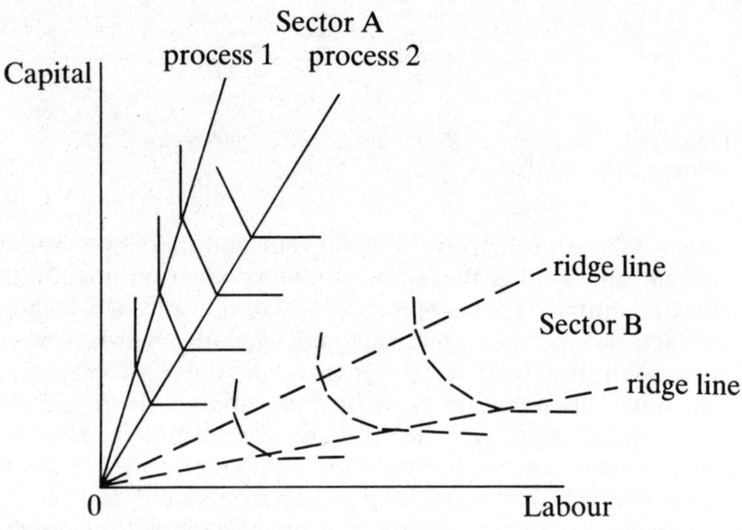

Figure 5.2: Two Sectors with Differing Substitution Possibilities
Source: Eckaus (1955)

Eckaus combines the two sectors in an Edgeworth–Bowley-type box diagram (not reproduced here) and traces the 'efficiency locus' defined by answers to the repeated

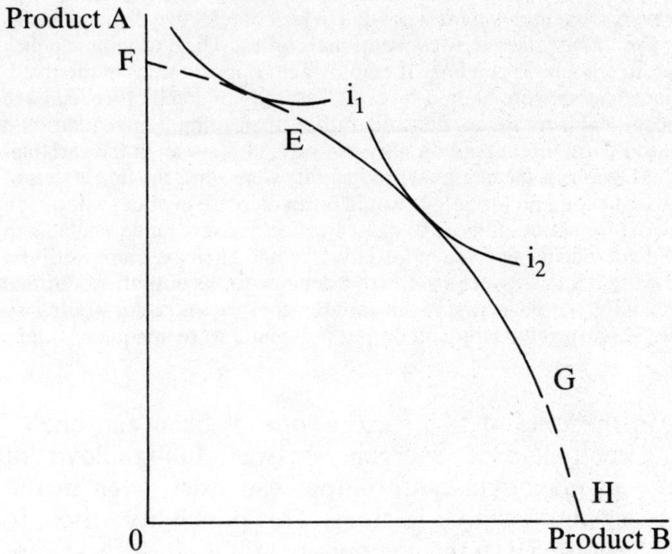

Figure 5.3: Production Possibility Curve with One Variable-coefficient and One Fixed-coefficient Sector
Source: Eckaus (1955)

question, 'For a given amount of good A what is the maximum amount of good B that can be produced?' This is then translated into a transformation (or production-possibility) curve diagram, showing the combinations of good A and good B that it is possible to produce, as in Figure 5.3. As can be seen, this curve has a range, EF, over which labour is a redundant factor, determined by the limits of substitution in the variable-coefficient sector and by the degree of labour-intensity in process 2 in the fixed-coefficient sector.[4]

Moreover, if the respective demands for output were such that a large part of the available capital is drawn into the more capital-intensive, fixed-coefficient sector A, this sector would be able to absorb little labour. In which case the relatively plentiful labour supply would be pushed into the variable-coefficient sector to the detriment of its marginal productivity in that sector, and possibly into open unemployment. As Eckaus comments:

> in this case . . . unemployment is not due to lack of effective demand and as a result cannot be relieved by conventional contracyclical economic policy designed to stimulate spending. If employment opportunities in the fixed-coefficient sectors were limited by capital scarcity or some other resource bottleneck, an increase in demand rather than stimulating additional output would only create inflationary pressures. Likewise, in the variable-coefficient sectors if the marginal productivity were zero, the first effects of an increase in demand for output would be an increase in prices without an increase in production. If more of the scarce factors were made available to the fixed-coefficient sectors, more labour could then be employed and would be used, if there were an effective demand for its output. Additional amounts of the scarce factors in the variable-coefficients sector would also increase labour productivity and output if demand were adequate[5] (*ibid.*: 371–2).

Thus, in the case of two sectors, one of fixed and one of variable coefficients, a divergence between full-employment output and maximum-value output can exist, even in the absence of market imperfections. This possibility arises, in terms of Figure 5.3, if the community indifference curves are like i_1, tangent to the transformation curve in range EF. If, on the other hand, the community indifference curves are like i_2, full-employment and maximum-value output can coincide.

The fixed-proportions assumption is applied by some development economists not only to labour in the economy as a whole but also to each occupation and each educational category in each industry and each sector. Thus 'manpower planners' (such as Harbison 1962, Correa and Tinbergen 1962) implicitly use versions of the following formula to derive estimates of the demand for workers of education level e in occupation j in industry i in sector s.

$$L_{ejis} = \mathrm{GDP}\left(\frac{\mathrm{GDP}_s}{\mathrm{GDP}}\right)\left(\frac{\mathrm{GDP}_i}{\mathrm{GDP}_s}\right)\left(\frac{L_i}{\mathrm{GDP}_i}\right)\left(\frac{L_j}{L_i}\right)\left(\frac{L_e}{L_j}\right)$$

where L is numbers employed and GDP is gross domestic product. With zero substitutability between different skills and categories, this clearly raises the possibility of a mismatch between demand, as thus estimated, and the supply of workers from the education and training system, and both surpluses and shortages of various categories would be explained primarily in these terms.

It also raises the possibility of the supply of skilled workers becoming a constraint on the growth of output, and thus of employment, separate from that of saving. Chenery and Strout (1966) put this slightly differently in terms of 'the absorptive capacity for additional investment', which they suggest is limited in any period by the supply of complementary inputs. They introduce the parameter ß, which they call the 'skill limit', reflecting the 'skill formation required of managers, skilled labour and civil servants in order to increase productive investment', and which defines the maximum rate of growth of investment made possible by skill formation. Thus

$$I^* = (1+\beta)\, I_{t-1}$$

where I is investment and I^* is the maximum level of investment possible in period t. The Harrod–Domar growth formula would then become I^*/k, rather similar to the 'natural' growth rate in the original Harrod model (see page 66). On these assumptions at least, training *can* create jobs, not only for those who receive it but for others also.

UNLIMITED-LABOUR-SUPPLIES MODELS

The early development economists saw surplus labour, thus generated by a shortage of capital, as an opportunity rather than a problem. For instance, the Lewis model which implicitly retains the Harrod–Domar growth formula[6] as its engine shows how unlimited supplies of labour in one sector contribute to the growth of output and employment in the other. The economy's assumed two sectors are a subsistence sector and a capitalist sector. His subsistence sector, where the surplus labour of 'negligible, zero or even negative' marginal productivity is to be found, consists not only of agriculture but also of petty retail trading, domestic service and 'the whole range of casual jobs—the workers on the docks, the young men who rush forward asking to carry your bag as you appear, the jobbing gardener, and the like' . . . in fact 'all that part of the economy which is not using reproducible capital'. In the other, capitalist sector the profit maximisation calculus applies and labourers are only employed up to the point where their marginal product is equal to their wage. As Figure 5.4 illustrates, the role of surplus labour in the subsistence sector is to allow accumulation and growth in the capitalist sector—and in this sense it should not be regarded as a problem.

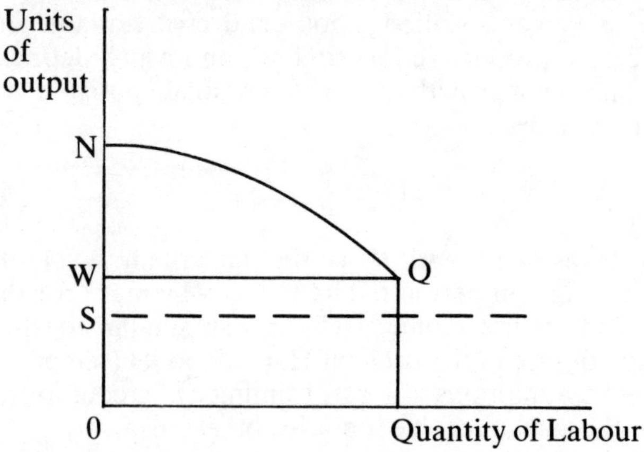

Figure 5.4: Demand and Supply in the Capitalist Sector's Labour Market
Source: Lewis (1954)

NQ is the marginal productivity of (and hence demand for) labour curve in the capitalist sector. OS is average product in the subsistence sector, which is assumed to set the *minimum* wage that the capitalist sector can offer. OW is the *actual* wage offered by the capitalist sector, including an incentive element to encourage the transfer of labour. Since this transfer can take place without affecting output in the subsistence sector it has no effect on the price of wage-goods produced by the subsistence sector. Thus an unlimited supply of labour is available when needed by the capitalist sector at a constant real wage. The resulting surplus (NWQ in Figure 5.4) is reinvested by profit-earners (the economy's only savers and investors) and growth and reinvestment become a continuous process. Indeed, since labour continues to be available at a constant wage of OW as NQ shifts outwards, 'if any part of profits is reinvested in productive capacity, profits will grow continuously relatively to the national income, and capital formation will also grow relatively to the national income'.

The obviously classical flavour of the model and of Figure 5.4 (compare it with Figure 2.1) is not accidental. Lewis proclaims that 'this essay is written in the classical tradition making the classical assumption, and asking the classical question. The classics, from Smith to Marx, all assumed, or argued that an unlimited supply of labour was available at subsistence wages. They then enquired how production grows through time. They found the answer in capital accumulation, which they explained in terms of their analysis of the distribution of income. Classical systems thus determined simultaneously income distribution and income growth, with the relative prices of commodities as a minor by-product' (*ibid.*: 400).

One difference between Lewis and Ricardo is that Lewis does not regard it as important to distinguish that part of the surplus which goes to landlords from that part which goes to capitalists. Ricardo did so distinguish (see Figure 2.1) because he believed that economic development inevitably increases the relative scarcity of land and thus pushes up rent (which is not reinvested). Lewis argues that technical progress in capitalist-sector agriculture will offset this tendency and thus hold up the rate of profit on capital.

However, the unlimited-labour-supply phase will not last for ever. At least two 'turning points' are implicitly identified. First, as the capitalist sector increases in size, relative to the subsistence sector, beyond a certain point, the terms of trade will turn against it. A shortage of the goods produced in the subsistence sector (wage goods for the capitalist sector) will push up their prices, which means that capitalists will have to pay higher real wages. In other words, the labour supply curve will begin to slope upwards. The second turning point occurs when average product in the subsistence sector (on which the supply price of labour to the capitalist sector is based) begins to rise as a result of the fall in the number of workers in the sector. Again the capitalists will have to pay higher real wages along the now upward-sloping supply curve of labour. The share of profits will no longer necessarily rise as output, income and employment grow. Indeed, as wages rise, unless technical change raises the productivity curve to keep pace, profits may no longer do more than cover the consumption needs of the profit earners. When that point is reached, the process of reinvestment and growth comes to an end.

To put the Lewis model in algebraic form runs the risk of violating the spirit of its flexible formulation but may expose its mechanisms more clearly. Its five main equations are as follows:

(1) Demand for labour in the capitalist sector: $L_c = L(W_c)$

(2) Supply price of labour to the capitalist sector:

$$W_c = \frac{Y_s}{L_s} \frac{P_s}{P_c} + \overline{G}$$

(3) Saving identity: $s = \dfrac{(1-\delta)\,(Y_c - W_c L_c)}{Y_c + Y_s}$

(4) Labour identity: $L_s = L - L_c$

(5) Growth rate: $\dfrac{\Delta Y}{Y} = \dfrac{s}{k}$

where L_c is the demand for labour in the capitalist sector;
W_c is the wage rate in the capitalist sector (expressed in units of capitalist-sector output);
Y_s is subsistence-sector output;
L_s is the subsistence-sector labour force;
P_s is the subsistence-sector price level;
P_c is the capitalist-sector price level;
$\overline{G}$ is the additional incentive element in the capitalist-sector wage necessary to induce transfer from one sector to the other;

s is the rate of saving;
δ is the proportion of their income consumed by profit-earners;
Y_c is capitalist-sector output;
L is the total labour force;
Y is total output; and
k is the incremental capital/output ratio.

As can be seen, with the growth rate determined by the Harrod–Domar formula (Equation 5)[6], anything which reduces the saving rate reduces the growth rate. Equation 3, in turn, shows that anything which increases the supply price of labour reduces the saving rate; and from Equation 2 it is clear that both an increase in average subsistence-sector product and an increase in subsistence-sector prices relative to those in the capitalist sector will push up the supply price of labour. Since the demand for labour in the capitalist sector varies inversely with the wage (Equation 1) this will have an adverse effect on employment, both through a movement along a given demand curve and through a reduction in the rate at which the curve moves outwards.

The advantages of Lewis's flexible (not to say loose) formulation became apparent when Ranis and Fei[7] tried (1961, 1964) to make the model more rigorous and precise. In the process they made some important changes to its specification. For one thing, the two sectors become food and non-food rather than subsistence and capitalist, moving the model closer to the question of migration from rural to urban areas. Secondly, accumulation takes place in the food as well as the non-food sector. Thirdly, in the precise form of their model, they assume a finite labour force without the possibilities assumed by Lewis of an endogenous increase in the participation ratio (particularly via the employment of the wives and daughters of the household) and in population (i.e. for Lewis L_s and L in Equations (2) and (4) are not fixed).

How their model works can best be shown with the aid of their two basic diagrams (Figures 5.5 and 5.6). In Figure 5.5, similar to Lewis' Figure 5.4, df is the marginal-product-of-workers-in-industry curve; SS′ is the supply curve of labour to industry. In Figure 5.6 (in which the position of the origin

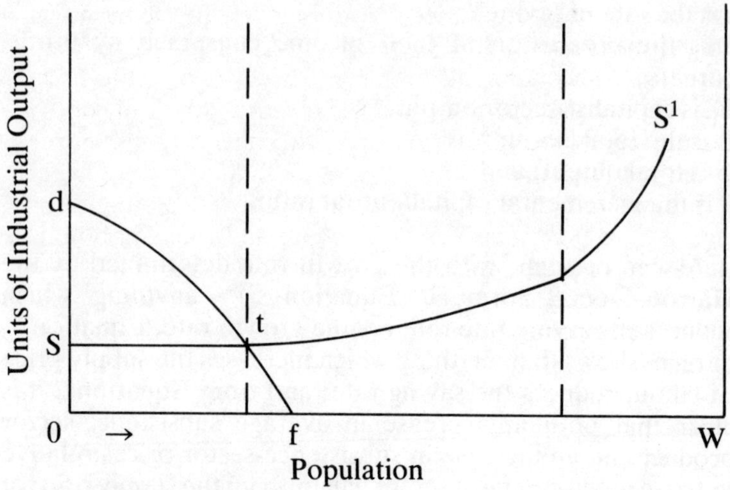

Figure 5.5: Industrial Sector

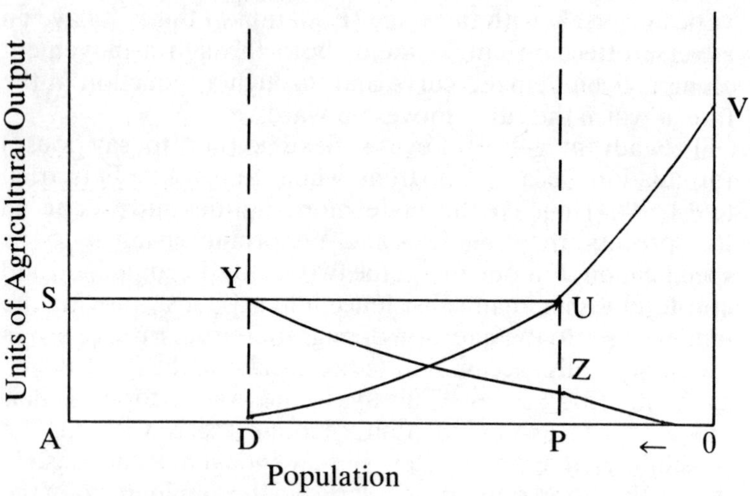

Figure 5.6: Food-producing Sector
Source: Ranis and Fei (1961)

should be noted), ADUV is the marginal-product-of-workers-in-food-production curve; AS is the 'institutional wage' (of which more in a moment); and SYZO is the average agricultural surplus curve (of which also more in a moment).

Starting from the point where the whole population is

employed in food production (OA in Figure 5.5) the authors identify three phases in the process of the allocation of labour from the food-producing to the industrial sector. In the first phase, AD in Figure 5.6, the marginal productivity of food-producing labourers is zero; in the second phase, DP in Figure 5.6, their marginal productivity is greater than zero but lower than the constant institutional wage that they are assumed to receive; in the final phase, PO in Figure 5.6, their marginal productivity is greater than this institutional wage.

When the whole population (OA) is in food production the whole of food output is consumed by food producers. But as labour moves out of food production a surplus of food output begins to appear. This is defined as the total agricultural surplus—'that portion of total agricultural output in excess of the consumption requirements of the agricultural labour force at the institutional wage'. The average agricultural surplus is the total agricultural surplus divided by the number of workers already allocated to industry. The shape of the average agricultural surplus curve (SYZO in Figure 5.6) is explained as follows. In phase 1, when marginal productivity in food production is zero, workers are able to leave agriculture without causing any drop in food output. The average agricultural surplus is thus constant; each allocated worker can be pictured as carrying his own subsistence bundle with him. In phases 2 and 3 however, marginal productivity rises and thus the average agricultural surplus falls until it finally disappears.

With the aid of these diagrams Ranis and Fei are able to analyse Lewis's 'turning-points' with elegance and precision. The first of the Lewis turning-points, which they call the 'shortage point', they identify as the boundary between phase 1 and phase 2 (point D in Figure 5.6). Up to this point an unlimited supply of labour has been available to the industrial sector at a constant wage. Beyond point D, however, as the average agricultural surplus begins to fall, the terms of trade turn against the industrial sector. A higher wage (in terms of industrial goods) has to be paid to attract workers from food production and the supply curve of labour to industry turns upwards.

The second turning-point, which they call the

'commercialisation point' (and which will not concern us so much) they place at the boundary between phase 2 and phase 3 (point P in Figure 5.6). At this point disguised unemployment in food production has disappeared altogether and the wage is equal to marginal product. This accentuates the upward movement of the wage in industry since industrial employers now have to compete with agriculture for labour.

The attempt to make the model more precise raises problems which have to be dealt with by special institutional assumptions if the authors' faith in the efficacy of the market mechanism is to be justified. In particular the question of leakage arises. In order that the prediction of an unlimited supply of labour to the non-food sector at a constant wage (with its consequence for accumulation and growth) should hold, average product in the food sector must remain constant as workers leave agriculture. But, as long as the total labour force is constant, *average* product will *rise* as workers leave, even where those who leave have zero *marginal* product; in effect a constant total product is being divided up between a progressively smaller number of people. If the whole of their average product is consumed by the food-sector workers and their households, the supply-price of labour to the non-food sector will be affected in two ways: (a) Since that supply price is set by the average product in the food sector[8] the supply curve will be upward-sloping rather than horizontal. (b) If average consumption in the food sector increases as average product rises, no agricultural surplus will be generated as workers leave the sector, food prices will rise relative to non-food prices[9] and, in order to maintain a constant exchange value, the wage in the non-food sector expressed in terms of that sector's goods will have to rise also. Thus further upward pressure will be put on the supply price of labour to the non-food sector.

Various ways of getting round this snag might be explored. For instance, the remaining food-sector workers might not increase their food consumption per head as average product rises, but might rather make surplus food available to those now working in the non-food sector in exchange for non-food goods. Unfortunately, this does not work. Surplus is now certainly being generated. But those in the food sector are now consuming the same amount of food as before *plus* the non-food goods received in exchange for their surplus. Thus, in terms of the model, their supply-price to the non-food sector has increased by an amount which depends on what has happened to the terms of trade. If the authors were less concerned to establish the power of the market mechanism, they might assume a role for the state at this point, taxing away the agricultural surplus as it emerges or even removing it by force. As it is they have to fall back on the assumed existence of a dualistic landlord/entrepreneur, on nineteenth-century Japanese lines, who squeezes the surplus out of the food sector by paying a constant 'institutional wage' and thus holding down consumption per head there.[10]

Since accumulation is assumed by Ranis and Fei to take place in both the non-food and the food sectors in response to market forces, and in such a way as to ensure 'balanced growth' between the sectors,[11] the landlord/entrepreneur has another role to play. He must be, 'on the one hand . . . an entrepreneur in the agricultural sector in whose hands rests the main responsibility for generating an agricultural surplus; and, on the other, an entrepreneur in the industrial sector responsible for a good share of the industrial investment activity simultaneously going forward'. Thus, as well as acting as a financial intermediary and being a well-behaved saver, he must be highly responsive to changes in profit opportunities in both sectors of the economy, so that a movement in the terms of trade between the sectors leads to an early change in the allocation of investment.

Accumulation in the food sector (as long as the resulting technological change is not labour-using) can prolong the phase of unlimited supply of constant-real-wage labour to the non-food sector. An increase in food productivity, *ceteris paribus*, allows a further transfer of labour, without a fall in the average agricultural surplus (the ratio of the total food surplus to the number of workers in the non-food sector), and thus without an increase in food prices. Given the existence of this class of landlord/entrepreneurs the market will ensure the prolongation of this phase. If too much capital goes into the non-food sector relative to the food sector, the resulting transfer of labour, fall in the average agricultural surplus and rise in the non-food sector wage and in food prices will increase the incentive to invest in food production. As the landlord/entrepreneurs respond to this incentive, food productivity and the average agricultural surplus increase and the phase of unlimited labour supply is restored.

In the absence of such a landlord/entrepreneur class, *unless* the tie between agricultural/subsistence productivity and the industrial/capitalist real wage is not absolutely rigid, or *unless* the size of the labour force is not given, or *unless* the state extracts the agricultural/subsistence surplus and holds down incomes in that sector—then the problem which such models imply for policy-makers is not, paradoxically, that of excess labour but of potential labour *shortage* in the capitalist sector, and of the need to take measures to ensure that the sector gets the labour it requires.

CONCLUSIONS

The models reviewed in this chapter are concerned not so much with surplus labour as a problem which needs to be alleviated as with the opportunity it provides for accumulation and growth of output and employment in the capitalist sector. If we ignore the significant differences of emphasis between them and lump them together they provide a *prima facie* case for government intervention in a primary producing economy to promote[12] import-substituting industrialisation on the basis of cheap and plentiful labour.

The case rests, of course, on the realism of the assumptions that underlie it—for instance, about income and price elasticities of international demand for and supply of primary products and manufactured goods, about the degrees of competition in export product and labour markets at the centre and at the periphery, about the external effects of industrialisation and about the existence of unlimited supplies of surplus labour.

On primary producers' international terms of trade positivist economists have been more concerned to test the prediction that they will inevitably tend to decline than to examine the individual assumptions underlying the prediction. While disputes about the evidence continue (for example, see Spraos 1983) and much depends on choice of period and commodity, recent studies suggest that the net barter terms of trade of non-petroleum primary commodities (*vis-à-vis* manufactured goods) have shown a significant downward trend, with interruptions for two world wars, between 1900 and 1982 (for example, see Sapsford 1984). The almost untestable dynamic arguments for intervention to rewrite comparative advantage also remain convincing. And, while on the strictest static assumptions the Lewis model can be shown not to 'work', realistic relaxations of those assumptions, such as those suggested by Sen (see pages 16-20) or by Lewis himself (page 29), easily rescue the unlimited-supplies-of-labour concept, which also looks consistent with data on international wage differentials.

Nevertheless, these models did appear to be overtaken by events during the 1960s. Their emphasis was on growth of output and on the contribution of surplus labour to this process; transfer of labour from one sector to another was assumed to be smooth, with no excess of job-seekers over capitalist-sector jobs. Such a perspective could hardly be maintained in the face of the growing evidence that the subsistence/agriculture sector was releasing labour at a rate far in excess of the rate at which the capitalist/industrial sector could absorb it. From the optimism of the surplus labour analysis the pendulum swung to the pessimism of the 'employment problem', with the emphasis particularly on urban unemployment. What this meant in analytical terms is reviewed in the next chapter.

NOTES

1. Later restated in Marxist language by Emmanuel and Amin.
2. These are the other aims that are particularly relevant to the rejection of specialisation according to the principle of comparative advantage. Redistribution of income, structural change, satisfaction of basic needs are among yet other aims discussed and planned for by development economists.

3. At 6 per cent of a national output of, say, 1,000 units, saving will be 60 units. Investment of 60 units, given an incremental capital/output ratio of 4, will yield an increase in output of 15 units, which is 1½ per cent of 1,000.
4. Analogously GH is a range over which capital is a redundant factor.
5. As will be discussed in Chapter 7 (pages 180-4), Nurkse suggests that labour productivity can be raised in the variable-coefficient sector *without* additional amounts of the scarce factors. Thus by him, also, surplus labour is seen as an opportunity.
6. However, Lewis does not explicitly assume that k is constant.
7. Ranis and Fei's version of the model is more neoclassical than classical in spirit. They do not properly belong to the category of 'development economists' as defined here. However, the problems raised by their attempt to make the model more rigorous are sufficiently interesting to merit discussion at this point.
8. Y_s/L_s in Equation (2) on page 128.
9. P_s/P_c in Equation (2) on page 128 will increase.
10. Thus, as Weeks points out (1971), the model is 'a marginalist translation of the Marxian model of capitalist development through "primitive accumulation"'.
11. Growth is balanced in two senses. On the output side each sector provides a market for the other's products and each must grow in such a way that the terms of trade do not turn against either thus affecting relative investment incentives. On the input side the food-producing sector provides workers for the growing industrial sector and, as a second condition of balance, the two sectors must grow in such a way that the non-food sector is able to absorb at a constant real wage the precise number of new workers freed by the food sector.
12. Promotion does not necessarily have to involve protection by tariffs and quotas. As neoclassical economists have pointed out, promotion by subsidising such industries and taxing primary poroducts would, if practicable, be preferable on resource allocation grounds. Nor is import substituting industrialisation a universally applicable prescription; it would not necessarily apply, for instance, to countries with very small populations or to extremely resource-rich or land-surplus economies.

6 Later Development Economics: Surplus Labour as a Problem

As, during the 1960s, urban populations grew at a considerably faster rate than modern-sector employment, the 'employment problem' began to be conceptualised in terms of open urban unemployment. In what sense this was seen as a problem depended on the point of view of the beholder. Governments and some international agencies were worried about the threat it posed to social stability and existing political arrangements. A more widespread concern was with the immediate implications for welfare or particularly the income and recognition aspects of unemployment (see Chapter One, page 9). However, capitalists and those concerned with accumulation presumably viewed it with equanimity. At any rate, its emergence raised all the analytical and definitional problems already discussed in Chapter One. The standard transnational definition of unemployment ('not working' and 'seeking work') was clearly inappropriate to the circumstances of the third-world city, with its mixture of modes of production and lack of public provision for social security. This led some (for example, Frank 1968) to argue, in a massive simplification, that all those without regular wage incomes derived from the modern sector might as well be classified as unemployed. Todaro implicitly embodied such an assumption in his probabilistic model of rural–urban migration, already discussed above (pp. 103-10). Others (for example, see ILO 1970, Turnham 1971), recognising such a definition as untenable, suggested the use of a 'minimum income' standard below which a person should be designated unemployed.

Calculations of this kind formed the basis of some extremely gloomy descriptions of the situation in third-world (particularly urban) labour markets. For instance, Singer reported in 1970 (p. 1) that 'all observers seem to agree on the high and rising unemployment figures in most developing countries, although precise quantification is not easy to come by, because of methodological difficulties as well as lack of data. Summarising the statistical evidence available, I have ventured to estimate that the true unemployment rate in developing countries is, today, of the order of 25 per cent, including the unemployment equivalent of clear underemployment, but excluding a good deal of disguised unemployment in the form of unproductive labour. This would mean the staggering total of approximately 250 million unemployed persons in the developing countries'. Such categorisation of almost all the poor as 'unemployed' seemed no more satisfactory than the highly restrictive concept of open unemployment. As Weeks pointed out (1974), on this basis 'unemployment' rates in many third-world cities might soon approach 100 per cent.

But, if it was now generally agreed among development economists that failure to get a modern-sector job did not automatically mean idleness and destitution for an individual, there was less agreement about definition and description of the alternative fate. Some of the labels that began to be applied to this 'sector' implied that it was necessarily lacking in dynamism. Todaro (1968), for instance, differentiated it only slightly from open unemployment, calling it 'the traditional sector', consisting of 'all those workers not regularly employed in the urban modern sector, i.e. the overtly unemployed or sporadically employed and those who grind out a meagre existence in petty retail trades and services' (*ibid.*: 139, fn). In similar vein Reynolds (1969) described it as 'the low-productivity urban sector'.

Other labels were rather more modest in their recognition of the extent of their ignorance as to what was going on in this sector. Weeks (1973) described it as the 'non-enumerated sector', Ghai (1972) even more frankly as the 'murky sector'. Rimmer (1970) distinguished the sector by the extent to which it was unaffected by government regulations, describing as the 'unorganised labour market' that which 'is attached in one way or another to small-scale enterprises engaged in distribution, other service trades, crafts and manufacturing. This part of the labour force includes self-employed persons, family labour, "learners" and apprentices, and also labour hired on terms which are not related to governmental decisions and which tend in fact to be below the minima legally or conventionally established by governments' (*ibid.*: 50–52).

THE INFORMAL SECTOR

All this groping around by economic theorists must have appeared strange to those who had done sustained field work in third-world cities and it is perhaps not surprising that the eventually seminal analysis came from a social anthropologist with several years of such experience in Accra who took the trouble to address himself to economists. Hart (1973) introduced 'the distinction between formal and informal income opportunities, . . . based essentially on that between wage-earning and self-employment. The key variable is the degree of rationalisation of work—that is to say, whether or not labour is recruited on a permanent and regular basis for fixed rewards'.[1] Hart almost inevitably remains agnostic about the crucial question of the development potential of the informal sector. While he poses the question, 'Does the "reserve army of urban unemployed and underemployed" really constitute a passive, exploited majority in cities like Accra, or do their informal economic activities possess some autonomous capacity for generating growth in the income of the urban (and rural) poor?'—he merely suggests that 'much more empirical research is required' before it can be answered.

The ILO/UNDP employment mission to Kenya, which enthusiastically took up the informal sector concept, had no hesitations about generalising on the basis of scant evidence, even in the absence of a clear analytical framework. In contrast to Hart, it uses a multidimensional definition (ILO 1972) of informal activities, describing them as a 'way of doing things, characterised by (a) ease of entry; (b) reliance on indigenous resources; (c) family ownership of enterprises; (d) small scale of operation; (e) labour-intensive and adapted technology; (f) skills acquired outside the formal school system; (g) unregulated and competitive markets'.[2]

Moreover, wage-earners as well as the self-employed are included in the sector—which is seen not only as a sector of economic activity but as a potential source of dynamism in the economy.

Discussion in terms of an informal sector represents an advance on the concept of 'unemployment' in the limited sense that it recognises the existence of a sector (not a geographical area or a number of people) which produces significant quantities of goods and services, and focusses attention on the role played by the small-scale, less-regulated productive units in that sector in the process of accumulation and distribution. But the concept as outlined in the ILO Kenya report is hardly adequate analytically to support the optimism expressed about it as a potential source of dynamism.

The reasons for this over-optimism seem to be the overemphasis placed by the ILO report on the role of the state in blocking the development of the informal sector and the underemphasis on the role of the market. The sector is characterised as 'largely ignored, rarely supported, often regulated and sometimes actively discouraged by the Government'. From this it follows naturally that if state harassment of the sector were to cease, if the policy of slum demolition were to be abandoned, if the system of trade and commercial licensing were to be altered, and if requirements for standardisation of specification and quality of products were to be relaxed, a great potential for growth of output and employment would be released. Indeed, the report's view of the role of the market is essentially as a benign and rationalising mechanism, so that it recommends the strengthening of links with the formal sector as the other main plank in its strategy for the sector. While it is true that the precise market relationship between the informal and formal sectors is widely variable, an explicit and much more substantial framework of analysis is needed before assertions concerning its generally benign or antagonistic nature and, even more, such optimistic leaps into policy prescription can be made.

The elaboration of an adequate analytical framework has hence become an active concern.[3] Some obervers, in discussing the constraints on the growth of the sector, see no need to go further than internal factors, such as lack of entrepreneurial attitudes and managerial ability (Kilby 1969, Stepanek 1960, Nihan *et al.* 1979), particularly if enterprises are run on a family basis. Lipton, on the other hand, sees internal factors as a source of strength rather than weakness, due to 'extended fungibility', i.e. the ability of the 'family enterprise to adapt to changed production conditions by adjusting not only its production behaviour, but also its consumption and reproduction decisions' (Lipton 1980: 2). On the basis of a review of the literature and of his own research in Brazil, Schmitz inclines towards Lipton's view (though with reservations) and suggests that 'insistence on the primacy of internal constraints on the sector's growth may serve an ideological function; emphasis on lack of entrepreneurship and managerial skills puts the blame for the failure of small enterprises on the people who run them rather than on the environment in which they operate' (Schmitz 1982: 445).

An analytical framework which emphasises external constraints on the sector is more convincing. For instance, by analogy with the two-sector models discussed earlier (pp. 125-34) at least two ways in which an informal sector relates to the formal sector can be identified. To begin with, it may perform a 'reserve army' role, setting the supply-price of labour to the formal industrial sector; whether or not it supplants the agricultural sector in this respect will depend on whether agricultural workers migrate directly to the formal sector or indirectly via the informal sector. Secondly, (one of the relationships emphasised by Leys in his trenchant critique (1973) of the ILO Kenya Report), it may share with the agricultural sector the role of producer of wage-goods (and services) for the employees of large firms. By analogy with Lewis-type models the extreme competition in the informal sector and resultant low prices will enable wages in the formal sector to be lower than they would otherwise need to be—an effect which will be reinforced if the formal sector has the power to manipulate the terms of trade in its own favour.[4] Its role in this respect will presumably be subordinate to that of the agricultural sector, given the actual consumption pattern of a typical wage-earner's household.

These two 'Lewis-model' types of relationship do not, of course, exhaust the relationships between the sectors. The informal sector shares several other roles with the agricultural sector *vis-à-vis* the formal sector. First, it may be a source of supplementary income to formal-sector workers and their households, making them available to that sector at wages that are lower than they would otherwise need to be. Secondly (another role emphasised by Leys), it may produce inputs for the formal sector at prices which the pressure of extreme competition will ensure are low and which the formal sector's monopsonistic buying power may push even lower. Thirdly, informal-sector workers and their households will be consumers of formal-sector products the prices of which may reflect the power of that sector to pass on cost increases.

All these relationships (as in the Lewis model) suggest ways in which surplus might be transferred from the informal to the formal sector, with the large-scale sector exploiting the smaller producers at one remove as suppliers of inputs, at two removes via the wage-good and supplementary-income effects, and as consumers, as well as maintaining the reserve army role of the informal sector by stimulating a high rate of rural–urban migration.

This raises the possibility that the ILO Kenya report's recommendation of strengthening links between the sectors, while perhaps allowing a limited increase in incomes in the informal sector, would mainly benefit surplus accumulation in the formal sector. In which case we would be back with the Lewis-model situation of growth being concentrated in the formal sector (and even there only if the surplus were reinvested rather than consumed or expatriated).

Moreover, so far we have considered only the way in which the informal sector complements, and is fundamental to accumulation in, the formal sector. We must consider the way also in which the two sectors *compete* with each other. Potentially, although their products look very different, the sectors are competing for markets. The goods and services that they produce represent different ways of meeting needs. In competition with the formal sector the informal sector is at a disadvantage in at least four ways. First, in many lines it has the unit cost advantage when markets are small because of its low labour costs but as markets grow economies of scale shift the cost advantage to mass-produced formal-sector goods (more so in manufacturing, less so in the case of most services). Secondly, the formal sector expends great effort and money to *redefine* consumer needs so that cost comparisons become less relevant. Thirdly, even in the absence of such expenditure, the growth of individualism and consumerism can shift the product-differentiation advantage towards the formal sector. Fourthly (and this is the aspect of the role of the state which *is* important) the formal sector obtains protection from competition from imports and other market entrants which enables it to make profits at lower-than-optimum outputs.

All this means that as soon as smaller less capital-intensive producers have developed a market to the extent that it is of interest then larger firms may move to take it over. Indeed, as the market grows, even the opportunities of gaining income (if not accumulation potential) from a subordinate relationship with the formal sector diminish. From the point of view of the large firm the exploitative purchase of cheap inputs from low productivity small producers is only preferable to purchase from other 'modern' firms, or to vertical integration, under certain specific conditions. That is, such an arrangement must offer advantages to the purchaser, on balance, in terms of unit cost, flexibility in response to an irregular demand for labour time, avoidance of supervisory problems and scope for monopolistic/monosonistic pricing. As the market grows the unit cost advantage of the small input producer will turn to disadvantage and may come to outweigh the three other continuing advantages. Similarly the changing logic of labour use (towards a low-turnover, more committed labour force—see Chapter four, page 90) in a growing formal sector may reduce the importance to capital as a whole of conserving the informal sector as a source of wage-subsidy via its wage-good and supplementary-income roles, particularly since it will continue to perform its reserve-army role.

While such an 'external-constraint' framework of analysis is useful, there is a need for caution in its application. Pockets of opportunity for accumulation by the informal sector exist in trades which, for any of the reasons discussed, are not yet profitable for the formal sector or in geographical areas not yet reached by it.[5] And in looking forward, as Schmitz warns, we must beware of resorting mechanically 'to deterministic and gloomy predictions, to the denial of all accumulative prospects and to a theory of marginalisation[6] as the general paradigm of small-scale production in the periphery . . . The issue is not *whether* small enterprises have growth and employment potential but *under what conditions*. This question cannot be answered by a mere listing of factors which favour or work against small producers'. (Schmitz 1982: 445).

Finally, doubts about the usefulness of the concept of the informal sector have been exacerbated by attempts to operationalise it. In this respect the results of survey work sponsored by the ILO in nine third-world cities (Sethuraman 1981) have been particularly worrying. Researchers, trying to decide whom to interview, were instructed to include any enterprise which satisfied at least one of the following 'criteria of informality': (a) It employs ten persons or less (all employees included). (b) it operates on an illegal basis, contrary to the government regulations. (c) Members belonging to the household of the head of the enterprise participate in the activity of the enterprise. (d) It does not observe fixed hours/days of operation. (e) It operates in a semi-permanent or temporary structure, or in a variable location. (f) It does not use any electricity. (g) It does not depend on formal financial institutions for its credit needs. (h) Output of the enterprise is not distributed through other enterprises. (i) Almost all the persons associated with the enterprise have fewer than six years of formal schooling.

The difficulties with such a list are enormous. One wonders whether there are any firms in developing countries which do not satisfy either conditions, b, c, or e. One wonders further about the analytical significance of such a classification. It does not appear to be designed to illuminate the question of growth potential. The results of the surveys were a largely unhelpful description of the characteristics of the enterprises which happened to be interviewed. One example of the confusions about definition (and possibly sampling procedure) is the small number of women who were identified as participating in the sector—a quarter or less of the participants in six of the cities surveyed. This leads to the conclusion that the 'dominance of males in the informal sector is, in general, noticeable in Africa, Asia and Latin America', which conflicts with widespread evidence from case-studies that women are disproportionately represented in the sector and, within it, in trading and food and beverage processing (for example, Heyzer 1981; Moser and Young 1981).

Such confusing results suggest that it would be better for researchers and policy makers to forget about the informal sector and to look at industrial branches and sectors as a whole, disaggregating as appropriate within each branch/sector. As Schmitz points out, 'what is of concern to the small-scale weavers are the actions of the larger weaving firms, not what the small shoemakers or streetsellers do'. Equally, family-based enterprises with unpaid family workers, small firms employing wage earners, domestic outworkers, low-paid casual workers, etc. have different problems and opportunities and it is not helpful to lump them all together.

FACTORS UNDERLYING THE EMERGENCE OF THE EMPLOYMENT PROBLEM

Development economists have suggested several reasons for the emergence of an urban employment problem in developing countries.

(a) Labour-Saving Accumulation

On the demand side it is widely believed that techniques used in the capitalist sector have not only been capital-intensive but increasingly so as accumulation has proceeded: 'although the Lewis model envisages sufficient capital-widening investment in the industrial sector to absorb the labour inflow the actual result has been a substitution of capital for labour in the modern sector' (Meier 1976: 174). Figure 6.1 illustrates how this might work. Rather than shifting outwards evenly as in the Lewis diagram (our Figure 5.4), the capitalist sector's demand-for-labour curve would shift unevenly as shown.

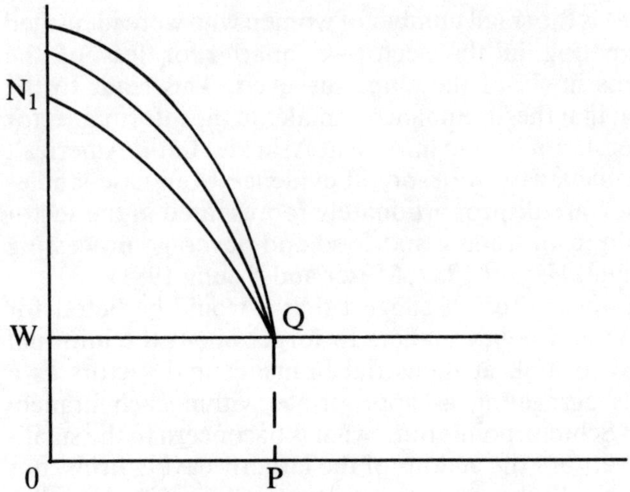

Figure 6.1: Labour-saving Accumulation in the Capitalist Sector

Employment would then remain unchanged, at OP, as would the wage bill, at OWQP, in spite of the increase in output and in profits.

In contrast to the neoclassical economists discussed in Chapter Four, 'structuralist' development economists tend to look beyond factor price distortions for explanations of this phenomenon. Some suggest that there is a link between income distribution and the demand for labour, via patterns of consumption. For instance, the ILO mission to Colombia, led by Seers, maintains that

> the main way in which income distribution affects the level of employment in Colombia is through its effect on the pattern of consumption. This works in two ways: the first is through the different import content of the expenditures of the rich and the poor; the second is through the different direct labour content of those expenditures (ILO, 1970: 138).

On the first point they argue that if the marginal propensity to consume imported goods is, as seems to be the case, higher for the rich than for the poor, the greater the degree of inequality in income distribution, the higher the demand for imported consumer goods and the less foreign exchange left over for the capital and intermediate goods needed to expand employment. On the second they suggest that 'the basic goods which are widely purchased by those on low incomes—essentially food and rather simple manufactures like clothing and footwear—are precisely the goods which are (or can be) produced with techniques considerably more labour intensive than those used in the production of the goods demanded by the rich' (*ibid.*: 140). They also suggest an effect on the labour supply side: 'since the poorer classes spend a high proportion of their income on food, the bigger their share of total income, the greater the demand for agricultural goods, and the greater the check on the pace of urbanisation—a check which we believe would help a full employment strategy' (*ibid.*: 140).

The proposition that the labour-intensity of the pattern of consumer demand varies inversely with the degree of income inequality can be illustrated on the Eckaus production-possibility-curve diagram (Figure 5.3). If the community indifference curves associated with a relatively unequal income distribution were shaped like i_1, full employment would be incompatible with the maximum-value output. If on the other hand income were redistributed and the community indifference curves associated with the more equal income distribution were shaped like i_2, it would be possible for full-employment output and maximum-value output to coincide.

Stewart (1974) refines the analysis further by exploring the source of the differences in the nature of products. she emphasises that technological development in industrialised countries leads to new and 'improved' products as well as to higher labour productivity in existing products. These new products reflect the society in which they are developed. The capital-intensive techniques required in their production (and if product characteristics are sufficiently finely specified only one process may be possible) reflect resource availability in that society; the specification of the products reflects its high income levels. Such products, she argues, may be 'inappropriate' to the developing countries to which they are transferred in the sense of having 'excessive characteristics and standards in relation to needs and income levels of the country in question' (*ibid.*: 402). Consumption of such products, including textiles with excessive standards of durability and strength as well as cars, washing machines and other consumer durables, *requires* an unequal income distribution in a poor country. And,

> once an unequal income distribution is established, emanating from the system of production, it is extremely difficult to make a radical change towards more appropriate products which are consistent with a quite different and more egalitarian income distribution. Traditional products, and those recently developed in and for the poorer sections of the community, are much more appropriate in characteristics and in methods of production. They are so by necessity. The labour intensity of traditional forms of entertainment, of housebuilding and of road construction, of carpentry and of spinning, arose from the fact that the people who used and developed them could afford only very limited amounts of capital (*ibid.*: 403).

Several authors strongly emphasise the link between the process of 'taste transfer' described by Stewart and the activities of multi-national corporations (MNCs). For instance, Langdon, on the basis of research in Kenya (Langdon 1980), suggests that import-substituting MNCs are primarily interested in the defence or penetration of markets for precisely the brand-differentiated quality-standardised products that they already sell in industrialised countries. He documents the way in which this product choice (the source of multinational oligopoly power in the world market) is heavily promoted by mass advertising.

Other labour-displacing characteristics of MNCs are also emphasised (see Vaitsos 1976). Some of these are shared with other large, oligopolistic firms, such as their capital-intensive techniques and tendency towards labour-saving innovation, ability to capture a disproportionate share of resulting increases in income, and power to negotiate generous concessions. Others, like the taste transfer effect, derive from the 'foreignness' and transnationality of the corporations. They include: income leakages through the remission abroad of oligopoly earnings; a relatively high propensity to import, reflected in low local linkages; and a tendency to pay higher wages and salaries than local firms of the same size, particularly at managerial and professional levels (see Abdin *et al.* 1983).

(b) Unequal Land Ownership

Another 'structural' factor underlying the emergence of urban unemployment is inequality in the ownership of land (for example, see Hunt 1984; Lipton 1974; Bhalla 1979). The less equal the distribution of land, it is argued, the smaller the population that can be 'carried' on a given area; and, as land ownership becomes more concentrated over time, workers and their families extruded from agriculture are forced to seek livelihoods in towns. Moreover, the process of concentration is not necessarily in favour of efficiency; many argue that small farms achieve higher yields per acre than large farms.

This is partly because of the difference in objectives, discussed earlier, between capitalist and non-capitalist farmers. The profit-maximising, wage-labour-employing, capitalist farmer will not increase his output and employment beyond the point where the marginal value product of labour is equal to the wage. The smallholding peasant farmer on the other hand, aiming to maximise or to achieve a given level of output rather than profits, will go on applying labour and increasing output well beyond this point (to the point where the marginal product of labour is zero if the family is an output maximiser)[7]. In addition, small farmers working their own land may give more careful attention to their task than hired managers on large farms and will not necessarily be less expert; and small farmers may cultivate a higher proportion of their land and may go in for more double cropping. Cases where yields on large farms are no lower or even higher than those on small farms are often explicable in terms of unequal access to research information or purchased inputs or of unequal use of socially scarce resources such as capital and foreign exchange.

These arguments have led to recommendations of land redistribution as a means of increasing employment, both directly and as an indirect result of 'the saving in foreign exchange as more labour intensive farming methods are introduced and . . . the expansion of the domestic market' (Hunt 1984: 281). Sceptics (for example, Byres 1974) point to the dangers of a fall in net marketed surplus accompanying a rise in output after land reform. But enthusiasts (for example,

Lipton 1974) do not regard such a fall as inevitable; even if the *proportion* of income saved and of output marketed by farmers were to fall, this would be likely to be more than offset by an increase in the *level* of income and output.

(c) Education

Structuralist development economists tend to emphasise the negative impact of education on the employment problem. For example, the 'white-collar hypothesis', whereby the curriculum of third-world schools is judged to lead to a disdain for manual labour and a desire for white-collar jobs, dies hard. The hypothesis has been advanced particularly strongly for Africa, where schools are criticised for being 'too academic' and 'insufficiently African'. Dumont, for instance, talks of 'this "colonial" education (which) in no way prepares students for the agricultural profession, but in fact turns them away from it . . . The schoolboy son of an agricultural worker is taught to have only one desire, to escape the land and his dependence on it' (Dumont 1966: 195). The remedy is to make first-level education primarily vocational. As Balogh puts it,

> elementary education must strive to impart directly available technical knowledge to the rural youth, enabling them to increase producion, . . . (and) above all . . . must cease to alienate pupils from their environment and render them unfit for the purpose to which education ought to be dedicated, namely, the rise in rural welfare. The reorganisation of elementary education ought to be so conceived as to create prestige and status for agricultural work (Balogh 1967: 98).

In the absence of such reorganisation, it is argued, educational expansion directly feeds the exodus from rural areas and the growth of urban unemployment.

The hypothesis has been refuted not only by surveys of occupational aspirations and expectations of school leavers but also by experience. The schoolboy son of an agricultural worker does not need to be *taught* to desire 'to escape the land and his dependence on it'. This is his reason for going to school, which is seen (by both children and parents) primarily as a means of escape from the traditional environment; it does not much matter to the individual what schooling consists of as long as it continues to perform this function. As the system expands, in final refutation of the white collar hypothesis, the level which performs this function rises. Although the process of adjustment has been long and painful, primary-school leavers, in spite of the non-agricultural things they still learn in the classroom, no longer bother to search for the urban jobs now reserved for secondary-school leavers. As Foster, the author of an authoritative study of education and social change in Ghana, says, 'the problem is not *curricular* in origin . . . Unemployment is not related to the character of the schools *per se* but is rather a dysfunctional consequence of the relationship between a rapidly expanding school output and a virtually stagnant economy' (Foster 1966: 138). He divides the process into three stages:

> In very early stages of educational development people with a few years of schooling may find it relatively easy to obtain jobs in the modern sector. As the outputs of the schools continue to grow, however, job opportunities are no longer commensurate with this growth. This second stage is where mass unemployment is likely to occur. The third stage is reached when primary schooling is so universal that it is recognised that all economic tasks require primary schooling (*op. cit.*: 139).

Recognition that what goes on outside the schools is more important than curricula in determining behaviour does not imply that response to changes in the labour market will be smooth. If attendance at school beyond a certain level (changing over time) is seen as a ticket to the town, having reached that level a school-leaver may feel it necessary to leave the village, irrespective of the current state of the urban labour market, because the acquisition of that level of education differentiates him from his age group to the extent that he feels himself to be in the 'migrant' category. Once in town, adjustment will take place to what is available, but this process of adjustment may be lengthy.

Moreover, even though the market for educated labour is thus deteriorating, the pressure to expand the schools does not diminish. On the contrary, according to the so-called screening hypothesis (Dore 1976), it becomes positively explosive (Rado 1973). In its extreme form the hypothesis is, first, that schooling in itself (i.e. what happens in classrooms) has no effect on productivity and income. Any observed correlation between years of schooling and income levels is attributed either to innate intelligence or to class background; the function of the school is merely to rank pupils according to ability, as measured in examinations, and the more 'able' survive longer in the schooling system. This conflicts directly with the neoclassical hypothesis (see pp. 107-8) that productivity and income differentials between the more and the less educated are to a large extent attributable to what is learned in school. It implies that the rate of increase in output and thus in opportunities for remunerative employment is determined exogenously (i.e. it is not affected one way or another by changes in educational provision). The second plank of the screening hypothesis is that employers, faced with an excess of applicants, select by level of education.

As Rado points out, if it is additionally assumed that the exogenously determined rate of growth of output and employment opportunities is lower than the rate of growth of the potential labour force, this hypothesis implies that, while the social return (in terms of additions to output and income) on additional investment in education is zero, private demand for extra education is very high. This is because 'the more unprofitable a given level of education becomes as a *terminal* point, the more demand increases for it as an *intermediate stage*; a precondition for the next level of education' (Rado 1973). This imparts an explosive quality to the expansion of private demand for education (based on the expected private rate of return—see page 107), which leads to pressure on governments to expand, staff and equip educational facilities and to a constant topping up of the pool of school-leavers looking for jobs for which their qualifications no longer suffice.

(d) Population Growth

The fundamental factor underlying the employment problem in many labour-surplus economies, in the opinion of some development economists, is their high rate of population growth. For instance, Reynolds has suggested that the labour-surplus model should be modified and redefined as a 'high population growth' model:

> If the problem were merely to absorb an initial labour surplus of, say, 15 or 20 per cent of the labour force, the task might not appear too difficult. The real difficulty is that the surplus is being continuously replenished by rapid population growth. Most of this population increase accrues in the countryside, which means that the farm labour force tends to increase rapidly. The question of what would happen to agricultural output if there were a net withdrawal of labour from agriculture is thus of only academic interest. The practical question is whether labour-using innovations can be introduced into agriculture fast enough to absorb the growing labour force without depressing marginal productivity. Unless this can be done, the amount of unused labour time in agriculture will rise. Underemployment in the urban trade-sector, and open unemployment in the cities, also seem likely to rise (Reynolds 1969).

The macroeconomic effects of rapid population growth (i.e. at a rate exceeding 2 per cent per year) are usually analysed in terms of its impact on savings per person, demand for capital, agricultural production and internal migration (see Cassen 1976, World Bank 1984). Rapid population growth would be expected to lead to a lower level of saving per head because it increases the burden of dependents on families. However, this effect is smaller in developing than in industrialised economies, since the majority of families are poor and in any case save little and banking and credit systems are not well established.

The impact on the demand for capital is likely to be more significant. For instance, in high-fertility countries school-age populations are expected to double or triple by the end of the century, posing a choice between spreading educational expenditure more thinly, excluding a growing number of children from school and diverting spending from other purposes towards education—each a threat, in its different way, to development and the growth of employment. In addition, the increase in the labour force which results (with a fifteen-year lag) from periods of high fertility raises the prospect of falling levels of capital per worker, delays in the transfer of workers from agriculture to non-agriculture and a particular problem of absorbing school-leavers into the labour force.

The impact on agricultural output and productivity (the point emphasised by Reynolds above) is most severe in the increasing number of countries which have reached or are reaching the limits of their cultivable land area. Such analysis is reminiscent of Malthus (see Chapter Two, page 34) and is open to Marxist charges that it confuses surplus population in relation to the means of employment with surplus population in relation to the means of subsistence (see Chapter Two, page 39). However, in an economy with a relatively small capitalist sector, for the majority of the population land is *both* the means of subsistence *and* the means of employment. And one does not have to believe in spurious neo-Malthusian 'eternal laws' to see that, if population/land and labour/land ratios are already high, then, other things being equal, the higher the rate of population and labour force growth the more difficult it is to absorb labour producively into agriculture (or, for that matter, into non-agriculture, as it is also more difficult to extract surplus from agriculture to feed non-agricultural workers—see Chapter Five, page 125). Escape routes exist (for instance, inputs such as fertilisers and improved seeds, improvements in marketing arrangements, land redistribution, irrigation, drainage), but they may be expensive or politically problematic.

Finally, high rates of population growth contribute to a particularly desperate type of rural–urban migration and to actual or supposed 'premature urbanisation' (see page 155), with its attendant problems for governments of urban unemployment, substandard housing, deteriorating public services, congestion, pollution and crime.

In the light of this analysis, it is difficult to disagree with Cassen's conclusion that 'of course population growth is not . . . responsible for unemployment in the Third World. That responsibility lies with inadequate access to public services, education and productive assets; with technological choices, fiscal policy and the pattern of demand for goods and services. These in turn depend on power structures, income distribution, the role of multinational corporations, the international economic order—all the much-analysed facets of the employment problem. But the likelihood that these circumstances will change rapidly is itself small, and all paths to speeding up that change are fraught with difficulty . . . Such being the case, the only arguments here are that rapid population growth makes the task of creating productive employment harder under any policies, however favourable; and that the abundance of labour may favour the *status quo* rather than threaten it' (Cassen 1976: 811).

RURAL–URBAN MIGRATION

The supply-side factors discussed in the previous section—concentration of land ownership, expansion of education and population growth—are obvious elements in any explanation of the process of premature rural–urban migration. In fact a distinctively development-economics analysis of this process has been slow to emerge. The Lewis model and its successors have little to say about it. Their implicit migration function focuses on the response to the difference between the urban wage rate and the average rural income. However, Lewis's later reflections show that he anticipated Todaro (see page 103) by emphasising not only this difference but also the probability of getting a job. 'Apart from full-time jobs this sector offers much casual employment (at the docks, in building, etc.) so everybody who looks for work stands some statistical chance of getting casual employment—whether for 5 or 10 or 20 days per month. Others can become self-employed, in retailing, or handicrafts, doing some business, though not much. The higher the wage, the greater the inflow, and the less work for each person, though presumably to each [ratio of capitalist wage to average non-capitalist income] there corresponds some degree of underemployment which would be enough to stop further migration' (Lewis, 1968, p. 28).

An alternative to Todaro's choice–theoretic analysis of the causes of rural–urban migration, and certainly more in the spirit of the development economists discussed in this chapter, is to see it as part of the process of structural change. This can perhaps best be illustrated by looking at this process, in an extremely abbreviated and stylised way, in a particular case—that of Kenya. The pre-colonial, pre-capitalist economy, with accumulation based only on raiding, looting and trading, was invaded by, and in the early part of the twentieth century interacted with, in the rural areas, large-scale European-owned farms and plantations and, in the emerging towns, a hierarchical colonial administration and associated services sector. Both the European farms and plantations and the administration used the subsistence economy to subsidise the extremely low wages they paid to their labour force and accepted a high rate of turnover, resorting on occasion to forced labour for public works and plantations.

This was the era of seasonal migration of the type still prevalent in southern Africa. Net rural–urban migration emerged on an increasing scale only from the 1950s onwards, as the removal of restrictions on the growing of certain cash crops and on the keeping of dairy cattle by Africans and the consolidation and registration of freehold individual landholdings were reflected in the spread of, first, commodity production, and secondly, capitalism in the countryside. With the emergence of a permanent agricultural wage-labour class, the process of rural differentiation and landlessness has accelerated. At the same time, in the towns, a new type of employer in import-substituting manufacturing has over the past few decades paid higher (although not necessarily 'high') wages to ensure the more stabilised labour force that he needs, and an increasing proportion of the surplus extracted directly and indirectly from primary production has gone to the formal schooling system and to support a growing bureaucracy.

A photograph of this process of structural change, frozen at a particular moment, might look something like Table 6.1, constructed from some heroic estimates of income distribution made by Crawford and Thorbecke for 1976. With such categories in mind, changes in the rate of rural–urban migration can be regarded as emerging from the interplay between the rural and urban processes of differentiation and class formation. In rural high-rainfall areas, as concentration of ownership becomes more pronounced, via the encouragement given to 'progressive' cash crop farmers and the operation of the land market, a few more smallholders' households climb into category 3 and a larger number fall towards category 5, either farming smaller areas of land or working for others if landless. In other areas, also, pressure of population leads to sub-division or landlessness, similarly swelling the ranks of category 5. As such changes take place, the number for whom even category 5 urban opportunities and comparable opportunities in marginal low-rainfall rural areas becomes attractive increases.

At the same time, rural parents, particularly those in categories 4 and above disproportionately influenced by urban salaries received by categories 1 and 2, which, along with recruitment by qualification, make it worthwhile to stay in school as long as possible, are diverting household expenditure to formal schooling for their children and to the construction of 'self-help' secondary schools, the current financing burden of which eventually falls on central government. As already emphasised, having acquired migrant status through the schools (a status for which the educational requirement rises over time) educated migrants may be relatively insensitive to the current state of that part of the labour market which is now relevant to them (again changing over time). There will be reluctance immediately to re-categorise oneself although, once in town, adjustment may take place to what is available.

Meanwhile in the towns also, polarisation is taking place. The output of large firms, often foreign-owned using modern technology, in the formal sector grows fast, displacing or stunting the growth of output of smaller firms in the informal sector. Formal-sector employment grows more slowly, however, and involuntary employment growth takes place in the informal sector. The fastest growth of income takes place in category 1 (from which land and property purchases are financed) while the growth in numbers, fed by migration, is in categories 4 and 5.

Moreover, as the number of rural households with kinsmen in the towns increases, migration acquires a built-in dynamic, somewhat independent of labour-market conditions. The disequalising effect of the whole process is offset, but only to a small extent, by migrants' net remittances from urban to rural and from rural to rural areas. The interaction of these various processes is reflected in a high rate of rural–urban migration (with the urban population expected to double every ten years) and of rural–rural migration (with the population of

Table 6.1 Rural and Urban Income Categories, Kenya 1976

Annual Household Income (Shs.)	Rural Category	Number ('000)	Urban Category	Number ('000
1. 30,000 or more	(a) Owners of large farms	23	(a) Owners of medium enterprises in commerce, industry and services	23
	(b) Rentiers		(b) Rentiers	
	(c) Professionals		(c) Professionals	
	(d) Managers and top bureaucrats		(d) Managers and top bureaucrats	
2. 20,000–29,999	(a) Skilled employees	59	(a) Skilled employees in formal sector	23
	(b) Owners of medium farms			
3. 6,000–19,999	(a) Clerical employees in formal sector		(a) Clerical employees in formal sector	
	(b) Semi-skilled employees in formal sector	271	(b) Semi-skilled employees in formal sector	214
	(c) More prosperous smallholders		(c) Owners of some informal sector enterprises	
	(d) Farmers on irrigation schemes			
	(e) Rural public sector employees			
4. 3,000–5,999	(a) Average smallholders	729	(a) Unskilled employees in formal sector	247
5. Below 3,000	(a) Squatters on large farms		(a) Informal sector employees and smaller entrepreneurs	40
	(b) Pastoralists	1,224	(b) Unemployed	
	(c) Landless			
	(d) Poorer smallholders			

Source: Crawford and Thorbecke (1976).

the low-rainfall, less-crowded marginal areas increasing at ten times the national average rate of increase).

This short illustration points the way to the alternative approach to migration, the essence of which is a concentration on class and other categories and on the way in which households and individuals are transferred by structural changes from one category to another—for instance, from average smallholder to poorer smallholder, from smallholder to landless, from insufficiently educated to sufficiently educated, from having-no-urban contacts to having-such-contacts, from responding-to-market-signals to politically mobilised and, for that matter, from bright-eyed rural school leaver to disillusioned, but thoroughly urbanised job-seeker.[8] Neoclassical economists, in contrast (see pp. 102-10), see migration as the aggregation of individual responses to marginal changes in key economic variables and emphasise the need to calculate precise migration elasticities. For instance, on the basis of their estimated income elasticity of migration for Tanzania, Barnum and Sabot (p. 120) suggest that a 10 per cent decline in urban real wages will induce a 7 to 20 per cent decrease in the migration rate and that a wage cut of at least 40 per cent would be needed to achieve balance between job openings and job seekers. But which urban income-earners should these cuts be aimed at? The professionals, bureaucrats and managers whose incomes disproportionately influence educational investment decisions? The informal sector wage-earners, comparison with whom may be most realistic for the majority of potential migrants? Or the modern sector wage-earners on whom policy discussions inspired by the Todaro model most often seem to concentrate?

The alternative to urban wage cuts implied by the estimated income elasticity is to raise rural incomes. But again, programmes to raise rural incomes are as likely to accelerate rural–urban migration as to reduce it, unless their impact on class formation, land ownership, political mobilisation, etc, is understood and controlled. In the Tanzanian case, for example, it may be more vital to know the trajectory of the Ujamaa village progress, whether towards successful communal self-reliance or towards demoralised disintegration, than to know precisely what is happening to rural incomes. In the Kenyan case, the more pressing question may be whether the peasantry is consolidating its position or whether it is threatened with proletarianisation by spreading rural capitalism. In ever country the answers to questions such as these may be more important to predicting the broad scale of migration and to deciding what can be done about it than the calculation of precise income and unemployment elasticities. It is the suggestion that, in many cases, perhaps nothing can be done about it which gives this structuralist analysis of rural–urban migration its pessimistic tone.

A COMPREHENSIVE LATER-DEVELOPMENT-ECONOMICS MODEL OF THE EMPLOYMENT PROBLEM

A model which in many ways epitomises the development-economics/structuralist approach, combining emphasis on MNCs, technology and income distribution with sectoral analysis, is that of Weeks (1975), based on his experience as a member of the ILO Kenya employment mission, with obvious echoes of Latin American experience and of the analysis of the ECLA school of development economists.

The economy is divided into three sectors: traditional, modern/formal and modern/informal. The label, 'traditional', has 'no behavioural connotation necessarily, but refers to the pre-colonial social and economic system. The term does not imply a static society, but a society in which the major mode of production was subsistence agriculture, settled or pastoral'. Similarly 'modern' describes a different model of production, without suggesting anything about the progressivity of values in that sector. The distinction between 'formal' and 'informal' is that of the ILO repoort described above (page 139), with the focus on the relationship with the state—the other characteristics of these two sectors being seen as a consequence of this relationship. The informal sector is not just less favoured by the state but often actively suppressed and discouraged.

The process of import-substituting industrialisation (ISI) is analysed as follows. In the initial pre-ISI situation the unequal distribution of income means that the pattern of consumption is biased towards imported goods that require capital-intensive methods of production. The policy decision is then taken that these goods should be produced locally. The technology to produce these goods is only available through foreign companies. In order to make such production profitable with these techniques, fiscal, monetary and other measures are taken which reduce the relative price of capital and give a favoured position to these foreign companies. The new consumer-goods industries require increased imports of capital and intermediate goods and as a result the balance-of-payments situation deteriorates.

The model contains several feedback mechanisms. The use of capital-intensive techniques of production yields high profits and involves the employment of a highly paid salariat; it also implies a relatively small wage bill, with high average wages. As a result, the elite pattern of demand is accentuated, the destruction of small local producers is accelerated and the bias towards capital-intensive production is increased.

Secondly, since innovation derives from research and development on new techniques in richer countries where capital is relatively cheap and labour expensive, there is a labour-saving bias in innovation over time. For instance, Figure 6.2 compares the path of employment over time with alternative techniques, K and L. The more capital-intensive technique, K, yields a higher surplus and, therefore, a faster rate of growth in employment. Eventually it would generate more employment than the more labour-intensive, L. However, repeated labour-saving innovation shifts the K line downwards.

Thirdly, (an element in the analysis with which neoclassicals would agree) tariff and other forms of protection for industry, with cheap imports of capital and intermediate goods, result in negative rates of effective protection on capital goods, thus discouraging the development of a local capital goods industry and of local technology. They also discourage exports by raising the prices of imports relative to exports and the prices of items which

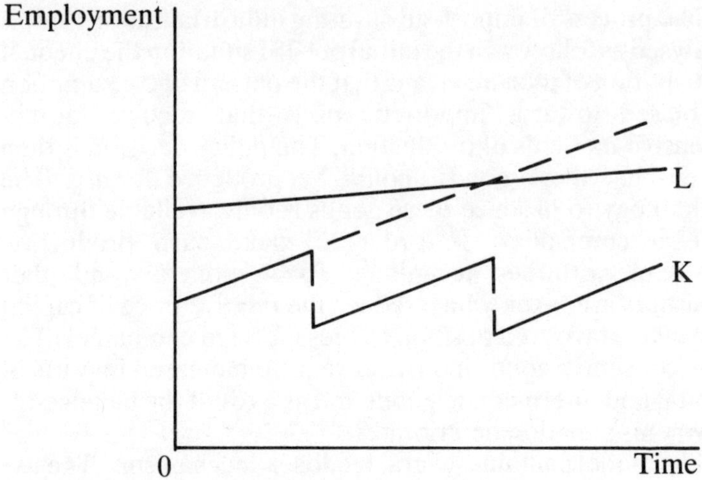

Figure 6.2: Growth of Employment over Time with Capital- and Labour-intensive Techniques
Source: Weeks (1975)

farmers buy relative to the prices at which they sell. Moreover, the chronic balance-of-payments crisis which is built into the process necessitates an intensification of import restrictions over time.

Fourthly, the elite-consumption strategy involves concentration of government services and infrastructure in the capital city, or perhaps in a few primate cities. These facilities represent external economies for new firms setting up, intensifying the tendency for them to be located in such cities and reinforcing the demand for infrastructure there. The capital city, with its concentration of formal-sector firms, is cumulatively attractive to rural–urban migrants but the high rate of migration does not dampen the growth of wage levels there, which continue to rise much faster than in the rest of the economy. With formal wage employment growing only slowly this implies a worsening of income distribution within the capital city, which feeds back on the structure of demand (increasing the tendency towards a capital-intensive product mix, centralisation of social services and deterioration in the balance of payments). It also implies an increase in the size of the informal sector but not of average incomes within it.

This model generates frightening predictions, for a relatively small import-substituting economy of this kind, of a 'Latin-American syndrome' (to emerge in Kenya's case before the end of the twentieth century). The components of the syndrome include: agricultural stagnation (as a result of adverse terms of trade, high rates of rural–urban migration and low rates of surplus and reinvestment), reflected in an urban food shortage and structural price inflation; continual balance-of-payments crisis, necessitating repeated devaluations and increased dependence on foreign finance; non-competitive local industry, in which trade unions push up wages to protect urban workers against rising import and food prices and protected industrialists pass these wage increases on to consumers in the form of still higher prices; and increased rural–urban migration, as agricultural terms of trade fail to improve, resulting in an explosive growth of shanty towns around the capital city.

CONCLUSIONS

The theorists discussed in this chapter share neither the complacency of the neoclassical economists nor the optimism of the pioneering development economists about surplus labour in underdeveloped countries. The basis of neoclassical complacency—the view of unemployment as essentially a voluntary condition (see pages 112-13)—is rejected; the urban unemployed are seen as involuntary victims of structural changes. The basis of the development economists' optimism—the hope that surplus labour in the subsistence sector would contribute to accumulation and growth of output and employment in the capitalist sector—is found to be undermined by a slower growth in demand for workers and a faster increase in supply than had been expected.

The resulting vision is bleak, even catastrophic—one of increasing poverty, unemployment and misery in the capitalist third world. The vision reflects the methodology of the structuralist development economists. Having shaken off the choice-theoretic obsessions of the neoclassicals, they are able to focus directly on the processes of growth and structural change, basing their assumptions on observation of third-world reality rather than on universal theorems. They are more at home also with disequilibrium and cumulative causation (as in the feedback mechanisms of the Weeks model).

However, their models are only as good as the assumptions that underly them; that there is a tendency towards capital-intensive techniques and labour-saving innovation; that the degree of income inequality and the labour-intensity of the pattern of consumer demand vary inversely; that multinational corporations are particularly labour-displacing; that small farms achieve higher yields per acre than large farms; that schools primarily perform a screening function, etc.

Some of these assumptions, such as the tendency towards labour-saving innovation (at least at process, plant or firm level) emphasised by Weeks and others, are reasonably well grounded in empirical research. Others are less so. For instance, the suggestion that the goods demanded by the poor are produced more labour-intensively than those demanded by the rich (see pages 146-7) has been enormously influential. Weeks is not the only economist to make it a central assumption of a model. Its empirical basis is very shaky, however. Its implication that a redistribution of income will feed back positively on itself by increasing employment has not, as far as is known, been unequivocally confirmed by any research which takes into account multiplier and dynamic effects. The most careful attempt to test the hypothesis, in a simulation using Indian data, does 'not provide much support for the "redistribution promotes employment" argument. The analysis suggests that even "radical" redistributions of private consumption expenditure would have no significant impact on the level of employment, either directly through increasing labour requirements or indirectly through reducing scarce resource requirements' (Berry 1981: 621). Similar doubts could probably be raised about other structuralist assumptions. This does not, of course, mean that the attempt to develop alternatives to the neoclassical theorems should be abandoned, merely that the realism of the assumptions on which they are based should be kept under constant surveillance.

NOTES

1. There is an obvious affinity with Rimmer's 'unorganised labour market', particularly as Hart allows the inclusion of the (by inference few) employees of small non-enumerated enterprises. Compare also McGee's (1974) classification of the 'proto-proletariat' on the basis of the mode of production in which they are engaged. McGee regards the urban proto-proletariat as fitting into the peasant mode of production, to which Hart's 'self-employment' presumably corresponds. Subsequent discussion of the informal sector has tended to put more emphasis on the wage employees and subordinate family workers within it.
2. There are interesting parallels with the concepts developed (in French) by Santos (*see* McGee 1974) of the upper and lower circuits of the urban economy, which have sixteen dimensions—technology, organisation, capital, hours of work, regularity of wages, inventories, prices, credit, benefits, relations with clientele, fixed costs, publicity, re-use of goods, overhead capital, government aid and direct dependence on foreign countries.
3. The following discussion owes much to Bienefeld and Schmitz (1976) and to Schmitz (1982).
4. One should distinguish here between movements in the real 'consumer wage' (i.e. money wage index ÷ relevant consumer price index) and movements in the real 'producer wage' (i.e. money wage index ÷ relevant product price index). A rise in the consumer wage does not necessarily mean a rise in the producer wage for a firm/sector which has the power to raise its own prices.
5. *See* King (1974) for a discussion of these two 'moving frontiers'.
6. *See* Chapter 8, pp. 190-200, for a discussion of the neo-Marxist 'marginalisation' school which overlaps substantially with the gloomier contributions to the informal sector debate.
7. *See* Sen (1962 and 1975) for further discussion.
8. *See* Godfrey (1973) for a more detailed discussion of the last point.

7 Development Economics: A 'Keynesian' Strand?

Development economists seem to agree that Keynesian employment theory has little or nothing to contribute to the analysis of the problems of underdeveloped economies. Lewis, for instance, (1954: 401) judges that, 'from the point of view of countries with surplus labour, Keynesianism is only a footnote to neo-classicism—albeit a long, important and fascinating footnote'. Kalecki implicitly agrees when he says that 'the problem of unemployment in under-developed countries differs fundamentally from that in developed capitalist economies. In the latter unemployment arises on account of inadequacy of effective demand. During periods of depression unemployed labour coexists with under-utilised equipment. The situation may, therefore, be tackled by measures designed to stimulate effective demand such as loan-financed government expenditure. Unemployment and under-employment in under-developed countries are of an entirely different nature. They result from the shortage of capital equipment rather than from deficiency of effective demand' (Kalecki 1968: 22).

In similar vein, Rao, a former student of Keynes, suggests that the Keynesian multiplier principle only works in the context of: (a) involuntary unemployment; (b) an industrialised economy where the supply curve of output slopes upwards towards the right but does not become vertical till after a substantial interval; (c) excess capacity in the consumption goods industries; (d) comparatively elastic supply of the working capital required for increased output. Where these assumptions do not hold, as in underdeveloped economies characterised by disguised unemployment, household enterprise, production for self-consumption, dominance of agriculture and deficiency of capital equipment and of technical knowledge, an increment in investment will lead not to an increase in real income and unemployment but to an increase in money income, in the form of a rise in prices and/or an increase in food consumption on the part of agricultural producers and/or an increase in imports or cash balances on the part of industrial producers (Rao 1952).

Yet there are development economists with at least a Keynesian flavour, in the limited sense that they emphasise constraints on the development process on the *demand* side rather than or in addition to those on the supply side[1]. Nurkse's vicious circles of poverty, for instance, ('a country is poor because it is poor') have both of these dimensions, although he recognises the paradoxical nature of the notion of demand deficiency:

> It may at first be surprising to hear that there can be anything wrong on the demand side of the problem of capital formation in underdeveloped countries. Can there be any deficiency in the demand for capital? Are not the backward areas, almost by definition, greatly in need of capital for the efficient use of their labour and for the exploitation of their natural resources? Is not the demand for capital in these areas tremendous? It may well be; and yet in terms of private incentives to adopt capitalistic methods in the productive process there is the difficulty that stems from the limited size of the domestic market in the early stages of a country's economic development. *The inducement to invest is limited by the size of the market* (Nurkse 1953: 5–6).

Myrdal, additionally drawing attention to the higher risk for investors in underdeveloped countries, concedes that 'capital is scarce in these countries; but the need for it does not represent an effective demand in the capital market. Rather, if there were no exchange controls and if, at the same time, there were no elements in their national development policies securing high profits for capital—i.e. if the forces in the capital market were given unhampered play—capitalists in underdeveloped countries would be exporting their capital' (1957: 53).

Rosenberg goes further and suggests that 'an adequate explanation of the general weakness of investment incentives and of the peculiar distribution of profit prospects in different sectors of underdeveloped economies would, *by itself*, account for many of the other apparent causes of low capital formation' (1960). He regards hoarding of assets such as jewellery as quasi-saving, evidence of willingness to refrain from consumption. The holding of assets in this form or in the form of cash or land, he suggests, is a reflection of the weakness of the inducement to invest. Thus lack of industrial investment is not necessarily a sign of shortage of capital.

Hirschman (probably the most important demand-side development economist) is similarly dubious about theories emphasising the primacy of one or other scarcity in explaining underdevelopment. Their cumulative impact, he suggests, is to 'raise doubts about the objective scarcity or outright absence of *any* of these specific factors; in fact, one is rather made to suspect that development is held back not so much by objective scarcities of specific factors of production as by subjective man-made difficulties in mobilising reserves in natural resources, capital, entrepreneurship etc. . . . that are potentially available and can be called forth in a variety of pressure situations, learning processes and inducement mechanisms' (Hirschman 1971:4).

DYNAMIC EXTERNAL ECONOMIES

Perhaps the most powerful analysis of potential demand constraints on the process of development is that in terms of pecuniary or dynamic external exonomies, associated particularly with Rosenstein-Rodan (1943), Scitovsky (1954) and Dobb (1960). Such external economies exist when the profits of one firm 'depend not only on its own output and factor inputs but also on the output and factor inputs of other firms' (Scitovsky 1954: 300). Consider, for instance, the situation in which firms in four industries (producing, say, bicycle frames, steel, bicycle tyres and cigarettes) are independently trying to decide whether or not to invest in further expansion. Even if all these firms have constant returns to scale (i.e. none of them enjoys internal economies), the proposition of the theory of dynamic external economies is that, left to themselves, market forces will produce a level of investment which is lower than is both possible and socially desirable.

The crucial factor here is what Dobb calls 'secondary uncertainty'—that is, uncertainty on the part of one decision-maker about other decision-makers' plans and about the effects of these plans on his own prospects. Such secondary uncertainty can be so great as to induce pessimism and caution on the part of entrepreneurs and so arrest the growth process entirely. In the case of our four industries, for instance, entrepreneurs in the steel, tyre and cigarette industries may be holding back because of uncertainty about the plans of bicycle-frame manufacturers for whom they produce, respectively, inputs, complementary goods and workers' wage-goods. The frame manufacturers, in turn, may be holding back because of uncertainty about the plans in the other three industries, the expansion of which affects the demand for frames. Figure 7.1 illustrates the interconnections between the industries.

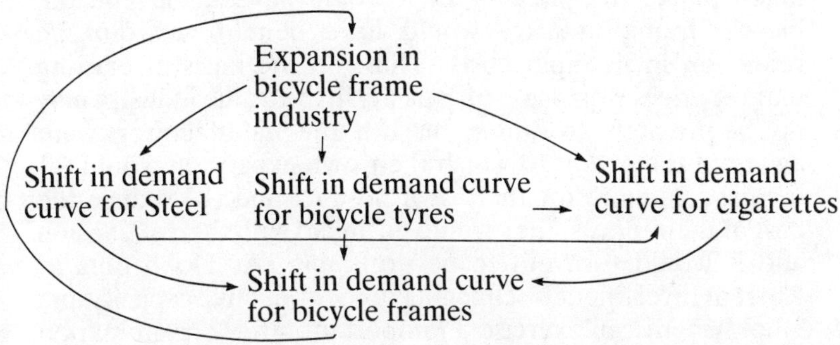

Figure 7.1: Demand Interconnections between Industries

Thus, if all the industries simultaneously invested in expansion their investment would turn out to be profitable, but secondary uncertainty may prevent any of them from undertaking such investment. Secondary uncertainty is not, moreover, evenly spread. The degree of uncertainty 'will be a function of the remoteness in time of a given investment decision from the final demand which it is designed to serve or from other sets of economic events which are its essential complement; and this time element will depend *inter alia* on the periods of construction and durability, which are likely to vary considerably in different types of industry' (Dobb 1960: 10). Those industries with a long time interval between investment and return will be particularly affected by secondary uncertainty—and so the expansion of basic industries and infrastructure will tend to lag behind that of low-risk sectors such as beer, cigarettes, clothing and other consumer goods. Thus, if the return to risk-taking is treated as a cost, the *ex ante, private* profitability of an expansion of our set of industries will be lower than its *social* profitability and the expansion will either not take place at all or will take place in the lop-sided way just outlines.

The divergence between private and social profitability would be even larger if returns to scale were not constant—if, say, in our example, the steel industry enjoyed internal economies of scale. Now the shelving of expansion plans would cause greater social loss because, if expansion *had* taken place, the price of steel would have fallen and the bicycle frame industry would have benefitted from the reduction in its input costs. Thus, on the basis of existing market prices expansion of capacity in the frame industry may not be privately profitable; but if frame manufacturers were aware of the extent to which their own expansion would (a) increase demand for their own product and (b) reduce the cost of their inputs, they would go ahead with their expansion and it would turn out to be profitable. As Dobb puts it, 'current investment by changing both productive capacity and employment can exercise an important influence on market prices . . . Accordingly the existing structure of market prices cannot be taken as a sure basis for forecasting what the future structure, and hence the return on any particularly investment project, will be' (*op.cit.*).

Leibenstein points to these external economies and interdependencies as one of the four factors[2] that determine the need for a 'critical minimum effort' in order to break out of the vicious circle of poverty. Both sides in the controversy of the 1950s and 1960s between the proponents of planned, balanced growth (for example, Nurkse 1953) and those who argue for unbalanced growth of industry (for example, Hirschman 1958) take them as their starting point; and they provide the analytical underpinning for one of the most interesting demand-oriented models of employment generation—the leading-sector model of Lauchlin Currie.

CURRIE'S LEADING-SECTOR MODEL

Currie argues strongly against the then dominant, Harrod–Domar-based school of development economists who find the effective constraints on growth to be on the side of supply and implicitly assume that 'no problem will be posed by lack of effective demand, which may therefore be safely neglected' (Currie 1974a: 1). He disputes their underlying assumptions that: factor proportions remain unchanged; demand exists for any increase in output; any addition to productive capacity will be utilised and, therefore, there is an unlimited market for whatever volume of savings the society cares to create. Factor proportions may be altered by changes in the pattern of demand or in physical productivity. And a combination of government-sponsored investment (for example, 'a road going from nowhere to nowhere'), inelastic demand (for example, for food) and poor mobility may lead to no increase in the value of output following a large investment.

In arguing the case for constraints on the side of demand rather than of supply he distinguishes carefully between Keynesian and Sayian demand. Aggregate money demand of the Keynesian type is *not* relevant to his case. An injection of money and an increase in Keynesian demand would be likely to leave the pattern of production and consumption unchanged and would therefore soon exhaust its effect in a generalised rise in prices. His concern, rather, is with the Sayian intersectoral demand for goods and services, on which the analysis of dynamic external economies[3] centres. The essence of this distinction is that 'in one case [Sayian] the increase in money demand is a *consequence* of an increase in real output; in the other [Keynesian], it may occur in the first instance independently of any expansion in real output. In the first case the pattern of production-consumption in real terms is changed; in the second, it may or may not be' (*op.cit.*: 4).

He does not deny that an expansion of Keynesian demand can be effective in stimulating an increase in real output under certain circumstances but suggests that these circumstances—open, available and usable unemployed factors of production—do not obtain in developing countries. In such countries there is certainly great slack in the system but 'this slack is a consequence of low mobility and low utilisation and there exist structural and institutional barriers to greater mobility and better utilisation' (*op.cit.*: 4). Like Nurkse and Myrdal he also distinguishes between need and effective demand for capital, and adds the point that low interest rates may ensure a 'demand' for all the credit available but that the satisfaction of this demand need not result in additional *productive capacity*.

He defines as 'leading sectors' those which have an 'unexploited or *latent* demand that can be actualized and a sufficiently *large* demand as to cause its satisfaction to have a significant impact on the whole economy' (*op.cit.*: 6). They must also (unlike 'following' sectors) be capable of exogenous increases in growth rate, independent of the current overall rate of growth of the economy. He distinguishes between latent demand and high income or price elasticity of demand. There may, in addition to high price and low income, be institutional barriers which keep demand for the products of a particular sector in a latent or unexploited state. However, the greater the elasticity of demand for such products the greater the extent of the latent market and the longer the period over which it can be exploited.

The ideal leading sector, in his view, in both developed and developing countries, is building, with its low import component and relatively high unskilled labour component. Demand is income-elastic and sufficiently price-elastic for a relatively small addition to the housing stock to have little effect on prices. Yet the effect on demand for the products of other sectors may be relatively large. Also, there is evidence of institutional obstacles—inappropriate financing systems, rent controls, 'Luddite' unions—the removal or reform of which might unleash a process of exogenous growth. 'The latent demand for more and/or better housing is so large that its satisfaction can lead to very high growth rates for extended periods without depressing the market' (*op.cit.*: 8).

Another candidate for leading sector, with high income elasticity of demand, is consumer durable goods. Currie rejects this candidate, however, on the grounds that the needs it meets are of lower priority than in the case of housing, because of its social side-effects and because in most countries such sectors are too small or require too high an import component to serve the purpose.

While the labour-intensity of the building sector is mentioned, this is not a primary reason for selecting it as a leading sector. Currie is very much against attempts to 'spread a limited number of jobs among more people by resorting to more labour-intensive (i.e. less efficient) techniques at low rates of pay' (*op.cit.*: 9). He looks to increased output and employment by exploiting a larger proportion of latent demand rather than to work-sharing methods. Building, as internal leading sector, could be combined with exports, as external leading sector, although, beyond suggesting that 'generally building and exports are not competitive for the same factors and can be complementary' (*op.cit.*: 13), Currie does not specify which type of exports he has in mind.

The whole analysis rests on the assumption that there is slack in the system in the sense already described. 'Lack of mobility' is assumed to result in disguised unemployment or employment with low productivity—'mal-use, misuse and under-use of human resources' rather than open unemployment (Currie 1971: 887). This is reflected in the enormous gap in productivity between commercial and traditional farming and between economic-sized and less than economic-sized agricultural units. Women, in particular, constitute a huge under-utilised labour force, available for work outside the home if it is offered. Under-utilisation of equipment is widespread, as a result of single-shift operation, frequent holidays and seasonality. Prestige investments show low rates of return, private or social. 'In view of all these observations and the possibility of increasing savings as income increases, it would appear safe to assume that all or nearly all developing countries could raise their rates of growth above levels now existing even within the constraints of existing exchange resources' (1974a: 12).

The removal of some barrier or the provision of some incentive can provide the initial impulse to a leading sector such as building but for sustained expansion a large and growing inflow of savings is needed. What Currie has in mind is finding some means of liquefying the large investment in existing homes of the upper working and salaried classes. he is *not* in favour of building houses for the very poorest groups and recent arrivals in cities, which in his opinion result in slums or impossible subsidies (Currie 1966: 102). His expectation is that those who are enabled to make down payments on new homes will sell their old homes to those slightly less prosperous than themselves, and so, 'by the familiar filtering process, provide homes for the poor groups' (Currie 1971: 893). At the same time highly capital-intensive processes could be used to break successive bottlenecks in the construction materials, transport and mass consumption goods industries, to prevent the whole process from being brought to a halt by shortages and inflation (*ibid.*: 894). As a means of ensuring that foreign exchange was available for this bottleneck-breaking purpose measures to restrict luxury expenditure and imports would be quite acceptable.

Currie's attitude to agriculture is ruthless. The ultimate aim is its complete conversion to 'commercial-type farming' (1966: 104). Thus rural–urban migration, and the resulting amalgamation of farms, is something to be encouraged rather than regretted. The existence of underutilised workers in agriculture is seen as an opportunity as well as a problem, their shift to industry being regarded as a gain no matter how inefficient that industry may be (*ibid.*: 112). Agriculture is unsuitable as a leading sector because of the inelastic demand it faces; any significant expansion in agricultural production would immediately cause a drastic fall in prices and agricultural incomes (1971: 892). However, it is recognised that 'responsiveness of agricultural production to increased demand is of course crucial to my argument' (*ibid.*: 901) and some space is devoted to arguing that, at least in the Colombian case, elasticity of agricultural supply is reasonably high (*ibid.*: 896–7).

THE LEADING-SECTOR STRATEGY IN PRACTICE

Currie had the unusual opportunity of overseeing the implementation of a strategy based on his theorising, in Colombia in 1971–1974. The centre point of the strategy was the establishment of private institutions, called *Corporaciones*, to channel savings into mortgages and construction, with *inflation-indexed* interest rates for both savers and borrowers. Savers were thus able to obtain a *real* return of at least 5 per cent from the *Corporaciones*, a return unequalled by any other financial asset (Ridler 1978: 56) and the range of potential borrowers was considerably extended by the resulting reduction in 'front-end loading' of mortgage payments. The *Corporaciones* were required to devote at least half of their mortgage funds to middle and lower income groups. The three other planks in the strategy, as applied to Colombia, were: the encouragement of exports, mainly through a continuation of the minor-exports promotion programme, initiated by the previous administration; increased agricultural productivity through improvements in inputs, such as fertiliser and seeds, and in administration, phased to *follow* the increase in demand for agricultural products; and income redistribution through progressive taxes and a marked reduction in tax incentives for industry (framed but largely unimplemented in the 1971–74 period) (Frankman 1977: 38–9, ILO PREALC 1976: 47–55).

Currie is in little doubt about the success of the experiment (abandoned in 1975 because of a change in government). Although he recognises that 'a longer period of trial would have been eminently desirable to test the strategy', he suggests that 'enough time has elapsed to be able to affirm that some of the assumptions have at least proved consistent with expectations' (Currie 1974b: 71). In particular he emphasises: the achievement of an annual average growth rate of between 7 and 8 per cent, which in his view indicates the large degree of pre-existing slack; the increase in savings, which indicates the inadequacy of previous savings; the fact that applications for loans persistently ran far ahead of rapidly increasing savings, which indicates the validity of the 'latent demand' assumption; the strong expansion in the proportion of industrial investment financed from internal cash flow, which suggests that industry can be relied on to respond to an increase in real as opposed to purely monetary demand; the demonstration that high rates of growth in consumption are compatible with increased saving and capital formation if real income is growing rapidly; and the absorption of a rapidly growing labour force by increased production rather than by work-spreading in the face of rapid technological progress and inflation. 'It would appear,' he concludes, 'that national governments and international agencies (as well as academic writers) might profitably devote serious study to the leading sector strategy as a means of accelerating growth' (*ibid.*: 72).

Some Colombian planners disagree strongly with this verdict, regarding the experiment as a 'four-year disaster', which proved extremely expensive to dismantle. Other observers, while not going as far as this, are slightly more cautious than Currie. For instance, Ridler (1978) judges that the strategy contributed to the acceleration in inflation rates and that supply elasticities in food and building materials production were overestimated. Prices of food, steel, cement, bricks and sand rose particularly fast. He is also tentatively dubious about its distributional impact, suggesting that labour's share of GNP may have increased but that the increase in prices of construction materials hit the poor and that the buildings constructed were principally of benefit to the wealthy. ILO PREALC (1976) also emphasises the contribution to inflation (adding that agriculture's slow response put extra pressure on the balance of payments) and the failure to improve income distribution. The increase in employment generated by the strategy is judged to have been too small to cope with expansion of the urban labour force as a result of rural–urban migration and rising participation rates (*ibid.*: 55).

Yet PREALC recognises the success of the strategy in mobilising resources within the modern sectors. Ridler spells this out in more detail. Between 1972 and 1974 the real value of building loans almost doubled and the new *Corporaciones* came to account for two thirds of the total. In a single year, 1973, more building was completed than in the entire previous twelve-year period. Employment in the construction sector rose by more than 50 per cent between 1972 and 1973 and in the whole of the strategy's four-year period almost a million jobs are estimated to have been created, 160,000 more than the increase in the labour force[4]. In spite of the reservations about effects on prices and income distribution, these achievements seem significant enough to 'merit more serious attention than has yet been the case'. (Frankman 1977: 41). Given the crucial role of the food and building materials industries a fruitful area of enquiry would seem to be the scope for increasing their supply response as demand generated by the building boom increases. To judge from Colombian experience this may require more intervention in production and distribution than Currie had envisaged. Alternatively, it could be suggested that the leading sector strategy is even more suited to industrialised economies where elasticities of supply are higher.

Finally, just how Keynesian is Currie's analysis and the strategy based on it? As has been seen, Currie himself is careful to deny that his approach is Keynesian. He calls it 'related to but in certain key respects quite different from the Keynesian approach' (1971: 898). Others are less hesitant. Frankman, for instance, says that to characterise Currie's model as Keynesian 'does strike at the heart of the matter' (1977: 40). Ranis calls his recommendation of a net increase in the level of effective demand directed towards urban housing 'just about as Keynesian as you can get' (1973: 204). While Ranis shrewdly identifies some apparent inconsistencies in Currie's analysis (for example, his emphasis both on barriers to mobility and on high supply elasticity) he does not really succeed in getting the Keynesian label (clearly not intended as a compliment) to stick. Currie's distinction between Keynesian and Sayian demand (see page 171) does seem to be important in this respect. Also the leading-sector model, like the dynamic external economies analysis to which it is related, is long run. It shows how the capacity to employ can be created by investment that can be induced by liquefying latent effective demand—in contrast to the Keynesian short-run exclusive emphasis on improving utilisation of existing capacity.

The issue of the Keynesian-ness or otherwise of Currie's strategy is not purely academic. In circumstances where the concept of the 'natural rate of unemployment' (see Chapter Three, page 73) holds sway in a large number of industrialised economies it may be important to present the strategy as a means of reducing a country's natural rate by institutional change rather than of bringing the actual and natural rates closer together by reducing the level of Keynesian demand-deficiency unemployment.

KNAPP'S FRUSTRATED SUPPLY AND VENT MANAGEMENT APPROACH

Rather similar to Currie's approach (and similarly neglected) but couched in more explicitly Keynesian terms is Knapp's analysis of 'frustrated supply', i.e. the situation in which lack of effective money demand lowers the incentive to invest and frustrates potential capacity to supply. To Keynes's historical examples of the types of projects that have eliminated frustrated supply by evoking the necessary incentive to invest (the building of pyramids, medieval cathedrals and monasteries and mansions) Knapp adds the demand for military supplies in time of war, the charting of new trade routes, the discovery of new sources of gold and silver, the opening up of new lands for settlement and development and the invention of new technology (Knapp 1956–7, quoted in Barratt Brown 1974). His approach, thus, in some respects resembles Myint's vent-for-surplus model, which analyses trade as providing new effective demand for the output of resources which would otherwise remain unused, particularly land (Myint 1958: Smith 1976).

His own proposal is for what he calls 'vent management', whereby governments, on the basis of preliminary resource surveys and studies of potential investment and consumer demand, would offer to buy and sell a wide range of specified goods and services at stated prices. This provision of a guaranteed market is seen as likely to increase the incentive to invest and produce. It might also enable farmers to borrow money to purchase simple agricultural implements and fertilisers. Or such equipment and inputs might be included in the list of goods on offer for sale and purchase. The re-equipping of farms in this way may raise labour productivity at the margin, thus increasing their demand for labour. Offers to buy and sell goods and services could also be located in remote unused areas, potentially suitable for cultivation if the market were enlarged, in the expectation that labour, entrepreneurs, finance, etc. would be attracted into the 'offer' area, where offers could include the new construction of transport and housing facilities.

As in the case of the Currie strategy, vent management is not intended to involve deficit financing; rather, the government's budget is expected to benefit on balance from the scheme. Moreover, it is quite possible that the authority which makes the sale and purchase offers will end up not having to buy or sell anything at all, 'since the expansion of employment and incomes associated with the increased investment and consumption expenditures generated by the offer, may, in a neatly designed set of offers, absorb all the increases in production generated by it' (Knapp 1969: 79). The scheme may be inflationary since prices offered would often (but not always) be higher than previous local prices and the repercussions may raise prices further. 'However, in-so-far as these price-developments were associated with a reduction of frustrated supply, they would be analogous to a price increase which occurs in the process of recovery from a slump' (*ibid.*: 79).

Unlike Currie, Knapp did not have the opportunity to put his strategy into practice although some schemes in Yugoslavia and India bear some resemblance to vent management (Barratt-Brown 1974: 314). The analysis underlying the two strategies is basically similar, but Knapp's relies more on the existence of an efficient and incorruptible civil service. The consequences for asset and income distribution of vent management will depend on the context but, as with the leading sector strategy, success in mobilising resources may not, in an economy where disequalising processes are strong, be accompanied by improvements in distribution. Nevertheless Knapp, like Currie, has the Keynesian appeal of offering something for nothing—improvements in output and employment without apparent sacrifice by anyone—and the approach that he suggests deserves further investigation.

NURKSE'S HIDDEN SAVING POTENTIAL ANALYSIS

Unlike the leading sector and frustrated supply models, Nurkse's analysis of the saving potential concealed in rural underemployment (Nurkse 1953) can hardly be said to have been neglected by development economists. For the thirty years since its publication it has been a major influence on theory and policy.

Its basis is the assumption that a large number of densely populated peasant economies, stretching from south-east Europe to south-east Asia, 'suffer from large-scale disguised unemployment in the sense that, even with unchanged techniques of agriculture, a large part of the population engaged in agriculture could be removed without reducing agricultural output'[5] (*ibid.*: 32). The changes in techniques that are excluded for the purposes of this definition comprise technological advance, more equipment, mechanisation, better seeds, improvements in drainage, irrigation and other such conditions. Changes in the manner and organisation of work, however, including possibly a consolidation of scattered strips and plots of land, are not excluded. In fact, as we have seen (pages 16–7), logic compels us to go further than this. If we are to avoid the implication that agriculturalists are applying their labour beyond the point that would be rational (assuming that work has some disutility) we must resist Nurkse's translation of his above definition of disguised unemployment into the statement that 'in technical terms, the marginal productivity of labour over a wide range, is zero' (*ibid.*: 33). More plausible, as Sen has shown (see pages 16–20) and still consistent with Nurkse's definition as originally stated, is the assumption that the marginal productivity of *workers* is zero over a wide range. Also, as we have seen (on pages 16–17), this definition of disguised unemployment logically implies a need for man-hours per worker in agriculture to rise after surplus workers have been removed, in addition to whatever changes in the manner and organisation of work are allowed.

Nurkse avoids casting doubt on employers' profit-maximising aims by stating categorically that 'the term disguised unemployment is not applied to wage labour', but 'denotes a condition of family employment in peasant communities' (*ibid.*: 33). In which case taking on extra workers beyond the point of equality between marginal cost and marginal revenue product, as long as they are either adding to output or reducing the number of man-hours per worker required to produce a given level of output, is quite consistent with the presumed aim of maximisation (or achievement of a given level) of output, rather than maximisation of profit or surplus.

Nurkse is cautious about quantifying the phenomenon of disguised unemployment. He says that it is not characteristic of the United States, nor of Latin America except for certain Caribbean regions such as Puerto Rico, but is typical of many countries in the area ranging from south-eastern Europe to south-eastern Asia.[6] In these countries between 66 and 80 per cent of the labour force work on the land and of this agricultural population perhaps between 15 and 30 per cent constitutes disguised unemployment. Even in countries where it is mainly a seasonal matter it still has important implications for capital formation, but in many countries it is more than seasonal, persisting throughout the year.

The simple, central point of Nurkse's analysis is that this disguised unemployment represents a hidden source of saving potential, in the sense that surplus peopls can be taken off the land and put to work on capital projects *without affecting agricultural output*. These surplus people, now working on capital projects, would continue to depend for their subsistence on the peasants remaining on the farms. None would be eating less than before, but all would now be productively employed. Thus Nurkse belongs to the school of development economists which sees surplus labour as an opportunity rather than a problem.

The difficulty lies, as Nurkse points out, in preventing leakages from the subsistence fund available for capital formation through increased consumption by the remaining peasants and/or by the new investment workers. The cost of transporting the food from the farms to the places where the capital projects are established constitutes another form of leakage. So does the provision of capital goods for the new investment workers to work with, in so far as these go beyond the simple tools that they could sit down and make for themselves. Complementary saving may be available from outside the system (foreign capital or domestic saving, voluntary or involuntary) but the 'need for preventing the leakages or holding them down to an absolute minimum' (*ibid.*: 43) is recognised. 'Some form of collective saving enforced by the state may prove to be indispensable' for this purpose, although the various mechanisms available—direct or indirect taxation of the peasants, land tax, taxation in kind, some form of requisitioning and controlled deliveries, collective farms—are discussed without much enthusiasm.

Nurkse is fairly vague about the types of projects to be undertaken. At one point (*ibid.*: 36) he mentions 'irrigation, drainage, roads, railways, houses, factories, training schemes and so on'. At another (*ibid.*: 46) he suggests that they may well be community development projects, especially designed to make use of local labour surpluses or of seasonal slack periods in the countryside. Initially most likely are social overhead capital projects, including public utilities, transport facilities and investment in human skill, education and health. The simple central idea of Nurkse's analysis is a powerful one, but the problems of political and social organisation that mobilisation of the hidden saving potential would involve are perhaps even more formidable than he recognises.

A sign of this is that the only economy in which a strategy resembling that of Nurkse has been implemented with any success is that of Maoist China. Here the strategy of using idle labour in wintertime for farmland and water conservancy capital construction was called 'labour accumulation'. Chinese experience of this strategy suggests that its main problem, inadequately emphasised by Nurkse in his discussion of leakages, is the provision of adequate incentives to peasants to participate in labour accumulation schemes. Indeed, it suggests that the strategy stands little chance of success unless agriculture is collectively organised[7]. A recent study identifies the 'use of a work point system' as 'the key to the superiority of collective agriculture in motivating peasant labour to participate in farmland and water conservancy capital construction without an immediate appreciable increase in the total of subsistence goods dispenses' (Nickum 1978: 275), i.e. without an appreciable Nurksean leakage.

Nickum emphasises the 'ability of the Chinese collective to use labour more extensively than under a private wage system, by relying on the distributional incentive of the work point system and by providing a close correspondence between those who do the work and those who reap the benefits' (*ibid.*: 284). In the latter respect choice of projects is also important. In the Chinese case these were mainly traditional farmland investment, such as the building of terraced fields, raised fields, canals, dikes and dams made of earth or stone, and the levelling of land to facilitate the use of water and sunlight, and the development of entire water systems. Thus, not only were those who participated in the labour accumulation schemes secure in their access to the requisite number of workpoints, but also the nature of the schemes was such as to contribute directly and significantly to an improvement in productivity and income in the whole community, including those who did the work. Where land is individually owned, on the other hand, and often not by those who are farming it, it is difficult enough to organise the transport of sufficient food to labour accumulation workers without leakage, even more difficult to ensure that the benefit of their work accrues even partially to the workers. Perhaps the most significant aspect of labour accumulation, as Nickum sums it up, is that 'it pays off for the peasant' (*ibid.*: 285).

This way of looking at it is perhaps relevant to the question of whether Nurkse's hidden saving potential analysis really belongs in the 'Keynesian' category. Nurkse's own judgement on this is that it stands 'midway between the classical and the Keynesian approach. In the Keynesian world of industrial unemployment, consumption as well as investment can be expanded at the same time. In the case now before us the situation differs from the Keynesian model in that it is impossible to expand both consumption and investment. On the other hand, it is possible to increase capital formation without having to cut down on the level of consumption' (*ibid.*: 38). At another point he notes that 'disguised rural unemployment differs in several ways from open industrial unemployment. It differs notably in that it cannot be absorbed by means of an expansion of monetary demand. The inelasticity of agricultural production makes this remedy quite ineffective' (*ibid.*: 36).

Yet the emphasis of this analysis, like that of Currie, is certainly on the demand side. The saving potential remains hidden, in a incompletely monetised economy where saving and investment are a matter of allocation of labour time by households, because of the weakness of the inducement to invest—in the sense of the absence of the political and social organisation that would make mobilisation of the potential pay off for the peasant. In this sense, though not Keynesian, Nurkse's analysis belongs in this chapter rather than in Chapter Five or Six.

CONCLUSIONS

This has been one of the more hopeful chapters in this book in the sense that by locating the problem on the demand rather than the supply side 'Keynesian' development economists make it look easier to solve. Almost by sleight of hand, latent effective demand can be liquefied (Currie), frustrated supply can be released (Knapp) and hidden saving potential can be mobilised (Nurkse), without any need for a sacrifice of consumption by anyone, to the benefit of the rate of growth of output and employment. The analysis underlying these suggestions is attractive, with the Currie/Knapp emphasis on the long-run consequences of an inadequate incentive to invest looking particularly relevant to the capitalist world in the recessionary eighties. The conditions for successful implementation are stringent: for Currie, for instance, slack and 'lack of mobility' must coexist with high elasticity of supply; for Nurkse, food must be transferred without leakage to labour accumulation workers and ways of making the work 'pay off' for the worker must be found. Moreover, the short-run question of the trade-off between unemployment and inflation (around which the debate centres in industrialised economies—see Chapter Three) is not addressed, nor is the Marxist question of the tendency towards crisis (see Chapter Two). Nevertheless, reformists in search of an alternative theory to the current orthodoxy could do worse than begin with a thorough review of these 'dynamic Keynesians'.

NOTES

1. In some cases (for example, Myrdal and Nurkse) development economists emphasise *both* the supply *and* demand sides in their theorising, so inclusion in this chapter does not imply membership of an exclusively demand-oriented school.
2. The other three are: internal diseconomies of scale due to indivisibilities in the factors or production; income-depressing obstacles that may be generated by the stimulants to growth; and culturally and institutionally determined attitudes that may inhibit growth.
3. Currie does not use this term, although he acknowledges Rosenstein-Rodan's 1943 paper and Leibenstein's critical minimum effort thesis.
4. Thus PREALC and Ridler disagree about the impact on employment.
5. For a more detailed discussion of the conceptual and measurement issues *see* Chapter One, pp. 16–20, and Chapter Four, pp. 110–12.
6. Cf. Lewis on the assumption of an unlimited supply of labour: 'it is obviously not true of the United Kindgom, or of North-west Europe. It is not true either of some of the countries usually now lumped together as underdeveloped; for example there is an acute shortage of male labour in some parts of Africa and of Latin America. On the other hand it is obviously the relevant assumption for the economies of Egypt, of India or Jamaica' (Lewis 1954: 401). *See* Chapter Five, pp. 125–35, for a detailed discussion of the Lewis model.
7. Analogous strategies could possibly work, even in capitalist economies, in the case of producer cooperatives that are owned and managed democratically by their members. With the experience of Mondragon particularly in mind, Levin points out that such producer cooperatives have the potential to create more jobs per unit of output and require less capital for the creation of each job than do capitalist firms (Levin 1983: 310 ff.).

8 Marxist and Neo-Marxist Theories of Surplus Labour and Underdevelopment

The development economists, discussed in the previous chapter, who question the emphasis on the supply of capital as the main constraint on the growth of output and employment and emphasise rather the inadequacy of the inducement to invest, have some affinity with the dependency school that emerged in Latin America during the 1960s.[1]

For, if the problem is seen to be on the side of the inducement to invest rather than of the supply of capital, then the logic of inviting an inflow of foreign capital is called into question. One such development economist, Hirschman (1971: 227), raised this question explicitly: 'Could the inflow of foreign capital stunt what might otherwise be vigorous local development of the so-called missing or scarce factors of production?' His view was that it could—sometimes in an absolute sense, for instance through the foreign takeover of local banks or businesses, more often in relation to what might have happened in the absence of the foreign investment. His evidence for this was the fact that during wars, depressions, national expropriations and international sanctions, the domestic supply of entrepreneurs, managers, technology and saving seems to be 'far more elastic than is ever suspected under business-as-usual conditions'. His conclusion that 'a policy of selective liquidation and withdrawal of foreign private investment' would be in the best interests of Latin America would be endorsed by most dependency authors.

THE DEPENDENCY SCHOOL

Where members of the dependency school part company from development economists (often their earlier selves) is in their rejection of modernisation theory; their analysis of the nation state not in isolation but in the context of the global evolution of capitalism: their incorporation of a strong historical dimension into their analysis; their endogenisation of the state as 'the crucial battleground between the different social groups' (Sunkel 1979: 29); their analysis of economic links with capitalist centres as antagonistic and exploitative rather than harmonious; and their use of a dialectical rather than an equilibrium mode of analysis. This difference in approach is reflected in the different set of questions addressed by them. The most important of these questions, assumed away by 'modernisationist' development economists, is: 'What are the limits on capitalist development at the periphery?'

The typical dependency answer to this question is, as already indicated, a gloomy one. None is more gloomy than Gunder Frank, perhaps unfortunately the author who has come to symbolise the dependency approach for readers outside Latin America. As Booth has pointed out (Oxaal *et al.* 1975) Frank's analysis is less mechanistic and metropole-oriented than is usually supposed, emphasising 'the impregnation of the satellite's domestic economy with the same capitalist structuree and its fundamental contradictions' as more important than 'the drain of economic surplus' from satellite to metropolis with which he is usually associated (Frank 1967: 10). However, he remains strongly insistent on the impossibility of capitalist development at the periphery:

> the economic basis of a developmentalist national bourgeois class . . . has been entirely eliminated or prevented from forming at all, thus precluding further or future development under capitalism . . . short of socialist revolution (Frank 1978: 10).

While critical of Frank, most of the more orthodoxly Marxian dependency authors share his scepticism about the prospects for capitalist development at the periphery. For example, Dos Santos (1973) would put more emphasis than does Frank on the elements within a nation which determine the effects of international situations upon national reality and on the assimilation of the national bourgeoisie by foreign capital in the role of 'dominated dominators' and less on the surplus drain. But he emphasises the inability of peripheral societies to develop a capital goods sector as a defining characteristic, and he would agree that capitalist development or at least 'autonomous' capitalist development is not possible and that a socialist path offers the only escape for peripheral societies.

Similar conclusions are reached via a different route to those who analyse the plight of the periphery in terms of 'unequal exchange'. Thus Amin (1978) describes his 'peripheral model', based on low-wage exports and (in the consequent absence of an internal mass market) on the production of luxury goods for internal demand, with 'new' mechanisms of domination by transnational corporations superimposed; and regards it as a 'dead end', with no possibility of transition to a 'self-centred' system based on production of mass-consumption and capital goods. He sees self-reliance, therefore, as a necessary strategy for transition to socialism. Marini (1972: 14) extends a similar analysis to 'subimperialism' (the form which dependent capitalism assumes upon reaching the stage of monopolies and finance capital) in Brazil. In this case the low-wage exports are of manufactured goods and the state takes an increasingly important role (in conjunction with foreign capital), but the whole system is crucially dependent on the superexploitation of labour. Successful pursuit of wage demands by urban and rural workers would 'close all exits for capitalist development in Brazil'.

The Caribbean dependency school is on the whole less pessimistic about the possibilities of capitalist development, as long as the plantation economy model is replaced by a localised or people's capitalism. A notable exception is Thomas (1974), who points to the way in which colonialism led to a separation of the pattern and growth of domestic resource use from the pattern and growth of domestic demand; and to divergence between domestic demand and the needs of the broad mass of the population. Even in the case of the most successful small capitalist economies at the periphery, he sees no real possibility of development 'beyond misleading rises in per capita income or indeed of even sustaining such advances on a long-term basis . . . unless a comprehensive socialist strategy is developed' (Thomas 1974: 105). He recognises, however, in 'some of the larger economies' the possibility of indigenous capitalist development of productive forces as a genuine alternative to socialism.

Perhaps the most complex and certainly the most impressive member of the dependency school, so critical in his more recent writing of most of its conclusions as almost to place himself outside it, is Cardoso. Like other *dependentistas*, he emphasises the absence of capital goods and financial sectors, the import of technology and penetration by foreign enterprises as characteristics of dependency, which he defines as the situation 'when the accumulation and expansion of capital cannot find its essential dynamic component within the system' (Cardoso and Faletto 1979: XX). However, he sees the relationship between external and internal forces as forming a:

> complex whole whose structural links are not based on mere external forms of exploitation and coercion, but are rooted in coincidences of interests between local dominant classes and international ones and, on the other side, are challenged by local dominated groups and classes (Cardoso and Faletto 1979: XVI).

Most important, he refuses to place theoretical limits on capitalist development at the periphery. He sees dependent capitalism as capable of growth and of transforming social relations of production, although not of resolving the employment and poverty problems of the majority of the population. He insists, however, on the need to analyse particular situations rather than to develop general theories:

> we do not try to place theoretical limits on the probable course of future events. These will depend, not on academic predictions, but on collective action guided by political wills that make work what is structurally barely possible (Cardoso and Faletto: 175).

THE NEO-MARXIST MARGINALISATION APPROACH

Perhaps the gloomiest vision within the dependency school belongs to the writers on whom the first part of this chapter is mainly focussing—who talk in terms of 'marginalisation' and 'marginal mass', such as Nun (1969, 1979) and Quijano (1974). They are neo-Marxist in the sense of basing their analysis on a critique of Marx's concepts of relative surplus population and industrial reserve army (see Chapter Two, pages 39–46). Thus Nun suggests that the forms of relative surplus population identified by Marx (floating, latent and stagnant—see pages 42–3) 'pertain to a specific historical period and not to theoretically universal forms' (Nun 1979: 10). Marx regarded the latent and stagnant manifestations of the surplus population as empirically important in the England he was writing about but as transitional forms. Therefore, he excluded them from his most abstract analysis of the general laws of motion of the capitalist mode of production which he organised around the floating form of the relative surplus population.

On the question of the subsequent fate of those who swell the ranks of the floating surplus population, according to Nun, Marx was not very precise but presented a series of images. Some redundant labourers would be forced to emigrate in search of employment, some would move into the 'last places of refuge' provided by domestic industry; some would become domestic servants or 'modern domestic slaves'; and others would sink into pauperism—'the hospital of the active labour army and the dead weight of the industrial reserve army'. But the dominant image, says Nun, was that of repulsion and attraction or of alternation between employment and unemployment as the collective destiny of a growing industrial proletariat. Moreover, this process was assumed to be taking place in a labour market that was moving towards ever greater homogeneity, with one proletarianised worker increasingly easy to substitute for another.

Nun regards this analysis as generally accurate for England and the USA in the last quarter of the nineteenth century but suggests that the intensification of the concentration and centralisation of capital since then affects the extent to which it any longer applies even to mature capitalist economies. The initial tendencies towards the growth and homogenisation of the industrial proletariat have been reversed and the resulting cleavage between monopolistic firms and other employers has been reflected in segmentation in the labour market, particularly in the USA (see pages 62–3 for a discussion of this literature). All this leads him to suggest that there is a need 'to reconceptualise Marx's problematic of labour surplus in this new context', (*ibid.*: 13) in central economies such as the USA and, even more so, in peripheral societies.

Quijano (1974: 417–421) adds an emphasis on the 'scientific technological revolution' and on the adverse impact of centre upon periphery to that of Nun on the differences between competitive and monopoly capitalism. He questions whether, in the current Latin American context, surplus population is any longer the 'lever of capitalistic accumulation', and the 'condition of existence of the capitalist mode of production' that Marx envisaged. In these conditions the link between surplus population and productivity increase is broken since rises in productivity are increasingly independent of competition between workers for employment and wages and more dependent on the quality of technical innovations embodied in the means of production.[3] The link between surplus population and wage determination is also broken, since workers in the monopolistic sector form a 'non-competing group'. Their higher skill level and the specificity of their skills make them more difficult to replace and increase their bargaining power. At the same time, monopoly capital's ability and willingness to pay higher wages is increased by labour-saving technical progress (which reduces the size of the firm's labour force) and by the high level of productivity per man employed. This analysis leads him to question the adequacy of Marx's 'industrial reserve army' concept in contemporary Latin America.

In place of the industrial reserve army this school suggests the concept of 'marginalised labour force' or 'marginal mass'. In Quijano's version marginalisation is a consequence of the grafting on to the previous Latin American production matrix of new sectors and new formations, derived from the dominant formations of the world system, without their incorporation as integral or coherent structural sectors.[4] The transition from one stage to another of capitalist expansion in Latin America is, thus, an abrupt one and is 'unable to generalise the effect of modernisation throughout the previous production matrix' (*ibid.*: 395). The insertion into the sub-continent's economy of the products of the scientific technological revolution (but not of the technology itself) brings the socio-economic matrix 'permanently to the edge of breakdown' (*ibid.*: 397).

Latin-American historical formations are 'structurally dependent' in the sense of having an 'overall structure incapable of attaining autonomy within the system'. But this is a dependence in which there is a 'basic congruence of interests between dominant social groups in both levels of development of the system' (*ibid.*: 398).

Two phenomena are identified as 'decisive'. (1) The generalising of industrial production of goods and services as a hegemonic sector of the economic structure as a whole. (2) The emergence of the monopolistic modality of organisation of the economic activity as a whole and especially of its hegemonic sector as the dominant modality' (*ibid.*: 400). These imply: concentration of control over capital, raw materials and technology; exertion of control over a significant high and middle-income market, via credit, obsolescence, model changes etc., leading to its 'qualitative widening'; a consequently increased concentration of incomes; a constant process of labour-saving technical change; an increase in the rate of capital accumulation and concentration of the surplus; and the reorganisation of financial institutions to perform a role of 'servicing the monopolistic organisations of production' (*ibid.*: 402).

At the other end of the scale from this hegemonic, monopolistic level lies the 'marginal pole' of the economy. 'In every basic sector of economic activity of Latin American countries, a level of activities and mechanisms of economic organisation which are continually losing the possibility of increased capital accumulation tends to expand and become differentiated,' such as 'artisanry, petty commerce, agricultural and livestock activities at the minimum level of productivity' (*ibid.*: 403). These forms of activity are 'devoid of all significant relationship with the basic means of production of the dominant forms and sectors of the economy'. They are not just a survival from the past but the product of new conditions (*ibid.*: 403). They operate 'around residual resources and, for the most part, residual activities . . . They are structured in an unstable and precarious way, they generate in turn extremely diminished incomes compared with their eqivalents in other levels, and serve a market formed by the population itself incorporated into this level of activity, incapable, therefore, of allowing for growing capital accumulation' (*ibid.*: 404).

In between the hegemonic level and the marginal pole an intermediate level of 'competitive capitalism' precariously survives. In the manufacturing sector this level though still the largest labour market, is declining fairly rapidly and is confined to the 'traditional' branches, such as clothing, food-processing and shoe-making, and to a semi-manufacturing form of organisation. The principal function of this level, which fluctuates in a way that is typical of competitive capitalism, is to 'supply the lowest levels of the market and transfer its surplus—by various mechanisms—to the monopolistic level of the sector and of the economy as a whole' (*ibid.*: 410).

These levels are not confined to the urban economy alone. Capitalist relations of production are expanding in the rural sector, in response to changes in the urban and international markets for rural products. The dominance of the rural hegemonic level, under the control of a few mainly urban-based groups, is being strengthened. Thus 'a growing contingent of manpower—increased by the very high rates of demographic growth which are higher here than in other sectors of the economy—is going to remain outside the labour market of the dominant levels of the rural economy. The new intermediate levels are not sufficiently extensive to absorb it and in this way it is forced to migrate geographically or to take refuge in a new rural 'marginal pole' constituted by what was previously called the 'subsistence economy', and by the complex of commercial and service activities of the lowest level with limited productive resources and on a precarious level of organisation' (*ibid.*: 413).

The crucial difference, then, between competitive and monopolistic capitalism as far as labour absorption possibilities are concerned is seen to lie in the differing effects of technical change. Under competitive capitalism, it is argued, technical change leads to a reduction in the price of commodities, an increase in demand for commodities and a derived increase in demand for labour; monopoly-capitalists, being price-makers rather than price-takers, on the other hand, take part of the productivity increase in the form of higher profits and pass part on to the 'hegemonic' labour force (increasingly 'specific' in various ways) in the form of higher wages, with the result that the demand for labour tends to stagnate. Since the link between surplus population and increases in productivity and the link between surplus population and wage determination in the hegemonic sector are broken (see page 191), the surplus can no longer be regarded as a *reserve* but should be seen as an *excluded labour force* which, 'as changes in the technical composition of capital progress, loses in a permanent and not in a transitory way the possibility of being absorbed into those hegemonic levels of production' (*ibid.*: 418).

Thus the marginalised labour force, or 'marginal mass' as Nun calls it, could be defined as surplus population over and above what is necessary to perform the functions of the industrial reserve army *vis-à-vis* the hegemonic level, i.e. as non-functional surplus population. Analysis in these terms is profoundly pessimistic, not merely questioning the employment-generating performance of peripheral capitalism but also denying its capacity to perform its historically progressive Marxian role.

MARX REAFFIRMED

Even within the dependency school there are those who feel that Marx's concept of industrial reserve army, although based on the experience of mature competitive capitalism, is still more or less adequate to explain the role of surplus population under monopoly capitalism. Cardoso, for instance (1971), questions the need to devise new concepts such as 'marginal mass' and to base on them catastrophic visions of the labour absorption possibilities in peripheral capitalist economies. He claims that, methodologically, the concept of marginal mass does not belong to the same universe of discourse as that of reserve army, being relevant to the theory of functionality of populations with respect to systems of production rather than to the theory of accumulation; Marx, in Cardoso's view, was more interested in the dialectical relationship between accumulation and surplus population, as a contradiction of capitalism, than he was in the question of functionality. Nor, in this version,[5] is the concept operational, since marginality is not seen as a shared social situation nor as a base for prediction of social or political behaviour but as a condition involving employed and unemployed alike.

Moreover, Cardoso accuses these theorists of not answering the empirical question which should have been their point of departure—does an increasing marginal mass really exist? For instance, Nun's talk about the 'tendency towards stagnation which the economy of the region has presented in the last two decades' (Nun 1969: 219) 'does not correspond to the facts, but to the vision of a "doomed developmentalism"' (Cardoso 1971: 164). Cardoso does not deny the existence of over-exploited surplus populations, such as a considerable proportion of North American blacks, Puerto Ricans, day-labourers and Mexicans, 'but this should not shock anyone familiar with the Marxist explanatory approach to accumulation, where the contradiction between wealth and indigence is fundamental' (*ibid.*: 169). In this respect, he suggests, the effects of capitalism in nineteenth-century England, as described by Marx, were similar if not worse. In contrast to Nun and Quijano he detects a 'pronounced dynamism in the creation of employment in monopoly capitalism', deriving from the relationship between the secondary and tertiary sectors—in Latin America as well as in the USA. Even in the secondary sector he suggests that the employment-reducing effects of changes in the production process are counterbalanced by the employment-creating effects of the creation of new products.

Bill Warren, perhaps the most influential Marxist critic of the dependency approach, is even more vigorous than Cardoso in his attack on the marginalisation concept. Indeed, he is careful to distance himself from the Brazilian sociologist, recognising 'Cardoso's substantial difference of emphasis [from that of the rest of the dependency school] as regards the dynamic character of Latin American development', but suggesting that this 'is not matched by an emancipation from the same theoretical framework' (Warren 1980: 162). In his own view a significant number of major under-developed countries have quite good prospects of successful capitalist development in the sense of 'development which provides the appropriate economic, social and political conditions for the continuing reproduction of capital, as a social system representing the highest form of commodity production' (Warren 1973: 4).

Warren's critique is primarily empirical. He disputes whether marginalisation is taking place, in the sense of increases either in unemployment or in underemployment of the labour force. He points to census and sample survey data[6] which show that rates of open urban unemployment in less developed countries are considerably lower than has generally been supposed, often comparable to rates in developed market economies and, if anything, falling rather than rising (between the mid-1960s and the mid-1970s). On underemployment he suggests that, since there is little evidence of a wide gap between 'hours worked' and 'hours available for work' in third-world cities, its existence must depend on the assumption that urban workers outside the modern sector are substantially underemployed only in the tautological sense of having low incomes or low productivity.

Warren inclines to the view that the informal sector 'comprises significant elements of internal dynamism in terms of innovation, accumulation and the upward mobility of the more successful operators', which implies the existence in the sector of an expanding wage-labour force, as opposed to being 'basically residual and stagnant' (1980: 216). It is not clear that the work force in the informal sector is rising proportionately to the urban labour force, nor that productivity is declining. Even if many of the incomes earned in the sector 'fall below some arbitrary dividing line demarcating the superior productivity or earnings of the rest of the urban labour force' (*ibid.*: 223) they are likely to be the result of a shift from less to more remunerative occupations and to have improved over time.

'The concept of marginalisation', Warren concludes, 'implies the effective disruption or weakening of the linkages of a growing number of the (generally urban) population with the central activities of the economy . . . In fact, so-called marginalisation is a way of referring to the anarchic, chaotic, unplanned sometimes brutal, but nevertheless vigorous fashion in which urbanisation expands the market, stimulates commercialisation of the whole of society (especially the agricultural sector) and thereby increases the division of labour and thus the *integration* of society, as Adam Smith noted long ago. The real process is just the opposite of that implied by the word; it is one of increasing *integration* . . . The rural-urban migration, together with the return flows to the villages, is a progressive force in breaking up subsistence activities, institutions and attitudes that held up material progress; rural life in general and agricultural practice in particular are consequently transformed. The growth of towns undermines relatively self-sufficient communities and leads to specialisation and reintegration of separate economic activities through the market, breaking down the economic isolation characteristic of precapitalist societies.' (*ibid.*: 223–4).

One might, then, summarise the views of Cardoso and Warren as minimising the differences, as far as generation and absorption of surplus population is concerned between the past experience of mature, competitive, capitalist economies and the present and likely future experience of peripheral economies under monopoly capitalism. In this view, surplus population is regarded as a contradiction fundamental to capitalism itself. Furthermore, the nature and scale of this problem is not significantly influenced by the fact of the internationalisation of capital in the twentieth century. This school is thus optimistic in the limited sense that it finds no reason to conclude from the current observation of surplus labour in peripheral economies that capitalism is not performing its historically progressive role.

CONCLUSIONS ON MARGINALISATION

The argument about marginalisation between different types of Marxist is, to some extent, an empirical one. Its resolution is, however, hindered by conceptual complexities. How, for instance, would one set about measuring the size of a marginal mass and how distinguish it in practice from a reserve army? Warren certainly does not resolve the debate by referring to meaningless open unemployment rates and narrow definitions of underemployment (see Chapter One, page 5); and his *a priori* optimism about the informal sector is no more convincing than that of some development economists (Chapter Six, page 140). Yet the careful empirical work that would be necessary to establish the validity of the marginalisation concept is also lacking.

The matter is made even more complex by the fact that the argument is about *trajectories* rather than situations. What is at stake is a comparison of the alternatives available to any particular society: a comparison of what open-door capitalism, along the lines promoted by Warren, has to offer with the best historically possible alternative. There is an initial confusion here, as Bienefeld (1980) points out, about the meaning of 'capitalist development'. If all that it means is the 'increase in the productive forces of social labour and the socialisation of that labour', then it is difficult to disagree with the conclusion of one influential review article (Palma 1980: 49) that 'to deny, as the "contemporary Narodniks" do, that capitalist development is taking place in some countries in Latin America and in some parts of the rest of the periphery is no less than absurd'.

The extreme stagnationism of such as Frank (see page 187) has clearly been refuted. Nevertheless, the important question remains as to where 'capitalist development', in this sense, is leading. Here Palma follows Cardoso and Warren in deriding those who hope that capitalism could ever produce a just distribution of income, wealth and power. Nevertheless the welfare implications of different possible trajectories *do* need to be analysed and compared. For instance, is the trajectory of peripheral capitalist development towards full-employment capitalism with a large role for the state and muted contradictions (of the kind enjoyed by industrialised economies during the 1960s)? Or is it towards a form of capitalism in which contradictions take a particularly acute form—fast growth perhaps, but combined with immiserisation and massive underemployment as far as the eye can see?

Even if it were possible to reach a fairly firm conclusion in any particular case about what open-door capitalism has to offer, it would still be necessary to compare this with the historically possible alternative. Virtually by definition this must vary from case to case. To overthrow capitalism and attempt a transition to socialism may, in a particular case, be premature in relation to the classical Marxist schema, but it may still stand a good chance of producing a preferable outcome in the longer run. Such an issue cannot be settled by appeals to general theory or to other countries' experience, but only through a careful study of the political economy in question. Political activists are constantly having to make decisions based on their judgement as to the balance of such comparisons, but there is a dearth of careful academic studies in this area.[7] Were they to be undertaken it is not at all obvious that they would inevitably lend support to the Warrenite position that disengaging socialism at the periphery is always 'premature'. Is it clear, for instance, that the Chinese would be better off today if the revolution had not occurred—or that post-Mao China could make effective use of imported technology without the earlier period of Maoist disengagement?

Insistence on the need for a case-study approach does not mean that we have to remain, with Cardoso and Palma, at the level of descriptive analysis of concrete situations. It is important to try to reach the highest possible level of generalisation in order to be able to predict outcomes rather than to invent *post hoc* explanations of them. Again, not much distance has been travelled along this road. Kaplinsky (1980) suggests that a distinction should be made between:

large economies with big internal markets (such as India), where sustainable accumulation is possible; labour-processing economies (such as South Korea, etc.) the prospects for which are debatable; and the small non-oil producing economies (such as Kenya) with limited prospects. Such typologising obviously needs to be much more subtle and to include many more dimensions (including, for instance, the coherence and administrative capacity of the state, the labour/land ratio, etc.) but it is preferable to the retreat from theory that an insistence on the uniqueness of each case represents.[8]

A NOTE ON SURPLUS LABOUR IN SOCIALIST ECONOMIES

Ultimately the argument between Marxists and Neo-Marxists about dependency and marginalisation is not about principle but about the most sensible timing of attempts to change the mode of production. Both sets of theorists would agree that, when socialism finally arrives, the employment problem as it is faced by a capitalist economy, industrialised or peripheral, will no longer exist.

This can be illustrated by an example of the choice of techniques for a single project. A planner is faced with a choice between two investment proposals, both involving the same amount of investment and producing the same annual output of a given product (say, textiles). The only difference between the two proposals is that one involves employing 1,000 workers, the other only 600. In a capitalist market economy with an employment problem the planner (choosing, say, between two foreign investment proposals) would probably have to choose the more labour-intensive method. In a socialist planned economy, even one which still had surplus labour, such a choice would not make sense. If the method employing fewer workers were chosen, (a) at worst, the 400 not absorbed in the textile factory could play football (or otherwise enjoy themselves) and subsist on transfers of income from the 600 employees; or (b) the work could be split up between all 1,000 and everyone could work shorter hours;

or (c) the excluded 400 could work on other socially beneficial projects of the kind discussed in the section on Nurkse's 'hidden saving potential' analysis in the previous chapter (page 180).

If the social organisation exists to pursue any of these three options, the economy faces not an employment problem but a productivity problem. The objective must be to raise productivity and sustain it at levels which will comfortably support all 1,000 and their dependents, however many or few are employed in the factory. In capitalist economies, where the social organisation to pursue options (b) and (c) does not exist and where even option (a) may be problematic, policymakers are forced to take an upside-down view and to try to organise production and technology to absorb as many people as possible rather than to economise on labour.

If, for any reason, employment is a concern in a planned economy (if surplus labour exists and there are problems in organising income transfers, work-sharing or labour accumulation) it does not necessarily make sense for a planner to choose a more labour-intensive production method for a process or plant. This is partly because of the indirect effects of an investment, which by breaking bottlenecks as efficiently as possible may generate employment in other processes and plants. It is partly because of the implications of bringing *time* into the analysis. A more capital-intensive technique, even within a single plant or process, may eventually (via reinvestment of surplus) generate a higher level of employment than a more labour-intensive technique. In the classic Galenson/Leibenstein (1955) formulation:

$$E_{t+1}=E_1\ (1+\frac{p-ew}{c})^t$$

where E is employment,
t is time period in years,
p is value added per machine,
e is number of workers per machine,
w is real wage rate, and
c is cost per machine.

Galenson and Leibenstein show that, on the assumptions (perhaps more realistic in a planned than in a market economy) that all surplus is reinvested, the wage rate does not vary between techniques, and wage earners do not save and are not taxed, employment generated by a capital-intensive technique soon overtakes that generated by a labour-intensive technique, as illustrated in Figure 8.1.[9]

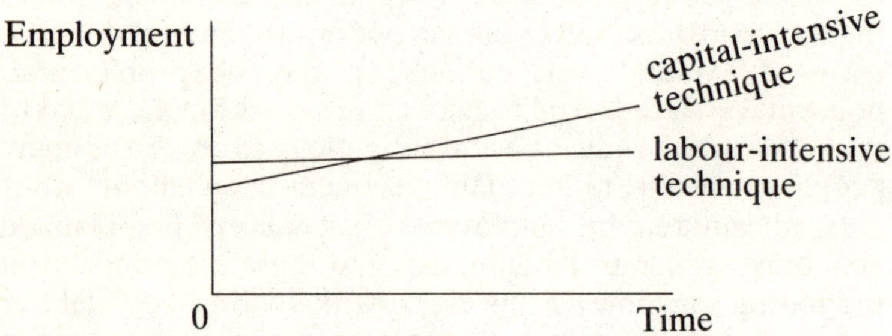

Figure 8.1: Choice of Techniques and Employment over Time

Ultimately, however, as Kornai (1980) convincingly argues, whatever policies are followed (with respect to overall investment rate, the composition of investment inputs, the composition of output and the choice of technology) a socialist system moves inexorably towards labour shortage.[10] He distinguishes between a demand-constrained and a resource-constrained labour market.

In a demand-constrained labour market (typical of an underdeveloped economy with a weak capitalist sector or of an advanced capitalist economy in a period of slow growth such as the 1980s) the participation rate remains low, so that there is always a large potential reserve of labour, only part of which appears in the unemployment statistics. Specific labour shortages are not eliminated (there are always some vacancies) but there is chronic unemployment in that the rate considerably exceeds the minimum rate caused by friction.

Even some of those 'used to employment' are unemployed. It is, thus, a buyer's labour market in which the employers are 'playing on their home ground' and in which job-searchers have to wait or accept 'forced substitution' in taking a job below their talent or training (*op.cit.*: 244).

In a resource-constrained labour market, on the other hand, the participation rate is high and near its tolerance limit. The potential reserve of labour (particularly independent small-scale producers and self-employed and women working in households) has been fully absorbed into the wage labour force. Unemployment is around the minimum caused by friction and chronic unemployment has been totally eliminated. Those 'used to employment' are in a situation of guaranteed employment and behave accordingly. Indicators of shortage in a pure resource-constrained labout market include: the extent to which the number actually employed falls short of the number initially demanded; and the frequency and extent of partial standstills in production, improvised modification of the composition of output and the substitution of other categories of labour for the category that is in short supply. This is a seller's market, with labour 'playing at home', in which the buyer has to bear the costs of adjustment, i.e. of searching, collecting information and waiting (*op.cit.*: 253).

The existence of shortage does not, however, imply the absence of underutilisation of labour—quite the contrary. The more frequent and intensive the shortage, the greater the *internal* labour slack—what Kornai calls 'unemployment on the job' (*op.cit.*: 255). This has several aspects. There is non-mobilisable slack, due to the non-availability of complementary inputs. There is slack due to the effect of labour shortage on workshop discipline, work quality and workers' diligence; assymmetry in the labour market forces managers to be indulgent and the circumstances conducive to a deterioriation in behaviour constantly recur. Finally, the hoarding of labour is encouraged by the labour shortage; thus shortage and unemployment on the job reinforce each other in a circular process. In another such process the intensity of the labour shortage is increased by the growth of the 'second economy', some of it illegal or semi-legal, the emergence and reproduction of which is encouraged by shortages. However, the growth of the second economy reduces the extent of the hidden labour slack (*op.cit.*: 256).

The ultimate absence of a demand constraint means that, even if a socialist economy starts from a situation of labour surplus, the potential reserve of labour must be absorbed sooner or later. And this is the result not of 'clever employment policies' but of the system. In the transition towards a pure resource-constrained labour market policy can influence the way the process develops, how long it lasts, its transitional and permanent features, the nature and distribution of the sacrifices made, etc. But, sooner or later, the economy will hit a resource constraint, managers will begin to regard labour supply as a serious problem and behavioural routines and regularities will change. Once economic growth has passed in this way from the 'extensive' to the 'intensive' period, reforms to encourage labour saving (such as the reorganisation of production, the tightening of labour discipline and changes in the form of wage controls) and the selection of labour-saving technologies cannot prevent shortage from chronically reproducing itself. 'Shortage cannot be eliminated by an increase in supply—as long as the innter regularities make demand almost insatiable' (*op.cit.*: 264).

To reverse the process requires not merely reform but a virtual change of system. This is illustrated by the experience of China since the death of Mao. The labour market of Maoist China appears to have exhibited at least some of the classic symptoms of Kornai's resource constrained case. 'Full employment' was ensured by labour accumulation schemes in collective agriculture (see Chapter Seven, page 182), the encouragement of collective enterprises organised by urban neighbourhoods, the expansion of the 'down to the countryside' movement to send unemployed urban middle-school graduates to rural production teams and the use of moral/political incentives to raise labour productivity. In short, as White (1982: 614) comments, 'on the one hand, urban surplus labour was being unloaded into the countryside, thus relocating the employment problem rather than solving it; on the other hand, there was widespread overmanning and "informal" unemployment in the cities' (in Kornai's terminology 'unemployment on the job' and the 'second economy').

The response of post-Mao reformers to this situation has been to press for 'destatification' of the process of labour allocation and the decentralisation of power to the enterprise. As White points out, to give enterprise managers the power of hiring and firing workers would raise the prospect of labour becoming a commodity. 'Regardless of labels, such as "state ownership" or "the hegemony of the working class", such a system would go some way in real terms towards creating a labour market and thus towards reproducing capitalist relations of procudtion' (*op.cit.*: 628). There have even been proposals for labour bureaux to provide a minimum standard of living for workers who have been dismissed, which, as he says, 'sound uncomfortably like a socialist form of the "dole".' Real democratisation of enterprises might be a way out of this dilemma (although it might merely increase the power of state sector employees to protect their own jobs and emoluments) but progress along this road has been limited and is likely to remain so.

Thus, ironically, governments of both socialist and capitalist countries are being driven, for somewhat similar underlying reasons, to search for labour market flexibility, which would increase the insecurity and vulnerability of workers. The possible dangers of this pursuit, in a labour market that is increasingly internationalised, will be explored in the next and final chapter.

NOTES

1. There is some dispute about the origins of the school. In the popularised version:

> 'two principal currents are generally cited: ECLA (the UN Economic Commission for Latin America) and the Marxian and neo-Marxian North Americans (Baran, Sweezy and Frank). It is added, at times, that the "dependentistas" . . . present different ideological standings, according to their proximity to ECLA (and to the "petty-bourgeois

nationalism" which is supposed to have derived from the ECLA studies) or to their more authentic opposition to capitalism, and hence their proximity to the thought of the Marxian economists referred to above' (Cardoso 1977: 2).

Cardoso justifiably objects to this version, which gives inadequate weight to the longstanding tradition of Marxian thought in Latin America, to internal political debates within Latin-American countries—and particularly within their Communist parties—on the role to be played by the national bourgeoisie, and to the influence of the Cuban revolution.

2. The question was never perhaps directly addressed at this level of generality by the *dependentistas*. Much of their work was geographically localised and historically circumscribed, but this is the general question implicit in that work.
3. Le Brun and Gerry (1975, p. 24) make a similar point, based on the experience of an African economy: 'Most urban Senegalese petty producers are confronted with a developed capitalist mode of production under which relative surplus value prevails, whereas European petty producers faced an emergent capitalist mode of production, wherein absolute surplus value was the rule. This distinction is crucial: in the case of early capitalisms the role or principal means of increasing the rate of surplus value was the lengthening of the working day. The limits of this were mainly those of working class organisation and resistance. But under advanced capitalism 'rational' labour processes and advanced technology enable increases in labour productivity to be made in other ways. The fact that petty production is faced with these advanced methods and technologies operating in the same exchange economy effectively blocks the transition of petty commodity production to capitalist commodity production, thus restricting and transforming the forms of social differentiation within an underdeveloped country.'
4. Cf. also Sunkel's (1973) concept of national disintegration which has rather wider implications: 'The process of modernisation incorporates into the new structures the individuals and groups that are apt to fit into the kind of rationality that prevails there; on the other hand, it expels the individuals and groups that have no place in the new productive structure or who lack the capacity to become adapted to it' (p. 169).
5. As opposed to those sociologists (not discussed here) who define marginals in terms of social mobility, social integration and socio-psychological characteristics (see Johnson 1979 for a discussion of this school).
6. Cf. our discussion on pages 2–5 above.
7. *See* Godfrey (1983) for a discussion of these issues in relation to Kenya.
8. Criticism of this aspect of Cardoso's approach is not intended to deny the richness of his analysis of specific societies in terms of class struggle and of the history of economic/political structures of domination (see particularly Cardoso and Faletto 1979).

9. This is the diagram that Weeks modifies to show the effect of a labour-saving bias in innovation over time (*see* Figure 6.2).
10. *See* Adam (1982) for a review of the experience of the USSR, Poland, Czechoslovakia and Hungary which is consistent with Kornai's analysis.

9 Conclusions: New Directions for Theory in a Changing World

At the end of Chapter One at least two inadequacies of theory, in the face of the new scale and structure of unemployment and under-utilisation of labour in industrialised and developing economies, were identified. Such theorising, it was suggested, is still kept largely in two separate compartments—short-run for mature capitalist economies, long-run for underdeveloped economies, and it is still usually conducted at a national rather than global level. The intervening chapters have tended to reinforce this view. In this final chapter we try to detect signs of change in theorising in either of these respects and, tentatively, to identify useful new theoretical directions in a changing world.

CONVERGENCE IN THEORISING?

Convergence in theorising about unemployment in industrialised and developing economies has so far largely taken the form of the export of static neoclassical theory from North to South. The consequences and limitations of the transfer of this (arguably inappropriate) technology were reviewed in Chapter Four. Interestingly, adapted forms of such theory are now being reexported to industrialised economies. For instance, Hall, whose two-sector model of unemployment in an industrialised economy (Hall 1975) is mentioned in Chapter Three (page 76), explicitly acknowledges his debt to the Harris–Todaro model of rural–urban migration in a developing economy (Chapter Four, page 103).

There are not many other examples of convergence, most of them achieved unintentionally. For instance, the literature on the informal sector in developing economies (Chapter Six, page 139) has proceeded without explicit reference to that on segmentation of labour markets in industrialised economies

(Chapter Three, page 62). And the more recent work on the informal or black economy in post-industrial society does not seem to relate much to that on the informal sector in the third world. Yet there are obvious parallels. For instance, Gershuny (Gershuny 1978; Gershuny and Miles 1983) identifies three categories of activity in the informal economy: the household, the communal and the underground.

The informal economy is defined as that outside the flows (of labour, goods and services, money wages and money payments between households and firms) captured by official surveys and enumerations. The household category of informal activity comprises flows within the household which are not based on any specific and explicit exchange of definite quantities of commodities but which represent the use of purchased goods as capital, in combination with household labour, in the production of services for final consumption. The communal category consists of the activities of voluntary or religious organisations, baby-sitting circles, transport cooperatives, housing-improvement cooperatives, etc., in which real money is not used as an indicator of exchange of value for value but, if at all, as a form of recognition. The third category, the underground, hidden or black economy, exists in the interstices of the formal economy and consists of economic activities which are hidden from the state authorities because of their illegality (for instance, through tax evasion or theft).

The rising cost of purchased services relative to that of domestic capital goods, Gershuny argues, leads to the export of jobs from the formal economy into the household and communal sectors of the informal economy. An increasing proportion of total demand is devoted to the products of the formal manufacturing sector, where productivity is growing fast, and a declining proportion to those of the formal services sector, where productivity is growing more slowly. In the absence (because of market imperfections) or wage flexibility in the formal services sector, unemployment increases, mitigated to some extent by the expansion of low-wage work in the underground economy, by definition free of external restrictions.

Gershuny identifies three options for government policy towards the informal economy; to ignore it, suppress it or exploit it. Neither of the first two options is regarded as particularly desirable, leading either to extreme dualism in the labour market or to excessively bureaucratic provision of public services. The third (preferred) option would involve the encouragement of community-based services, the reduction of tax and other pressures on very small companies and of effective tax rates on low wage-earners, some form of protection for full-time workers in the informal economy and the promotion of simultaneous participation in both the formal and the informal economies.

All this, with its echoes of Hart's emphasis on the illegality of many of its activities (Hart 1973) and of the ILO's belief in the dynamic potential of the sector once government harassment is replaced by encouragement (ILO 1972), will appear familiar to students of the literature on the informal sector in developing countries. Unfortunately also familiar is the *a priori* optimism about the capacity of the sector to absorb large numbers of people at acceptable wage levels. If this optimism is unwarranted the process that Gershuny describes would generate increased unemployment rather than growth of the informal sector. Of course, government measures to ecourage the sector could be accompanied by cuts in unemployment benefit along the lines recommended by Minford (Chapter Three, page 77) but that would amount to a blurring of the distinction between employment and unemployment rather than a cure for unemployment. The two literatures, at present parallel but largely separate, undoubtedly have much to teach each other.

Another example of accidental convergence is the recommendation of import controls as a means of achieving a sustained expansion of domestic output and, ultimately, full employment in an industrialised economy, such as Britain, suffering from a growing lack of competitiveness. The arguments for such controls (for example, in Ward 1981) are similar in many ways to those advanced for protection of import-substituting industry in a primary-producing economy (see Chapter Five, page 116). In Britain's case they are regarded by the Cambridge Economic Policy Group as 'the only feasible means of removing the balance of payments constraint on demand expansion and of avoiding prolonged stagnation with mounting unemployment'. Ward documents the steady deterioration in the trade performance of British manufacturing industry since the last quarter of the nineteenth century and the accelerated process of industrial decline from the 1970s onwards, when the divergent growth paths of exports and imports necessitated the restriction of output below its full employment level. In this context he argues that the case for an import control strategy is based not on conventional international trade theory, which would be concerned with shifting resources towards products in which Britain had a comparative advantage, but on dynamic analysis of the process of arresting industrial decline and generating recovery.

The parallel with development economics is again obvious, although in this case the argument has a more Keynesian flavour. A sustained expansion of aggregate demand is needed in order to generate the growth in output necessary to bring down unemployment. For this purpose a 'major and continuing fiscal stimulus' will have to be combined with import controls to secure a substantial rise in net exports. Across-the-board controls are preferred to selective controls since the main objective is not to 'protect existing jobs in particular industries, a policy which is unlikely to achieve lasting success, but to ensure, through expansion, that new jobs are created to replace those lost as the economy evolves and to provide employment for new members of the labour force as well as those currently unemployed' (*op. cit.*: 103).

The development economists' arguments in favour of protected import-substituting industrialisation, in contrast, have usually implied selective controls intended to raise the incentive to invest in certain sectors but not in others. However, the emphasis on dynamic rather than static efficiency is common to both sets of theorists. Ward regards efficiency in the allocation of resources between productive units at a particular point in time as 'by far the least important in quantitative terms'; the efficiency with which productive units use the resources allocated to them is 'somewhat more important'; and the rate at which efficiency improves over time is 'the most important aspect'. Import controls are intended to secure the high rate of output growth which is necessary to achieve dynamic gains in productivity arising from the introduction of new plant and the adoption of new methods of working (*op. cit.*: 105).

The circumstances of a deindustrialising mature capitalist economy and of a developing economy, with a large pre-capitalist sector, intent on industrialisation are obviously very different. Yet the two debates on import controls could usefully be brought together. The experience of protected import-substituting industrialisation in developing countries and the critiques of that experience, from both neoclassical economists (Chapter Four) and dependency theorists (Chapter Seven), could yield useful lessons for deindustrialising economies contemplating a similar path. On the whole countries which have successfully rewritten their comparative advantage have combined import controls with much more purposive state intervention than appears to be contemplated by Ward, while the dangers of fostering industries that are inefficient (in Ward's second sense), low-technology, multinational-dominated and primarily adept at bargaining with (and where necessary bribing) government are widely demonstrated. This is not an argument against import controls as such but avoidance of such dangers needs to be built into the design of any scheme.

A final example of convergence that is apparently unintentional (in the sense that neither author makes reference to the other) is the case for the indexation of mortgage contracts that is being made by economists at Massachusetts Institute of Technology (MIT), particularly Modigliani.

Modigliani (1976: 100) suggests that, where the traditional level-payment mortgage is the prevailing vehicle for financing residential housing and where financing through this instrument is provided by specialised savings or mortgage banks or building societies, a high rate of inflation will tend to curtail the demand for housing. This occurs because the high nominal rates of interest which result from the addition to the 'real' rate of interest of a premium roughly equal to the expected rate of inflation have the effect of increasing the level of the annual payment relative to the rate of earnings in the early years of the mortgage contract. Thus, at a 6 per cent rate of inflation and a real intrest rate of 3 per cent, the annual nominal payment on a $30,000 thirty-year mortgage has to be $2,895. By year 12 the real value of this payment (at year-1 prices) has been reduced by inflation to $1,525 and by the terminal year to $524. Since the income of the typical home buyer can be expected to rise at a rate at least equal to the price index this means that someone with an annual income of $10,000 will be devoting 29 per cent of it to mortgage payments in the initial year but that this proportion will fall steadily to 5 per cent in the terminal year. Indexation of mortgage contracts would reduce this 'front-end-loading' of interest payments and thus expand the market for mortgage financed housing to include those further down the income scale.

This, as will be obvious, was precisely the logic underlying the index-linked mortgage rates of the Currie-inspired *Corporaciones* in Colombia (discussed in Chapter Seven, page 174). However, in Modigliani's case, the wider framework of dynamic external economies and of the argument in terms of a leading-sector strategy is lacking. This may be one reason why, whereas Currie's strategy has been implemented, Modigliani's scheme has attracted little interest since it was first proposed to the White House in 1977, even though the extent of untapped demand for housing in industrialised economies is considerable (Merritt 1982: 185). Thus this is another example of the likely benefits to be gained from a more explicit convergence of the two literatures, perhaps more striking in this case in that the leading sector strategy seems to be more suited to an industrialised economy than to the developing economy in which is was implemented.

AN OPEN-ECONOMY LEWIS MODEL

As for the internationalisation of the labour market, a useful starting point for analysing its implications is provided by the relatively neglected 'open-economy' section of Lewis's paper on unlimited supplies of labour (Lewis 1954) discussed in

Chapter Five (page 125). The Lewis model, as we have seen, shows how the availabiity of an unlimited supply of labour in the subsistence sector of an economy gives rise to profits in the capitalist sector which consequently enjoys a continuous process of growth and reinvestment. In a closed economy this process comes to an end when capital accumulation catches up with the labour supply, the labour surplus is exhausted and wages begin to rise. However, as Lewis points out, if the closed-economy assumption is dropped capitalists can escape from the consequences of labour shortage either by encouraging immigration or by exporting their capital to other countries where abundant labour is still available at a constant real wage.

In analysing the consequences of immigration, Lewis distinguishes between 'relatively small' and 'mass' immigration. 'If 100,000 Puerto Ricans emigrate to the United States every year, the effect on US wages is negligible. US wages are not pulled down to the Puerto Rican level; it is Puerto Rican wages which are then pulled up to the US level.' On the other hand, 'if there were free immigration from India and China to the USA, the wage level of the USA would certainly be pulled down towards the Indian and Chinese levels' (*op. cit.*: 436). This is why trade unions in high-wage economies press for restrictions on immigration except of people in special categories. Such restrictions keep wages higher than they otherwise would be and profits, capital resources and total output smaller than they otherwise would be.

The effects of the export of capital to labour-surplus economies, as Lewis analyses them, depend on what type of competition there is between the capital-exporting and the capital-importing countries. If there is neither competition nor trade between high-wage country A and low-wage country B, the effect of the export of capital from A to B is merely that wages in A cease to rise, as they would have if the exported capital had instead been invested at home. And this pause in the upward movement of wages in A will continue until capital accumulation in B has wiped out B's labour surplus.

If the countries do not compete but do trade with each

other, the outcome depends on what types of goods they produce. If each country only produces one good—and that a different good from the other—export of capital from the high-wage country A to the low-wage country B *may* benefit workers in A through its effect on the international terms of trade. As Lewis puts it, 'capital export may benefit the workers [in A] on balance if it is applied to increasing the supply of thjings they import' (*op. cit.*: 441). The result becomes determinate if we add the assumption that both countries also produce food but do not trade in it. Investment by A's capitalists in B's commercial export sector adds to B's employment and tax revenue but does not raise wages in that sector; 'the whole benefit of increasing productivity in the commercial sector goes to the foreign consumer'. This is the 'unequal-exchange' effect already discussed in Chapter Five (pages 117-18).

When the two countries produce (in addition to food) the *same* things and trade with each other, investment by A's capitalists in B's export industry lowers the price of the exports, to the benefit of *consumers* in A but to the detriment of *workers* in that industry in A whose jobs are threatened. Finally, if the two countries produce the same goods and compete in third markets, the export of capital to increase productivity in the exporting sector of the capital-importing country strikes a double blow at workers in the capital-exporting country. They are hit, 'first by the reduced capital accumulation at home, and then again by the fall in their rivals' prices' (*op. cit.*: 447).

INTERNATIONALISATION OF THE RESERVE ARMY

Lewis's analysis can be used to throw light on the changes in the world economy since he wrote his classic paper in the early 1950s. At that time industry producing for the world market was located only in the high-wage, labour-shortage economies of the North. Production in the South for the world market consisted only of primary products (inputs for Northern industry and wage-goods for Northern workers). In addition, the capitalist sector included a certain amount of import-substituting industry, producing for a protected domestic market. This broadly corresponds to Lewis's two-countries, three-goods case, just discussed[1]. At that time, also, migration of labour from South to North was negligible. Thus the huge reserve of surplus labour in the South was only indirectly relevant to Northern capitalists, through its effect on input and wage-good prices.

The two-sector diagram of the unlimited-labour-supplies model (Figure 5.5, page 130) can be adapted and 'globalised' to illustrate the situation, as in Figure 9.1. The curves $N_N Q_N$ and $N_S Q_S$ show the demand for labour in the capitalist sectors of the North and South respectively. The curves $M_N P_N$ and $M_S P_S$ show the marginal productivity of workers in the subsistence sectors of the North and South respectively. (The position of the origin in the subsistence-sector diagrams should be noted.) In the North there is no surplus labour in the subsistence sector; at the wage OW_N, OE workers are employed in the capitalist sector (defined in the usual Lewis-model way), leaving OF workers in the subsistence sector. If productivity rises in the capitalist sector, given the supply curve of labour $S_N L_N$, wages will rise also. In the South, on the other hand, there is $P_S H$ surplus labour in the subsistence sector and until that surplus is absorbed unlimited labour is available to the capitalist sector at the wage OW_S. Thus, if productivity were to rise in the capitalist primary production sector, signified by an outward shift in $N_S Q_S$ (as a result say, of Northern investment), this would not affect wages in that sector, which would remain at OW_S. However, the resulting fall in prices of the primary products would benefit workers and capitalists in the Northern capitalist sector, since the exchange value of a given unit of the sector's output would increase.

Since Lewis wrote, however, the internationalisation of the labour market has increased considerably, along the lines described in Chapter One. Industrial production for the world market has come to be located in the low-wage economies of the South, and Northern capitalists have made use of immigrant workers from the South, both on a modest but significant scale. This broadly corresponds, as far as export of capital is concerned, to Lewis's final case, where

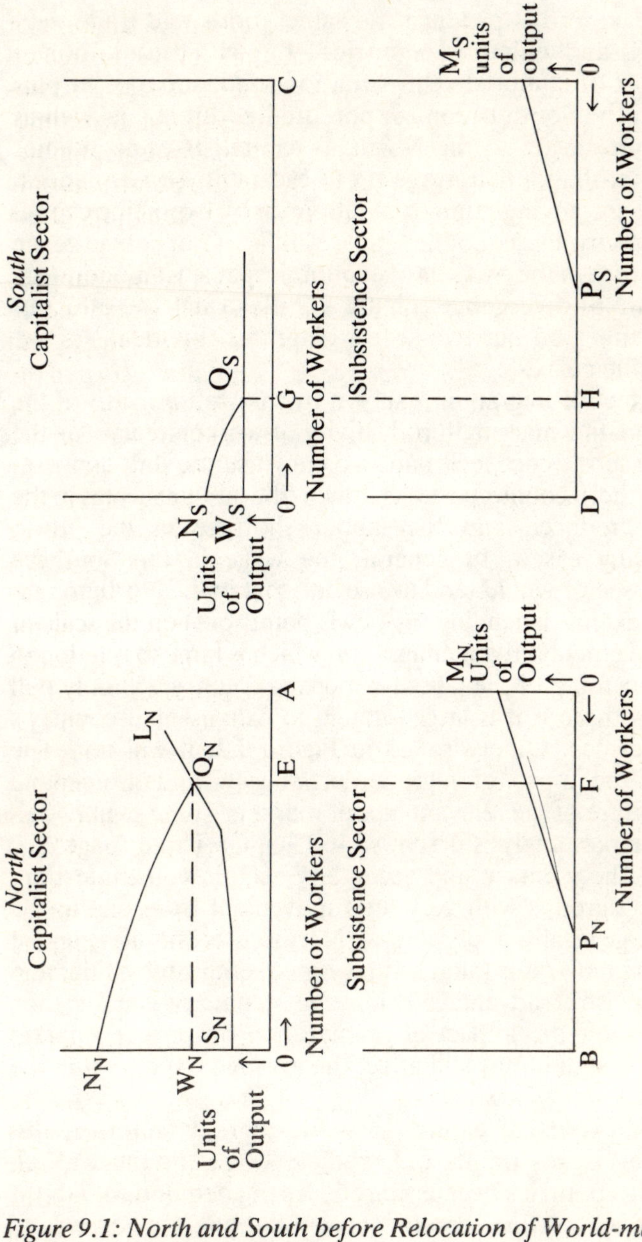

Figure 9.1: North and South before Relocation of World-market Industry and without Migration

countries A and B produce the same goods and trade with each other and with third countries—but with the addition of the import of labour. In this situation the reserve of surplus labour in the South becomes, potentially, directly as well as indirectly relevant to the North. If capitalists in economies running into labour shortage try to escape its consequences, either by employing immigrant labour or by exporting capital to labour-surplus economies, the result is, if not convergence of wage rates in the two sets of economies, at least moderation of the rate of divergence. Figure 9.2 illustrates the effect of these changes on our two-sector diagrams (by means of the broken-line curves).

The effect of migration is shown by the shift *inwards* of the origin and the marginal-productivity-of-workers curve in the Southern subsistence sector and a commensurate shift *outwards* in its Northern counterpart. As drawn, the labour surplus in the South is reduced and the labour shortage in the North substantially eased. In general, the wage in the Southern capitalist sector would tend to rise and that in the North to fall, with the extent depending (as Lewis points out) on the scale of these movements. Even emigration which is large in relation to the labour force of the labour-exporting country will only pull up wages there if it is large enough to exhaust that country's labour surplus. Otherwise, as in Figure 9.2, it will not. The extent of the impact of migration on wages would also depend on the nature of the relevant labour markets. If the segmented-labour-market analysis described in Chapter Three (page 62), whereby the primary and secondary sectors constitute non-competing groups with very little movement from one to the other, is generally applicable to Northern economies; and if unskilled immigrants (along with women, ethnic minorities and the otherwise disadvantaged) join the secondary market; then this will limit the impact of immigration on primary-market wages although it may still affect the average wage level in the capitalist sector as a whole.

As for export of capital to world-market factories, this would, as Lewis points out, reduce wages in the capital-exporting countries because it reduces the demand for labour directly by cutting capital accumulation at home and indirectly by raising productivity and lowering prices in

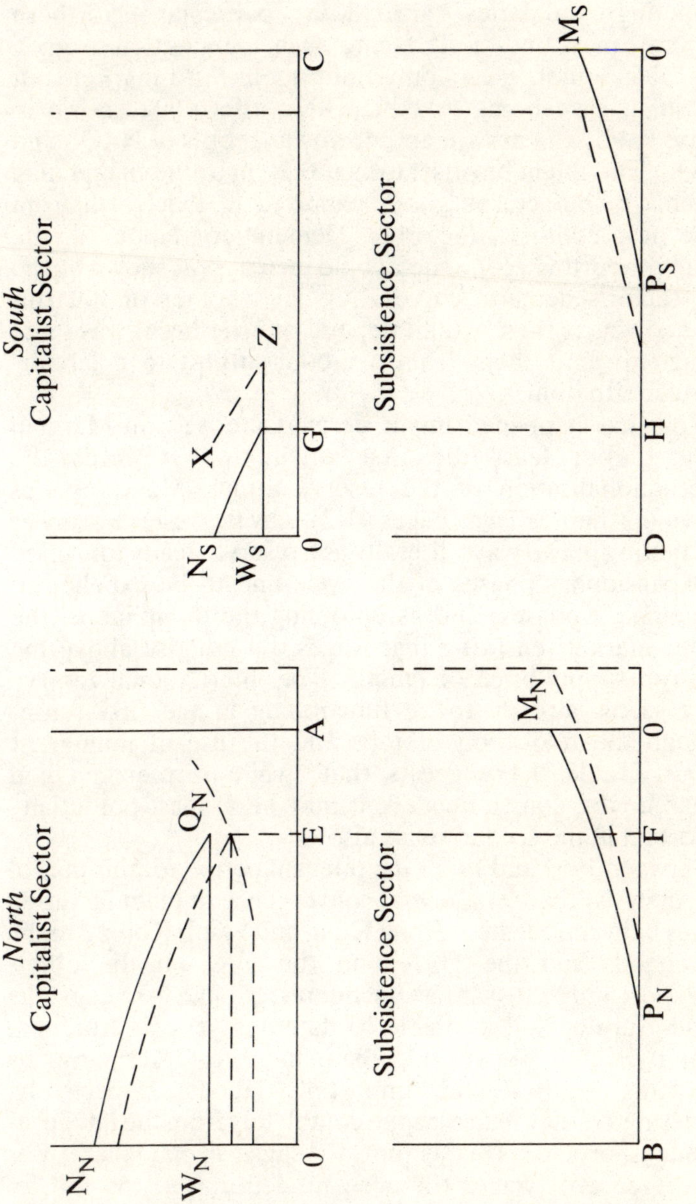

Figure 9.2: North and South after Relocation of World-market Industry and with Migration

competing industries abroad—a particular Northern economy may find itself facing such competition from a particular Southern economy not only in third markets but also in its own home market. These effects are shown in Figure 9.2 by the inward and downward shifts of N_NQ_N and W_NQ_N. This might be offset to some extent by the cheapening of some manufactured goods exported to the North from these new Southern factories. Demand for labour in the capital-importing economies would increase (as shown by the new sector's demand curve ZX) but whether or not this affected wages there would depend on whether it was large enough to shift them from a labour-surplus to a labour-shortage situation.

What has happened might be characterised, in Marxian terms, as at least the first small steps towards the 'internationalisation of the reserve army'. Marx, as was shown in Chapter Two (pages 41-2), saw the reserve army as functioning in two ways: literally as a reserve, ready for action in expansionary phases of the cycle and to be expelled in recessionary phases; and as enforcing the discipline of the labour market, ensuring that wages did not rise above the long-run supply-price of labour. The international reserve army seems already to be functioning in the first sense, through the relocation of jobs and the use of immigrant labour. Table 9.1 suggests that, while further detailed research is of course needed, it may be at least potentially important in the second sense also.

Between 1964 and 1978 (the relevant period for this part of our analysis) there was actual convergence in manufacturing wages between Mexico, Hong Kong and South Korea, on the one hand, and the USA and the UK, on the other. Singapore's growth was fast but not fast enough to exhaust the labour surplus still available to its employers (untroubled, also, by union pressure). Japan and West Germany, by exporting capital and importing labour respectively, moderated rather than escaped completely from the impact of labour shortage. This is not to suggest that there was convergence of wages (or even moderation in the rate of divergence) between industrialised and developing countries as a whole. Its occurrence in some instances does, however,

Table 9.1 Trends in Real Manufacturing Wages in Selected Industrialised and Newly Industrialising Countries, 1964–1982

	Index (1964=100)			*Annual average rates of change*		
	1972	*1978*	*1982*	*1964–72*	*1972–78*	*1978–82*
Mexico[a]	116.8	151.2	147.0	+2.0	+4.4	−0.7
Hong Kong[b]	167.4	183.2	192.4	+6.7	+1.5	+1.2
South Korea[c]	254.2	453.1	497.5	+12.4	+10.1	+2.4
Singapore[a]	94.1	100.3	126.2	−0.8	+1.1	+5.9
USA[a]	110.3	114.6	106.6	+1.2	+0.6	−1.8
Japan[c]	183.5	220.7	230.1	+7.9	+3.1	+1.0
West Germany[a]	149.7	180.0	183.4	+5.2	+3.1	+0.5
UK[d]	134.3	138.6	139.9	+3.8	+0.5	+0.2

[a]Hourly earnings. [b]Daily rate. [c]Monthly earnings. [d]Hourly earnings (males only).
Source: ILO, *International Yearbook of Labour Statistics.*

suggest that this approach to the analysis of the international labour market may be worth taking further.

OTHER OPTIONS FOR CAPITAL

While classical[1] Marxist analysis, in terms of unlimited labour supply and reserve army, can thus be seen to be potentially fruitful at a global as well as national level, mechanical versions, which ascribe unique functionality to the international reserve army have to be avoided. For instance, Paine reports the view of Nikolinakos (1973) that, for Western Europe, 'foreign workers constitute the modern reserve army of labour whose presence is essential for sustained accumulation: their availability has rescued the capitalist system from crisis. Indeed, the import of the last foreign workers would "mark the gravestone of capitalism" ' (Paine 1974:21). Paine justifiably criticises this analysis as crude. Use of the international reserve army was only one of a number of options open to Northern capitalists in the sixties and seventies, in the face of several new developments which were workinng to offset the normal centralising tendencies of capitalist development (Murray 1972).

These developments included the following. Wages had been rising faster in the North than in the South during the

1950s and early 1960s, widening the already large wage differential. Technical change was allowing the decomposition of productive processes, so that more or less unskilled workers working with modern equipment could achieve similar levels of productivity in some processes regardless of location. Labour in the North (and particularly in the USA and Britain) was becoming increasingly difficult to control—less flexible; less willing to be fitted into shift-working, staggered rota, fast assembly line and other such arrangements; less predictable; more insistent on participation in decisions and more difficult to lay off. Transport and communication costs were falling. And Southern governments were going out of their way to attract foreign capital, particularly into export manufacturing, with export processing zones and other concessions (Bienefeld, Godfrey and Schmitz 1977).

In this situation at least three options, in addition to those of importing labour or exporting jobs, were open to Northern capital in labour-intensive industries such as textiles, clothing, electronics, sports goods, toys, furniture and plastics. The first was to recruit national female labour. Table 9.2 shows the varying extent to which this option was taken up in a number of industrialised economies. The number of women in civilian employment in all OECD countries rose from around 34 per cent of the total in 1960 to 36 per cent in 1973 to almost 39 per cent in 1981. Interestingly, employers in countries which increased their use of immigrant workers particularly quickly during this period, such as France and West Germany, made less use of this option, as did those in countries such as Italy and Ireland which still had sizeable national, male reserve armies. The fall in the relative importance of women in Japanese civilian employment may reflect Japan's use of the capital-export option but also increases in education enrolment rates and the rapid decline in importance of agricultural activities.

A reserve-army approach is useful in analysing this option also. For instance, Humphries argues that women in this period represented a *latent* labour reserve, with a role analogous to that of precapitalist agriculture in an earlier era (see Chapter Two, page 42, for Marx's definition of this

Table .9.2 Women as a Percentage of All Civilian Employees, Selected Industrialised Economies, 1960, 1973 and 1981

	1960	*1973*	*1981*
Belgium	30.7	34.0	35.9[a]
Denmark	31.8	41.1	43.6
France	35.2[b]	36.0	38.0[a]
W. Germany	37.8	37.2	38.7
Ireland	26.6[c]	26.6[d]	28.5[a]
Italy	30.1	28.7	32.3
Japan	40.7	38.5	38.7
UK	34.4	37.6	40.3
USA	33.3	38.5	42.8

[a]1980 [b]1968 [c]1961 [d]1971
Source: ILO, *World Labour Report 1*, 1984.

category):

> Housewives like precapitalist agricultural workers initially constituted a pool of unexploited labour hidden in the sense of not representing a drain on the capitalist surplus, but able to respond to the demands of the economy. This is obviously what socialist feminists have in mind when they identify women with the 'reserve army'. Again capital could work on both the demand for and the supply of this labour. Capital's infiltration of household production has, at least partially displaced household workers making them available to industrial production (Humphries 1984: 13).

However, here too a mechanically functionalist use of reserve-army analysis has to be avoided. By the 1980s, Humphries argues, the identification of women workers with a latent reserve army had become anachronistic. Housewives cannot be permanently maintained as a temporary supplement, since unlike traditional agriculture the household cannot reabsorb workers without a collapse of productivity. Thus the increase in women's employment shown in Table 9.2 represents in part, especially in recent years, a secular process of assimilation of women into the labour force and of substitution of female for male labour. And, increasingly women in industrialised economies are joining men in the ranks of the *floating* reserve army, i.e. in (measured and unmeasured) open unemployment (see Chapter Two, pages 42 and 50).

The second additional option open to Northern capital in

this period was to introduce technical changes aimed at increasing both the productivity and flexibility of labour. The latter involved reducing skill specificity and increasing the range of output levels achievable with a given labour force.

The third and final option was that of trying to integrate workers more efficiently into production, for instance through programmes of job enlargement and enrichment, sometimes moving completely away from flowline production to the creation of autonomous groups of production workers, and the establishment of worker councils and employee representation on boards of directors. In this way workers' resistance to the intensification of the labour process could be reduced by associating them with the supervisory function. However, this option is not an easy one. In some countries, particularly Britain and Italy, workers have often opposed such a blurring of the line between capital and labour. Also, many managements are still wary of a development with such unclear long-term political consequences. Thus, even in the era of labour shortage in the North, resort to the international reserve army was only one of the options available to capital. Nevertheless its latent availability was an important new feature of the international economy.

EMERGING TRENDS: SLOW GROWTH AND LABOUR-SAVING TECHNOLOGICAL CHANGE?

As Chapter One made clear, the international economic climate has drastically deteriorated since the early 1970s. Rates of ecoomic growth in market economies, particularly industrialised economies, have been much lower than they were in the 1960s. Rates of inflation have increased and, most important for our topic, unemployment in the industrialised economies has risen to levels and rates unheard of since the 1930s (see Table 1.1, page 2). Thus, since 1973 and particularly since 1979, Northern capital has no longer been faced with a shortage of labour in its national markets. At the same time large increases in the price of oil unbalanced world trade and payments and generated excess demand for labour in oil-producing economies. This is the context in which growth rates in developing countries' GDP and manufactured exports began to falter and in which, while migrant workers in Western Europe have been returning home, this was more than compensated for until recently by the increase in migration to the Arab region.

In spite of the gloomy trends of the past decade, some economists are indomitably cheerful about the growth prospects of the world economy. Balassa, for instance, in a recent projection of demand for manufactured goods from developing countries (Balassa 1980), has assumed an annual average growth rate in GDP in the industrial countries during the 1980s considerably higher than the rate achieved in the 1970s. This allows him to hope that the Far Eastern countries that have a relatively high educational level may increasingly take the place of Japan in exporting skill-intensive products while Latin-American countries may expand the exports of relatively capital-intensive products. countries at lower stages of industrial development, in turn, may take the place of the newly-industrialising countries in exporting products that chiefly require unskilled labour (Balassa 1980: 37).

This is similar in spirit to the 'high-case' projection in the World Bank's 1984 *World Development Report*, of an annual average growth rate in GDP for industrialised economies in 1985–95 of 4.3 per cent, almost as high as that achieved in 1960–73, and a steady fall in unemployment. This would imply a return to near 1960s growth rates for developing countries also, with particularly exciting opportunities for manufactured exports. The snag is that achievement of the high-case targets depends on improvements in policy in industrialised countries; they need to overcome 'the rigidities and inflationary fears that slowed them down in the past ten years' (*op. cit.*: 48). In particular, they need to bring budget deficits under control, turn away from protectionist policies and take concerted international initiatives to liberalise trade and enlarge flows of finance to developing economies. In the absence of such improvements the alternative 'low-case' scenario offers a growth rate of only 2.5 per cent in the industrialised economies, virtually the same as between 1973 and 1979, and continued high unemployment.

Such a combination of slow growth and high

unemployment in the North might be expected to reduce the pressures behind the global search for cheap labour. This is so whether the primary motive of capital is minimisation of unit labour cost (Bienefeld 1983) or avoidance of difficulties in controlling labour (Murray 1980), since Northern wages might be expected to grow more slowly and labour to become more docile. As Table 9.1 shows, rates of increase in manufacturing wages in the main industrial economies were already much lower in 1978–82 than in 1972–78, and although rates of increase were also lower in many NICs (apart notably from Singapore which has reached the end of its surplus-labour phase) the process of convergence was continuing. Nevertheless, weaker capitals would still be under strong pressure to find some way of increasing their rate of profit and the continued availability of a huge latent reserve army in the South would still represent a tempting option for them.

An additional complicating factor is technological change. Radical new developments in microelectronic technology are expected by many researchers to erode the comparative advantage of surplus labour economies in labour-intensive manufacturing and to increase the technological gap between North and South (Hoffman and Rush, 1980; Kaplinsky 1982). Textiles, garments and electronic goods are among industries in which microprocessor-based automation is thought to be saving labour. There is not complete agreement that this will reverse the trend towards relocation; Froebel (1980), for instance, points out that automation economises on skills, which may continue to favour location in low-wage economies. Some of the front-running Newly Industrialising Countries (NICs) will certainly be in a position to make use of the new technologies. However, the conclusion of a recent, careful review of the literature on microelectronics-related innovation is that:

> ultimately, because of the unevenness of diffusion of these best-practice techniques, and also because of variation in the political structures which surround their introduction, there is likely to be a reordering of global trade patterns. This will lead to employment being more likely to take place near final markets (Kaplinsky 1985: 52).

There is also the question of whether these new technologies are likely to displace labour in industrialised economies. There is a tendency in the literature towards gloomy macro-generalisation based on sector, firm-, plant- and even process-level studies, which ignores the fact that 'unemployment is a general equilibrium phenomenon' (Nickell 1982: 10). There is much to be said for the view of Freeman, Clark and Soete (1982) that, 'even though gains in labour productivity, or the introduction of new products and services may lead to temporary job losses, these can be compensated, on the one hand by the growth of demand, which may often outstrip the growth of labour productivity, with sufficiently high price and income elasticities, and on the other hand by the emergence of entirely new opportunities for employment. A dynamic and efficient economy will always simultaneously experience a process of job loss compensated to some degree by growth of new employment'. However, as they recognise, this compensation mechanism will not be instant, simple, painless and automatic. Uneven diffusion across countries, sectors and labour market segments will bring variations in its specific impact. Having weighed the evidence and accepting the Freeman/Soete point about compensation mechanisms, Kaplinsky still believes that 'far-reaching changes in the pattern of industrial organisation' will cause 'significant labour displacement . . . in the major industrial economies especially in Europe and North America' (*op. cit.*: 52).

If Kaplinsky is right, this, along with the slow growth assumed in the 'low-case' scenario, would be likely to reinforce pressures for increased protection against imports and control of immigration in the North. If governments of industrialised countries acceded to such pressures, the World Bank has calculated that it would reduce the 'low-case' growth rate in developing countries from 4.7 to 4.3 per cent in 1985–95, with particularly unhappy consequences for low-income Africa where GDP per head would fall by 7 per cent over the ten-year period.

Even some of those who are sceptical about the gloomier predictions of changes in comparative advantage and the trend towards protectionism suggest that the quantitative impact of further relocation of production is likely to be limited. For instance, Froebel questions the interpretation of automation as the inevitable 'reply of the industrial countries' to relocation and suggests that there is 'no discernible political force which is both willing and able to impose a drastic reduction in the international freedom of movement of commodities and capital' (*op. cit.*: 38). Nevertheless he suggests that, although relocation will continue to grow in importance, 'this process simply does not possess the potential to reduce unemployment in the developing countries in whole or in part' (*op. cit.*: 41).

In addition to the general factors affecting the search for cheap labour there are some special factors affecting international migration. In Europe the onset of the recession, reducing the demand for immigrant labour, has coincided with the 'maturing' of the immigrant population, making it more difficult for employers to treat indigenous and immigrant labour as 'non-competing groups' and more necessary for governments to increase provision of social infrastructure. The number of young Europeans entering the labour force has also been abnormally large. As unemployment has risen, political tensions, nurtured by right-wing organisations, have grown. During the 1970s several European governments followed a policy of 'stabilisation', restricting new immigration, offering financial grants to those who wished to leave permanently and trying to integrate those who remained. Moreover, during the 1980s, Portugal and Spain, both of them labour-surplus economies (with over 900,000 migrant workers in the EEC in 1980) are lkely to join Greece as full members of the Community (Wedell, 1979). All these factors suggest that while intra-EEC movement of labour may continue on a limited scale, the age of massive immigration into Western Europe is over.

In the capital-surplus oil exporting countries expectations about growth rates in output and demand for labour have been hit by the fall in oil prices during 1983 and 1984. Even before this happened several new influences on their demand for immigrant labour were discernible (World Bank 1979). The construction phase of their development has subsided and the demand for skilled workers and technicians is showing signs of growing in importance relative to that for unskilled and semi-skilled workers. At the same time, the number of unskilled and semi-skilled nationals of oil-producing countries entering the labour market is tending to increase. Thus the demand for unskilled and semi-skilled immigrants is likely to be much less buoyant than in the past and some labour-surplus economies can expect a net return flow of such migrant workers.

On the 'low-case' assumption of continued recession in the North and on a pessimistic view of the likely impact of technological change, then, the emerging international labour market may look something like Figure 9.3. Growth in the Northern capitalist sector would be slow and, in spite of some re-relocation of processes from the South, relatively jobless (signified by the shift and change in slope of N_NQ_N). In the South, world demand for primary products would fall (signified by the inward shift of N_SQ_S and while a few front-running NICs might 'vacate space' by moving higher up the technological scale this would result in only limited opportunities for labour-surplus economies (how limited depending on the impact of labour-saving technical change on location of production). At the same time there would be a net return flow of migrants from North to South (signified by the shifts in the axes and the M_NP_N and M_SP_S curves). As a consequence the size of the labour surplus in the South would increase (from $P_{S1}H_1$ to $P_{S2}H_2$ in terms of Figure 9.3), while a high rate of unemployment persisted in the North. To an extent, having developed a sizeable reserve army of its own, Northern capital would have less need of an international reserve army. Neo-Marxists might now want to characterise it as an 'international marginal mass' (see Chapter Eight, page 190). It would probably be more accurate to describe it as a 'latent' reserve army in relation to Northern capital, and gaining importance in this role from the assimilation of women into the labour forces of the industrialised economies (discussed on page 222).

One consequence of the increase in the size of the Northern reserve army which further tips the balance in favour of capital is the increasing segmentation of labour markets *within* firms. In a process which has only been documented in

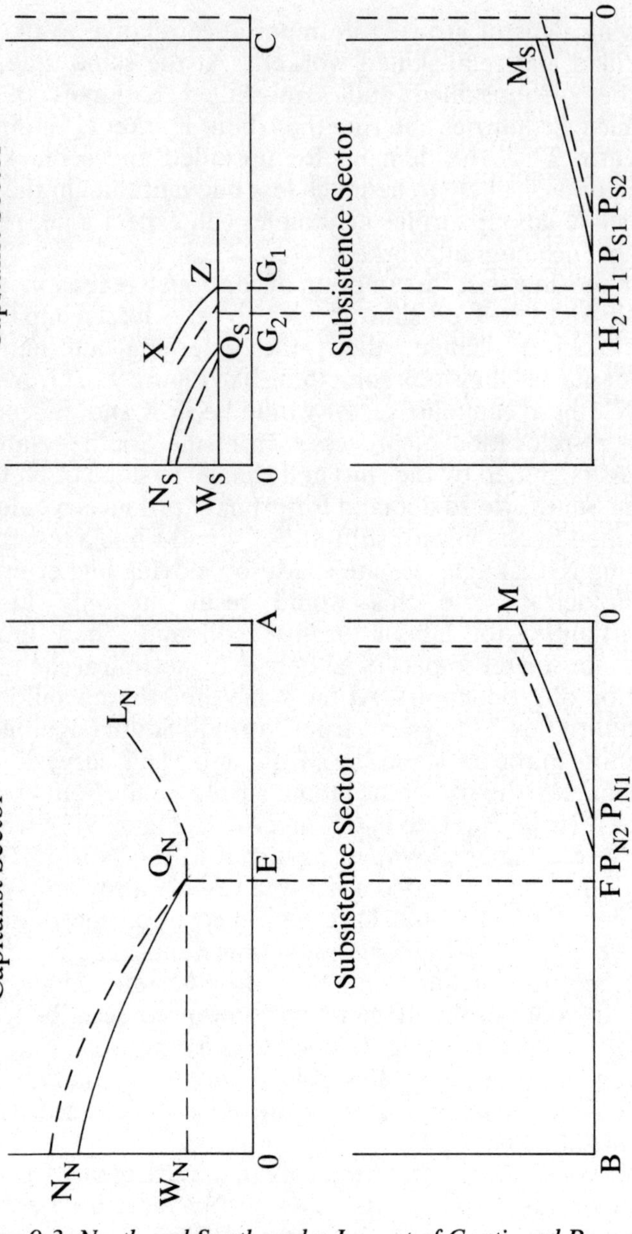

Figure 9.3: North and South under Impact of Continued Recession and Radical Technical Change

the case of the UK (Atkinson 1984) but which is probably common to all industrialised market economies employers are beginning to reorganise their manpower systems into fixed (primary or core) and variable (secondary or peripheral) components. Most firms contain both primary (stable, career-oriented, male-dominated) and secondary (high turnover, with little career progression, involving little training) forms of employment. Atkinson points out that the primary jobs are also those in which employment does not vary immediately with changes in output, whereas in secondary jobs it does. He argues that the internal labour market of many firms is fragmenting into 'increasing peripheral, and hence numerically variable, groups of workers, clustered around a numerically stable core group of employees, responsible for the key, firm-specific activities of the organisation' (*op. cit.*: 6).

Peripheral groups include not only those on full-time 'permanent' (but dead-end and less secure) contracts but also part-time and job-sharing employees, those on short-term contracts, probationers, public subsidy trainees, etc. In addition, extensive and increasing use is made of external groups, such as agency temporaries, outsourcing, subcontracting and self employment. This process, itself a response to recession in product and labour markets, increases the vulnerability of the growing number of secondary workers, restricts their career and training prospects and adversely affects their conditions of employment. It emphasises the increasing extent to which Northern employers are, as Kornai put it, playing on their home ground and the need to look beyond unemployment statistics for a measure of deterioration in labour markets.

CONCLUSIONS

In this context theories which attribute the growth of mass unemployment to wages being too high and which imply a need for downward wage flexibility become potentially dangerous. As Bienefeld (1982: 52) has pointed out, 'if one assumes that the competitive process could be extended internationally to its logical limits, so that the nation state was superceded as the effective social and political base for capital, then in the absence of global full employment the conditions of labour would be equalised downwards, since in so far as labour was thrown into one large market suffering from excess supply the competitive principle would produce a progressive downward pressure on the wage *irrespective* of the average productivity of labour, a conclusion which follows equally from neoclassical, classical or specifically Marxist perspectives'. In other words, if, in terms of our Figure 9.3, accumulation and growth were never fast enough to close the gap between H_2 and P_{S2} in the Southern subsistence sector and to eliminate Northern unemployment, the average international real wage would fall. There might be pockets of labour shortage in the world which would enjoy rising real wages for a while (producing the convergence discussed on page 220) but the general pressure would be downward.

Measures to increase downward real wage flexibility would accelerate this process—but with no guarantee that the eventual outcome would be global full employment. Competitive wage cuts around the world would result in movements along labour demand curves (N_NQ_N, N_SQ_S and XZ in Figure 9.3) but also in inward shifts in such curves as purchasing power and the incentive to invest were adversely affected. The interest-rate, real-balance and real-net-tax-burden effects (see Chapter Three, page 57) might exert some offsetting outward pressure on the demand curves, but at the global level the fallacy of composition would operate and prevent wage cuts from giving any stimulus to total exports. Ultimately, also, there is a limit, set by the need for the survival and reproduction of the labour force, on the extent to which the international real wage can be allowed to fall, which may be higher than what is necessary to produce global full employment via wage cuts.

Of course, as Bienefeld also points out (*op. cit.*: 52), a pure, competitive labour market of this kind could never exist. Sections of labour will always be able to insulate themselves from the rest of the labour market and, in the larger-scale, capital-intensive, technologically advanced sectors, employers will continue to find it in their interests to offer wages that are higher than would be necessary to attract merely the minimum number of workers required (see Chapter Four, page 89). And the examples of Japan and South Korea remind us that capital has a national as well as international character, which implies a need for it to keep the social formations from which it derives at a certain level of viability and internal cohesion (Bienefeld *et al.* 1977: 429). Nevertheless the strong pressures for downward wage flexibility in many industrialised economies do raise the prospect of heightened dualism within the labour markets of such economies and an increase in the size of their flexible-wage sectors and of their secondary forms of employment and at least the possibility of a fall in the average international real wage, without much diminution in the level of unemployment and underutilisation of labour around the world.

This argues the need for a change in direction in the theorisation of unemployment, away from the exclusively choice-theoretic emphasis of the neoclassical economists towards a more eclectic approach.[2] Such an alternative would need to be dynamic and long-run, with capital accumulation and growth at its centre, rather than static and short-run. It would need to be concerned with rapid structural change rather than equilibrium, with shifts in curves rather than moves along them. It would need to be global rather than national in the reach of its analysis, avoiding the fallacy of composition in its policy prescriptions.

In this respect the analytical framework used so far in this chapter, derived from Lewis's 'classical' development-economics model and Marx's reserve army analysis, is at least a starting point. It seems useful, also, particularly in current global conditions, to see the constraint on the rate of accumulation and growth of output and employment in a capitalist economy as being on the demand rather than the supply side. Specifically, the useful focus is on the incentive to invest.

Here the dynamic external economies approach discussed in Chapter Seven (page 168) looks highly relevant. Its analysis of the demand interconnections between industries suggests a variety of ways in which the incentive to invest can be maintained by a development-oriented government, of which Currie's (page 171) and Modigliani's (page 212) index-linked-mortgage scheme is only one. This emphasis also encourages a positive view of technological change as a macroeconomic means of increasing demand and thereby investment incentives, whatever its impact at process and plant level (page 227).

However, even if all the world's states were developmental and actively involved in programmes to maintain the incentive to invest (rather than, as is the case, predominantly involved in programmes which effectively reduce it) this would not necessarily open up a smooth path to global full employment nor banish the spectre of falling international real wages. For one thing, in a world of free trade and movement of capital, the distribution of the gains and losses of the process would be uneven, between countries, regions, sectors, labour market segments and genders. Technical progress destroys specific types of jobs in specific industries in specific locations; variations in investment incentives mean that the new jobs created by accumulation may be of other types in other industries and other locations. This raises internal restructuring problems for national governments. More seriously, it raises the possibility that governments of countries which appear likely to be net losers from the global process will want to protect themselves against its consequences (for example, the proposals for import controls in deindustrialising economies discussed above, page 210). In short, even under the most favourable circumstances it would be difficult to sustain such a process.

In the much less favourable *actual* circumstances of the 1980s Bienefeld argues that 'nationally oriented strategies' represent the only hope for most countries of 'mobilising domestic resources in a dynamic and effective manner on a national (or regional) basis, and trading with the outside world, in so far as that is possible, without allowing the social conditions of production and the adequate (for economic survival) level of productivity to be determined by those established somewhere else, irrespective of short-term social or economic consequences' (Bienefeld 1982: 56).

Even within such a nationally oriented strategy, however, if it were still based predominantly on investment by private capitalists in response to opportunities for profit, the problem of maintaining indefinitely the incentive to invest at an adequate level (discussed in Chapter Two, page 43) would remain. And even if this were possible (through judicious leading sector and technological change strategies, for instance) industrialised economies in which wages were determined by free collective bargaining would still face the short-run problem of reconciling high levels of employment with price stability. The conclusion of Chapter Three (page 79) was that, whether or not the 'natural rate' hypothesis is accepted in its entirety, there is clearly a ceiling on employment compatible with non-accelerating inflation, in economies with free wage bargaining, which is well short of full employment. Thus, unemployment could be regarded as an 'inherent vice' of this type of capitalism. Instant solutions such as work-sharing, early retirement or shorter working weeks will not work in this context since they merely redefine full employment and the point (still well below it) at which inflationary pressures begin to be exerted. The dilemma is only partly resolvable by a willingness to accept a hgher rate of inflation since it is the avoidance of *accelerating* inflation which is at issue. Nothing less than a fundamental change in the way in which wages are determined would be needed to restore the possibility of full employment capitalism. There is, of course, nothing new in this diagnosis. Kalecki was saying these things over forty years ago. His message was obscured by the false dawn of the sixties but it remains sufficiently important for him to be given the final word:

> Full employment capitalism will have, of course, to develop new social and political institutions which will reflect the increased power of the working class. If capitalism can adjust itself to full employment a fundamental reform will have been incorporated in it. If not, it will show itself an outmoded system which must be scrapped (Kalecki 1943: 429).

NOTES

1. If the Southern import-substituting industrial sector is ignored, which it can be for the purpose of this analysis.
2. This is not to deny that neoclassical theory may have something to offer on the question of the *incidence* of unemployment, by region, education level, gender, age, etc. *See* Chapter Four for further discussion.

References

R. Abdin, P. Bennell, O. Fajana, B. Hamdouch and M. Godfrey, *A World of Differentials: African Pay Structures in a Transnational Context* (Hodder and Stoughton, London 1983).

G. Ackley, *Macroeconomic Theory* (Macmillan, New York 1961).

G. Ackley, *Macroeconomic Theory and Policy* (Macmillan, New York 1975).

J. Adam, 'Similarities and differences in the treatment of labour shortages', in *Employment Policies in the Societ Union and Eastern Europe*, ed. J. Adam (Macmillan, London 1982).

G. Akerlof and H. Miyazaki, 'The implicit contract theory of unemployment meets the wage bill argument', *Review of Economic Studies*, vol. 47 (1980).

Samir Amin, *Unequal Development* (Harvester, Brighton 1978).

J. Atkinson, 'Manning for Uncertainty: Some Emerging UK Work Patterns', mimeo. (IMS, Sussex 1984).

C. Azaridis, 'Implicit contracts and underemployment equilibria', *Journal of Political Economy*, vol. 83, no. 6 (1975).

M.N. Baily, 'Wages and unemployment under uncertain demand', *Review of Economic Studies*, vol. 41, no. 125 (1974).

B. Balassa, 'The process of industrial development and alternative development strategies', *World Bank Staff Working Paper*, 438, October (1980).

H.M. Barnum and R.H. Sabot, 'Education, employment probabilities and rural–urban migration in Tanzania', *Oxford Bulletin of Economics and Statistics*, vol. 39, 2, May (1977).

H.N. Barnum and R.H. Sabot, 'Migration, education and urban surplus labour: the case of Tanzania', *Employment Series*, no. 3 (OECD Development Centre Studies, Paris 1976).

M. Barratt-Brown, *The Economics of Imperialism* (Penguin, London 1974).

P.T. Bauer, *Equality, the Third World and Economic Delusion* (Methuen, London 1981).

P.T. Bauer and B.S. Yamey, *The Economics of Underdeveloped Countries* (CUP,. Cambridge 1957).

D.K. Benjamin and L.A. Kochin, 'Searching for an explanation of unemployment in interwar Britain', *Journal of Political Economy*, vol. 87, no. 3, June (1979).

T. Balogh, 'The economics of educational planning: sense and nonsense', in *The Teaching of Development Economics*, ed. K. Martin and J. Knapp (Frank Cass, London 1967).

A.R. Berry and R.H. Sabot, 'Labour market performance in developing countries: a survey', *World Development*, vol. 6, nos. 11/12 (1978).

R. Berry, 'Redistribution, demand structure and factor requirements: the case of India', *World Development*, 9.7, July (1981).

S. Bhalla, 'Farm size, productivity and technical change in Indian agriculture', in *Agrarian Structure and Productivity in Developing Countries*, ed. R. Berry and W. Cline (Johns Hopkins 1979).

M. Bienefeld, 'Dependency in the eighties', *IDS Bulletin*, 12.1 (1980).

M. Beienefeld, 'The international context for national development strategies: constraints and opportunities in a changing world', in *The Struggle for Development*, ed. M. Bienefeld and M. Godfrey (John Wiley, Chichester 1982).

M. Bienefeld, H. Schmitz and M. Godfrey, 'Trade unions and the "new" internationalisation of production', *Development and Change*, October (1977).

M. Bienefeld and H. Schmitz, 'Capital accumulation and employment in the periphery—a programme of research', *IDS Sussex Discussion Paper*, 98 (October 1976).

M. Blaug, *Economic Theory in Retrospect* (Richard D. Irwin and Heinemann Educational Books, London 1968).

M. Blaug, *An Introduction to the Economics of Education* (Penguin, London 1970).

M. Blaug, *Education and the Unemployment Problem in Developing Countries* (ILO, Geneva, 1973).

T. Byres, 'Land reform, industrialisation and the marketed surplus in India', in *Agrarian Reform and Agrarian Reformism*, ed. D. Lehmann (Faber, London 1974).

F.H. Cardoso, 'Comentario sobre os conceitos de superpopulação relativa y marginalidade', *Revista Latino-Americana de Ciencias Sociales*, 1.2, June–December (1971).

F.H. Cardoso, The consumption of dependency theory in the United States', *Latin American Research Review*, XII.3 (1977).

F.H. Cardoso and E. Faletto, *Dependency and Development in Latin America* (University of California Press, Berkeley, Los Angeles and London 1979).

R. Cassen, 'Population and development: a survey', *World Development*, 4.10/11 (1976).

H.B. Chenery, 'The role of industrialisation in development programmes', *American Economic Review*, May (1955).

H.B. Chenery and A.M. Strout, 'Foreign assistance and economic development', *American Economic Review*, 56.4 (1966).

W. Cline, 'Can the East Asian model of development be generalised?', *World Development*, vol. 10, no. 2 (1982).

R.W. Clower, 'The Keynesian counter-revolution: a theoretical appraisal', in *The Theory of Interest Rates*, eds. F.H. Hahn and F.P.R. Brechling (Macmillan, London 1965).

G. Correa and J. Tinbergen, 'Quantitative adaptation of education to economic growth', *Kyklos* (1962).

E. Crawford and E. Thorbecke, *Employment, Income Distribution, Poverty Alleviation and Basic Needs in Kenya* (ILO, Geneva 1978).

J.S. Cubbin and K. Foley, 'The extent of benefit-induced unemployment in Great Britain: some new evidence', *Oxford Economic Papers*, vol. 29, March (1977).

L. Currie, *Accelerating Development* (McGraw Hill 1966).

L. Currie, 'The Colombian plan 1971–74: a test of the leading sector strategy', *World Development*, 2. 10–12, October–December (1974b).

L. Currie, 'The exchange constraint on development: a partial solution to the problem', *Economic Journal*, vol. 81, no. 324 (1971).

L. Currie, 'The leading sector model of growth in developing countries', *Journal of Economic Studies* (New Series), 1.1. May (1974a).

L.A. Dicks-Mireaux, 'The interrelationship between cost and price changes, 1946–1959', *Oxford Economic Papers*, Vol. 13, October (1961).

M. Dobb, *An Essay on Economic Growth and Planning* (Routledge & Kegan Paul, London 1960).

M. Dobb,*Theories of Value and Distribution since Adam Smith: Ideology and Economic Theory* (Cambridge University Press, Cambridge 1973).

P. Doeringer and M.J. Piore, *Internal Labour Markets and Manpower Analysis* (Heath, Lexington, Mass. 1971).

E. Domar, 'Capital expansion, rate of growth and employment', *Economica*, vol. 14 (1946).

R. Dore, *The Diploma Disease* (Unwin, London 1976).

T. Dos Santos, 'The crisis of development theory and the problem of dependence in Latin America', in *Underdevelopment and Development*, ed. H. Bernstein (Penguin, Harmondsworth 1973).

R. Dumont, *False Start in Africa* (Deutsch, London 1966).

Z. Ecevit and K.C. Zachariah, 'International labour migration', *Finance and Development*, 15.4, December (1978).

R.S. Eckaus, 'The factor proportions problem in underdeveloped areas', *American Economic Review*, 45.4, September (1955).

G.S. Fields, 'Rural-urban migration, urban unemployment and underemployment, and job search activities in LDCs', *Journal of Development Economics*, vol. 2, no. 2, June (1975).

P. Foster, 'The vocational school fallacy in development planning', in *Economics of Education*, ed. M. Blaug (Penguin, Harmondsworth 1966).

A.G. Frank, *Capitalism and Underdevelopment in Latin America* (Monthly Review Press, London and New York 1967).

A.G. Frank, *Dependent Accumulation and Underdevelopment* (Macmillan, London 1978).

C.R. Frank, 'Urban unemployment and economic growth in Africa', *Oxford Economic Papers*, vol. 20, no. 2, July (1968).

M. Frankman, 'Employment policy for Colombia: towards full employment and the four strategies', *Manpower and Unemployment Research*, 10.2 (1977).

C. Freeman, J. Clark and L. Soete, *Unemployment and Technical Innovation*, (Frances Pinter, London 1982).

M. Friedman, 'Unemployment versus inflation?', *Occasional Papers*, no. 44, Institute of Economic Affairs, London (1975).

Folker Froebel, 'The Current Development of the World Economy', mimeo. (Max Planck Institut, Starnberg 1980).

W. Galenson and H. Leibenstein, 'Investment criteria, productivity and economic development', *Quarterly Journal of Economics*, August (1955).

W.R. Garside, *The Measurement of Unemployment: Methods and Sources in Great Britain 1850–1979* (Basil Blackwell, Oxford 1980).

J.I. Gershuny, 'The informal economy: its role in post-industrial society', *Futures*, February (1979).

J.I. Gershuny and I.D. Miles, *The New Service Economy: the Transformation of Employment in Industrial Societies* (Pinter, London 1983).

D.P. Ghai, 'Employment performance, prospects and policies in Kenya' in *Prospects for Employment in the 1970s*, ed. R. Robinson and P. Johnston (University of Cambridge Overseas Studies Committee, 1972).

M. Godfrey, 'Measuring the removable surplus of agricultural labour in low-income economies', *The Journal of Economic Studies*, Spring (1967).

M. Godfrey, 'Economic variables and rural–urban migration: some thoughts on the Todaro hypothesis', *Journal of Development studies*, 10.1 (1973).

M. Godfrey, 'Kenya: African capitalism or simple dependency?' in *The Struggle for Development: National Strategies in an International Context*, ed. M. Bienefeld and M. Godfrey (John Wiley, Chichester 1983).

M. Godfrey, 'Rural–urban migration in a 'Lewis-model context', *Manchester School of Economic and Social Studies*, September (1979).

D.F. Gordon, 'A neo-classical theory of Keynesian unemployment, *Economic Inquiry* (1974).

P. Gregory, 'An assessment of changes in employment conditions in less developed countries', *Economic Development and Cultural Change*, vol. 28, no. 24 (1980).

S. Grossman and O.D. Hart, 'Implicit contracts, moral hazards and unemployment', *Cambridge University Economic Theory Discussion Paper*, 37 (1980).

H.G. Grubel and A.D. Scott, 'The international flow of human capital', *American Economic Review*, 56.2, May (1966).

L.R. Hadley, 'The migration of Egyptian human capital to the Arab oil producing states: a cost benefit analysis', *International Migration Review*, vol. 11, Fall (1977).

R.E. Hall, 'The rigidity of wages and the persistence of unemployment', *Brookings Papers on Economic Activity*, vol. 2 (1975).

F.H. Harbison, 'Human resources development planning in modernising economies', *International Labour Review*, 85.5, May (1962).

J.R. Harris and R.H. Sabot, 'Urban unemployment in LDCs: towards a more general search model', in *Migration and the Labour Market in Developing Countries*, ed. R.H. Sabot (Westview Press, Boulder 1982).

J.R. Harris and M.P. Todaro, 'Migration, unemployment and development: a two-sector analysis', *American Economic Review*, vol. 69, no. 1, March (1970).

R.F. Harrod, 'An essay in dynamic theory', *Economic Journal*, vol. 49 (1939).

K. Hart, 'Informal income opportunities and urban employment in Ghana', *The Journal of Modern African studies*, vol. 11, no. 1 (1973).

N. Heyzer, 'Towards a framework of analysis', *IDS Bulletin*, 12.3, July (1981).

A. O. Hirschmann, *A Bias for Hope* (Yale University Press 1971).

A.O. Hirschman, *The Strategy of Economic Development* (Yale University Press, 1958).

K. Hoffman and H. Rush, 'Microelectronics, Industry and the Third World', mimeo. (SPRU, University of Sussex 1980).

C. Holt, 'Job search, Phillips wage relation and union influence: theory and evidence', in *Macroeconomic Foundations of Employment and Inflation Theory*, ed. E.S. Phelps (W.W. Norton, New York 1970).

M. Hopkins, 'Employment trends in developing countries, 1960–80 and beyond', *International Labour Review*, 122.4, July/August (1983).

J.J. Hughes, 'How should we measure unemployment?' *British Journal of Industrial Relations*, XIII, 3 (1975).

J. Humphries, 'The emancipation of women in the 1970s and 1980s: from the latent to the floating', *Capital and Class*, 20 (1984).

D. Hunt, *The Impending Crisis in Kenya: the Case for Land Reform* (Gower, Aldershot and Brookfield 1984).

ILO, *Towards Full Employment: a Programme for Colombia* (ILO, Geneva 1970).

ILO, *Employment, Incomes and Equality: a Strategy for Increasing Productive Employment in Kenya* (ILO, Geneva 1972).

ILO, *Sharing in Development: a Programme of Employment, Equity and Growth for the Philippines* (ILO, Geneva 1974).

ILO/PREALC, *The Employment Problem in Latin America: Facts, Outlooks and Policies* (ILO, Santiago 1976).

H.G. Johnson, 'An "internationalist" model', in *The Brain Drain*, ed. W. Adams (Macmillan, New York 1968).

R. Kahn, 'Unemployment as seen by the Keynesians', in *The Concept and Measurement of Voluntary Unemployment*, ed. E.D.N. Worswick (Allen and Unwin, London 1976).

N. Kaldor, 'Alternative theories of distribution', *Review of Economic Studies*, vol. 23 (1955).

M. Kalecki, 'Full employment by stimulating private investment', *Oxford Economic Papers*, New Series, 7 (1945).

M. Kalecki, 'Political aspects of full employment', *Political Quarterly*, vol. 14 (1943).

M. Kalecki, *Selected Essays on the Dynamics of the Capitalist Economy* (Cambridge University Press 1971).

M. Kalecki, *Theory of Economic Dynamics* (Allen and Unwin 1965).

M. Kalecki, 'Three ways to full employment', in *The Economics of Full employment*, six studies in applied economics prepared at the Oxford University Institute of Statisics (Oxford University Press, Oxford 1944).

M. Kalecki, 'Unemployment in underdeveloped countries', in *Employment and Unemployment*, ed. V.K.R.V. Rao (Allied Publishers Private Ltd, Bombay 1968).

R. Kaplinsky, 'Capitalist accumulation in the periphery: the Kenyan case reexamined', *Review of African Political Economy*, vol. 16 (1980).

R. Kaplinsky, *The Impact of Microelectronics on the International Division of Labour—the Illustrative Case of Computer Aided Design* (Frances Pinter, London 1982).

R. Kaplinsky, *Microelectronics and Employment Revisited* (ILO, Geneva, 1985).

J.M. Keynes, *The General Theory of Employment, Interest and Money* (Macmillan, London 1936) (1960 edition).

P. Kilby, *Industrialisation in an Open Economy: Nigeria 1949–1966* (Cambridge University Press, Cambridge 1969).

K. King, 'Kenya's informal machine makers: a study of small-scale industry in Kenya's emerging artisan society', *World Development*, vol. 2, nos. 4/5 (1980).

L. Klein, foreword to G. Feiwell, *The Intellectual Capital of Michal Kalecki* (University of Tennessee Press 1975).

J. Knapp, 'Some Aspects of Economic Development', mimeo. (1956/7).

J. Knapp, 'Vers une analyse Keynesienne des sous-developpement et des points de croissance', *Le Tiers Monde*, 10.37, January–March (1969).

J. Kornai, *Economics of Shortage*, vol. A (North-Holland, Amsterdam, New York, Oxford 1980).

D.E.W. Laidler, 'The end of "demand management": how to reduce unemployment in the 1970s' in 'Unemployment versus inflation?', ed. M. Friedman, *Occasional Papers*, vol. 44, Institute of Economic Affairs, London (1975).

D. Lal, 'The poverty of development economics', *Hobart Paperback*, no. 16, Institute of Economic Affairs, London (1983).

S. Langdon, *Multinational Corporations in the Political Economy of Kenya* (Macmillan, London 1980).

O. Le Brun and C. Gerry, 'Petty producers and capitalism', *Review of African Political Economy*, 3 (1975).

H. Leibenstein, *Economic Backwardness and Economic Growth* (John Wiley and Sons, New York 1957).

A. Leijonhuvud, *On Keynesian Economics and the Economics of*

Keynes: a Study in Monetary Theory (Oxford University Press, New York 1968).

A. Leijonhuvud, *On Keynesian Economics and the Economics of Keynes: a Study in Monetary Theory* (Oxford University Press, New York 1968).

H.M. Levin, 'Raising employment and productivity with producer cooperatives', in *Human Resources, Employment and Development*, vol. 2, ed. Paul Streeten and Harry Maier (Macmillan, London for the IEA, 1983).

W.A. Lewis, 'Economic development with unlimited supplies of labour', Manchester School of Economic and Social Studies, vol. 22, no. 2, May (1954).

W.A. Lewis, 'Four steps to full employment', *International Development Review*, 14.2 (1972).

W.A. Lewis, 'Reflections on unlimited labour', *Discussion Paper 5* (Woodrow Wilson School, Princeton University, Development Research Project, 1968).

C. Leys, 'Interpreting African underdevelopment: reflections on the ILO report on employment, incomes and equality in Kenya', *African Affairs*, vol. 72, no. 289 (1973).

R.G. Lipsey, 'The relation between unemployment and the rate of change of money wage rates in the United Kingdom, 1862–1957: a further analysis', *Economica*, vol. 27, February (1960).

M. Lipton, 'Labour and poverty', *World Bank Staff Working Paper*, 616 (1983).

M. Lipton, 'Towards a theory of land reform', in *Agrarian Reform and Agrarian Reformism*, ed. D. Lehmann (Faber, London 1974).

I.M.D. Little, 'The experience and causes of rapid labour-intensive development in Korea, Taiwan Province, Hong Kong and Singapore; and the possibilities of emulation', in *Export-led Industrialisation and Development*, ed. Eddy Lee (ILO, Geneva 1981).

I. Little, T. Scitovsky and M. Scott, *Industry and Trade in Some Developing Countries* (Oxford University Press, London 1970).

A. Maddison, 'Measuring labour slack', ch. 7 in *Human Resources, Employment and Development*, vol. 3. ed. B. Weisbrod and H. Hughes (Macmillan, London for IEA, 1983).

D. Maki and Z.A. Spindler, 'The effect of unemployment compensation on the rate of unemployment in Great Britain', *Oxford Economic Papers*, vol. 27, November (1975).

T.R. Malthus, *Principles of Political Economy* (Murray, London, 1820).

T.R. Malthus, *An Essay on the Principle of Population as it Affects the Future Improvement of Society* (Macmillan, London 1826; 1966 edn.).

R.M. Marini, 'Brazilian sub-imperialism', *Monthly Review*, 9, February (1972).

A. Marshall, *The Economics of Industry* (Macmillan, London, 1879).

A. Marshall, *Principles of Economics* (Macmillan, London 1920; 1952 edn.).

K. Marx, *Capital*, vol. 1 (Lawrence and Wishart, London 1867; 1954 edn.).

K. Marx, *Principles of Economics* (Macmillan, London 1867; 1954 edn.)

T.C. McGee, *The Persistence of the Proto-Proletariat: Occupational Structures and Planning for the Future of Third World Cities* (Comparative Urban Studies, School of Architcture and Urban Planning, University of California, Los Angeles 1974).

R.K. McKinnon, *Money and Capital in Economic Development* (Brookings Institute, Washington D.C. 1973).

R.L. Meek, *Marx and Engels on the Population Bomb* (Ramparts Press, Berkeley 1971).

S. Mehra, 'Surplus labour in Indian agriculture', *Indian Economic Review*, 1 (1966).

G.M. Meier, *Leading Issues in Economic Development* (Oxford University Press, London 1976).

G. Merritt, *World Out of Work* (Collins, London 1982).

J.S. Mill, *Principles of Political Economy*, Book III (Longmans, London, 1848).

P. Minford, *Unemployment: Cause and Cure* (Roberson, London, 1983).

F. Modigliani, 'Some economic implications of the indexing of financial assets with special reference to mortgages', in *The new Inflation and Monetary Policy*, ed. M. Monti (Macmillan, London 1976).

C. Moser and K. Young, 'Women of the working poor', *IDS Bulletin*, 12.3, July (1981).

R. Murray, 'Imperialism and the Labour Process', mimeo. (IDS, Sussex 1980).

R. Murray, 'Underdevelopment, international firms and the international division of labour', in *Towards a New World Economy* (Rotterdam University Press 1972).

G. Myrdal, *Asian Drama* (Penguin Books, Harmondsworth 1968).

G. Myrdal, *Economic Theory and Underdeveloped Regions*

(Methuen, London 1957).

S.J. Nickell, 'The effect of unemployment and related benefits on the duration of unemployment', *Economic Journal*, vol. 83, March (1979).

S.J. Nickell, 'The determinants of equilibrium unemployment in Britain', *Economic Journal*, vol. 92, September (1982a).

S.J. Nickell, 'Research into unemployment: a partial view of the economics literature', London School of Economics, Centre for Labour Economics, *Discussion Paper*, no. 131, June (1982b).

J.E. Nickum, 'Labour accumulation in rural China and its role since the Cultural Revolution', *Cambridge Journal of Economics*, 2.3, September (1978).

G. Nihan, E. Demol and C. Jondoh, 'The modern informal sector in Lome', *International Labour Review*, 118.5 (1979).

M. Nikolinakos, *Politische-Oekonomie der Gastarbeiterfrage* (Rowohlt Reinbekbei, Hamburg, 1973).

J. Nun, 'Dismissals in the Argentine automobile industry: a case study of the floating surplus population', *Labour, Capital and Society,* 12.2, 1979.

J. Nun, 'Superpoblacion relativa, ejército industrial de reserva y masa marginal', *Revista Latinoamericana*, 5.2 (1969).

R. Nurkse, *Problems of Capital Formation in Underdeveloped Countries* (Basil Blackwell, Oxford 1953).

I. Oxaal, T. Barnett and D. Booth (eds.), *Beyond the Sociology of Development* (Routledge & Kegan Paul, London 1975).

Howard Pack, 'Employment and Productivity in Kenyan manufacturing', in *Essays on Employment in Kenya*, eds. D. Ghai and M. Godfrey (Kenya Literature Bureau, Nairobi 1979).

Howard Pack, 'Policies to encourage the use of intermediate technology', in *The Struggle for Economic Development*, ed. Michael P. Todaro (Longman, New York and London 1983).

S. Paine, *Exporting Workers: the Turkish Case* (Cambridge University Press, London 1974).

G. Palma, 'Dependency and development: a critical overview', in *Dependency Theory: a Critical Reassessment*, ed. D. Seers (Frances Pinter, London 1981).

M. Parkin, 'Unemployment and inflation: facts, theories, puzzles and policies', in *Unemployment in Western Countries*, eds. E. Malinvaud and J. P. Fitoussi (Macmillan, London 1980).

E.S. Phelps, 'Money wage dynamics and labour market equilibrium', in *Microeconomic Foundations of Employment and Inflation Theory*, ed. E.S. Phelps (W.W. Norton, New York 1970).

A.W. Phillips, 'The relationship between unemployment and the rate of change of money wage rates in the United Kingdom', *Economica*, vol. 25, November (1958). Reprinted in *Readings in Macroeconomics*, ed. M.G. Mueller (Holt, Rinehart and Winston, London 1969).

A.C. Pigou, *The Theory of Unemployment* (Macmillan, London 1933).

A.C. Pigou, *Employment and Equilibrium* (Macmillan, London 1941).

M.J. Piore, *Birds of Passage: Migrant Labour and Industrial Societies* (Cambridge University Press, Cambridge 1979).

M.J. Piore, 'The dual labour market: theories and implications' in *Readings in Political Economy: an Urban Perspective*, ed. D.M. Gordon (Heath, Lexington, Mass. 1971).

J. Power, 'The role of protection in industrialisation policy' *IDS Nairobi Working Paper*, 32 (April 1972).

R. Prebisch, 'Commercial policy in underdeveloped countries', *American Economic Review*, papers and proceedings, 49.2 (1959).

G. Psacharopoulos, *Returns to Education: an International Comparison* (Elsevier Scientific, New York 1973).

A. Quijano, 'The marginal pole of the economy and the marginalised labour force', *Economy and Society*, 3.4 (1974).

E.R. Rado, 'The explosive model', *Manpower and Unemployment Research*, 8.1 (1975).

G. Ranis, 'The exchange constraint on development—a partial solution to the problem: a comment', *Economic Journal*, March (1973).

G. Ranis, 'Unemployment and factor price distortions', in *Third World Employment Problems and Strategies*, ed. R. Jolly (Penguin, London 1973).

G. Ranis and J.C.H. Fei, 'A theory of economic development', *American Economic Review*, vol. 51, no. 4, September (1961).

G. Ranis and J.C.H. Fei, *Development of the Labour Surplus Economy* (Richard Irwin, Homewood, Illinois 1964).

V.K.R.V. Rao, 'Investment income and the multiplier in an underdeveloped economy', *Indian Economic Review*, February (1952).

L.G. Reynolds, 'Economic development with surplus labour: some complications', *Oxford Economic Papers*, March (1969).

D. Ricardo, *The Principles of Political Economy and Taxation*

(Dent, Everyman's Library, London 1821; 1973 edn).

N.B. Ridler, 'Employment policy for Colombia, 1971–74', *Manpower and Unemployment Research*, 11.1 (1978).

D. Rimmer, 'Wage politics in Africa', *Occasional Paper* no. 12, University of Birmingham, Faculty of Commerce and Social Science (1970),

J. Robinson, *Essays in the Theory of Employment* (Macmillan, London 1937).

J. Robinson and F. Wilkinson, 'What has become of employment policy?' *Cambridge Journal of Economics*, 1 (1977).

N. Rosenberg, 'Capital formation in underdeveloped countries', *American Economic Review*, 50.4 (1960).

P. Rosenstein-Rodan, 'Problems of industrialisation of Eastern and South-Eastern Europe', *Economic Journal*, June/September (1943). Reprinted in A. Agarwala and S. Singh, *The Economics of Underdevelopment* (Oxford University Press, New York 1963).

R. H. Sabot, *Economic Development and Urban Migration: A Study of Tanzania* (Clarendon Press, Oxford 1978).

D. Sapsford, 'Some Further Evidence in the Statistical Debate on the Net Barter Terms of Trade between Primary Commodities and Manufactures', mimeo. (University of East Anglia and IMF, August 1984).

M. Sawyer, *Macroeconomics in Question* (Wheatsheaf, Brighton 1982).

H. Schmitz, 'Growth constraints on small-scale manufacturing in developing countries: a critical review', *World Development*, 10.6, June (1982).

T.W. Schultz, *Transforming Traditional Agriculture* (New Haven, 1964).

T. Scitovsky, 'Two concepts of external economies', *Journal of Political Economy*, April (1954). Reprinted in A. Agarwala and S. Singh, *The Economics of Underdevelopment* (Oxford University Press, New York 1963).

A. Sen, *Choice of Techniques* (Basil Blackwell, Oxford 1960).

A.K. Sen, 'An aspect of Indian Agriculture', *Economic Weekly*, vol. 14 (1962).

A. Sen, *Employment, Technology and Development* (Oxford, London 1975).

A. Sen (ed.), *Growth Economics* (Penguin Books, Harmondsworth 1970).

S.V. Sethuraman (ed.), *The Urban Informal Sector in Developing Countries—Employment, Poverty and Environment* (ILO,

Geneva 1981).

H.W. Singer, 'The distribution of gains between borrowing and investing countries', *American Economic Review, Papers and Proceedings,* vol. 11, no. 2, May (1950).

H.W. Singer, 'Brief note on unemployment rates in developing countries', *Manpower and Unemployment Research in Africa*, 3.1 (1970).

A. Smith, *The Wealth of Nations* Modern Library, New York 1776; 1937 edn).

S. Smith, 'An extension of the vent-for-surplus model in relation to long-run structural change in Nigeria,', *Discussion Paper in Economics, University of Liverpool,* July 1975.

R.W. Solow, 'A contribution to the theory of economic growth', *Quarterly Journal of Economics*, 70, February (1956).

J. Spraos, *Inequalising Trade?* (Oxford University Press, New York and London 1983).

L. Squire, *Employment Policy in Developing Countries: a Survey of Issues and Evidence* (Oxford University Press for the World Bank, Washington 1981).

G. Standing, *Labour Force Participation and Development* (ILO, Geneva 1978).

G. Standing, 'The notion of structural unemployment', *International Labour Review*, vol. 122:2, March–April (1983).

G. Standing, 'The notion of voluntary unemployment', *International Labour Review*, vol. 120:5, September–October (1981).

J.E. Stepanek, *Managers for Small Industry: an International Study* (The Free Press, Glencoe, Illinois 1960).

F. Stewart, 'Technology and employment in LDCs', *World Development*, March (1974).

M.T. Sumner, 'The history and significance of the Phillips curve', in *Macroeconomics*, David Demery *et al.* (Longman, London 1984).

M.T. Sumner and R. Ward, 'The reappearing Phillips curve', *Oxford Economic Papers*, 35.4 (1983).

O. Sunkel, 'The development of development thinking', in *Transitional Capitalism and National Development*, ed. J. Villamil (Harvester, Brighton 1979).

O. Sunkel, 'Transnational capitalism and national disintegration in Latin America', *Social and Economic Studies*, 22.1 (1973).

T. Swan, 'Economic growth and capital accumulation', *Economic Record*, November (1956).

J. Taylor, 'A note on the comparative behaviour of male and female unemployment rates in the UK, 1951–76', University of Lancaster (1977) (mimeo.).

C.Y. Thomas, *Dependence and Transformation* (Monthly Review Press, New York and London 1974).

M.P. Todaro, 'The urban employment problem in less developed countries: an analysis of demand and supply', *Yale Economic Essays*, Fall (1968).

M.P. Todaro, 'Migration and economic development: a review of theory, evidence, methodology and research priorities', *Occasional Paper*, 18, IDS, Nairobi (1976).

V.E. Tokman, 'Labour market dynamics and income distribution in Latin America', ch. 9 in *Human Resources, Employment and Development*, vol. 4, ed. V.L. Urquidi and S. Trejo Reyes (Macmillan, for International Economic Association, London 1983).

D. Turnham, 'The employment problem in less developed countries: a review of evidence', *Employment Series*, no. 1, OECD Development Centre, Paris, June (1971).

UNECAFE, *Programming Techniques for Economic Development* (Bangkok 1959).

C. Vaitsos, 'Employment problems and transnational enterprises in developing countries', *ILO WEP 2–28, Working Paper 11* (October 1976).

J. Viner, 'Some reflections on the concept of "disguised unemployment"', *Contribucoes a Analise do Desenvolvimento Economico* (1957).

T. Ward, 'The case for an import control strategy in the UK', in *Socialist Register*, ed. D. Currie and R.P. Smith (Merlin, London 1981).

W. Warren, 'Imperialism and capitalist industrialisation', *New Left Review*, September/October (1973).

W. Warren, *Imperialism: Pioneer of Capitalism* (Verso, London 1980).

G. Wedell, 'The enlargement of the European Community: implications for employment and free movement of workers', *Manchester Business School and Centre for Business Research Working Paper*, 38 (1979).

J. Weeks, 'Imbalance between the centre and periphery and the "employment crisis" in Kenya', in Oxaal *et al.* (*op. cit.*) (1975).

J. Weeks, 'The political economy of labour transfer', *Science and Society* (1971).

J. Weeks, 'An exploration into the nature of the problem of urban imbalance in Africa', *Manpower and Unemployment Research*

in Africa, vol. 6, no. 2 (1973).
J. Weeks, 'A brief note on the unemployment crisis in poor countries', *Manpower and Unemployment Research in Africa*, 7.1 (1974).
J. Weeks, 'Policies for expanding employment in the informal urban sector of developing economies', *International Labour Review*, vol. 3, no. 1, January (1975).
G. White, 'Urban employment and labour allocation policies in post-Mao China', *World Development*, 10.8, August (1982).
World Bank, *Accelerated Development in Sub-Saharan Africa: an Agenda for Action* (IBRD, Washington, D.C. 1981).
World Bank, 'Research project on labour migration and manpower in the Middle East and North Africa', *Interim Report* (Washington 1979).
World Bank, *'Sub-Saharan Africa: Progress Report on Development Prospects and Programmes'* (Washington 1983).
World Bank, *World Development Report* (IBRD, Washington, D.C. 1984).

Index